Ministry of Agriculture,
Fisheries and Food

National Food Survey 1996

Annual Report
on
Food Expenditure, Consumption and
Nutrient Intakes

LONDON : THE STATIONERY OFFICE

©Crown copyright 1997. Published with the permission of the Ministry of Agriculture, Fisheries and Food on behalf of the Controller of Her Majesty's Stationery Office

Applications for reproduction should be made in writing to:-

    The Copyright Unit,
    Her Majesty's Stationery Office,
    St Clements House,
    2 – 16 Colegate,
    Norwich,
    NR3 1BQ.

ISBN 0 11 243031 7

Preface

The National Food Survey (NFS) is a well established source of information on food purchases and the nutritional value of the domestic diet in Great Britain. In 1996 the survey was extended to cover Northern Ireland thus allowing results for the United Kingdom to be presented for the first time.

This report gives the results of the Main (household purchases) part and the Eating Out part of the Survey for 1996. The Main Survey provides comparisons of food consumption and expenditure with the previous year and with a decade ago. In addition, there is a special section presenting an analysis of regional results, showing regional patterns of expenditure, consumption and nutrient intakes and trends in regional consumption over the last ten years.

The fieldwork and sample selection was carried out by the Office for National Statistics and, in Northern Ireland, the fieldwork was undertaken by the Northern Ireland Statistics and Research Agency. The Ministry of Agriculture, Fisheries and Food would like to express its gratitude to these organisations and to all the households who participated in the Survey. Thanks are also due to the National Food Survey Committee, whose members give their time freely. Their advice on the analysis and presentation of results and other aspects of the Survey is invaluable.

In February, Professor Chesher presented a paper to the Royal Statistical Society on the subject of estimating nutrient intake – age relationships from the household food purchases data recorded in the Survey. The paper was published in the RSS Journal (Series A, volume 160, Part 3, 1997). An article on changes to the design of the NFS sample appeared in the January 1997 edition of the Survey Methodology Bulletin published by the Office for National Statistics.

Summary NFS data can now be found on the Internet. Details of additional analyses obtainable from the Ministry of Agriculture, Fisheries and Food are given at the end of this report.

John M. Slater

(Chairman - National Food Survey Committee)

The National Food Survey Committee 1996/97

John SLATER BSc, MS, PhD
    Ministry of Agriculture, Fisheries and Food, Chairman

John BEAUMONT, BSc, PhD
    Institute of Grocery Distribution

Caroline BOLTON-SMITH, BSc, PhD
    University of Dundee

Jim BURNS, BA, MSc
    University of Reading

Professor Andrew CHESHER, BSocSc
    University of Bristol

Susan CHURCH, BSc
    Ministry of Agriculture, Fisheries and Food

Jil MATHESON, BA
    Office for National Statistics

Stuart PLATT, BSc
    Ministry of Agriculture, Fisheries and Food

Robert PRICE, BSc
    Food and Drink Federation

Tom STAINER, BA, Dip (Agric)
    Department of Agriculture for Northern Ireland

Roger WHITEHEAD, CBE, BSc, MA, PhD, FIBiol
    MRC Dunn Nutrition Group

Professor Martin WISEMAN, MB, MRCP
    Department of Health

Secretary

Stan Speller, FIS
    Ministry of Agriculture, Fisheries and Food

Report of the National Food Survey Committee, 1996/97

The National Food Survey (NFS) Committee consists of officials from Government Departments with an interest in the Survey and outside experts with specialised knowledge of economics, statistics, nutrition and the food industry. Its purpose is to recommend such changes to the Survey as appear desirable and to advise on the publication of annual and other reports. It generally meets once a year.

The Committee met once during the year, in February 1997. It considered the proposed content of this annual NFS report and the current and future development of the Survey. The 1996 report contains several new features. The extension of the Survey in 1996 to cover Northern Ireland means that results for the United Kingdom and Northern Ireland are presented for the first time. However, in order to retain continuity the Report is still largely based on Great Britain. Other new features agreed by the Committee include the addition to the report of a summary of the year's NFS results; a shorter section on eating out and information about standard errors and non-response. The Committee also discussed alternative definitions of convenience foods but concluded that such an aggregation was difficult to define and was probably not meaningful. However, to maintain continuity, this report presents the usual (limited) data using the existing NFS definition of convenience foods.

Consideration was given to basing the special analysis section of the report on NFS results by income group. However, it was decided instead to provide an analysis by Standard Statistical Region as these regions will be replaced by the new Government Office regions in the next annual report. The report for 1997 will also be the first to present results using a smaller, but better designed sample, introduced from the beginning of 1997.

In response to the Committees recommendation of mounting a separate one-off survey of sources and the amount of food purchased (for consumption inside and outside the home) but not consumed, the Ministry published a specification for a pilot study and are currently evaluating proposals. Such a survey will help improve the NFS-based estimates of nutritional intakes (which currently allow for household wastage on the basis of the results of previous studies).

The Committee considered certain sampling and design issues. The Ministry will continue to consider the need for weighting results to correct for differential non-response and is participating to some extent in the move towards greater harmonisation of government household surveys, with the introduction of standard wordings for certain questions in 1998. However, whilst the Committee agreed that this was desirable, it reiterated its concern that the standard household definition used for many surveys would not be suitable for a survey of household food consumption and expenditure.

Contents

		Page
Section 1	**Introduction and Summary of Results**	1
	Summary of results	3
Section 2	**Household Food: Expenditure and Consumption**	5
	National Averages	6
	Regional Comparisons	15
	Income Group Comparisons	18
	Analysis by Household Composition	23
Section 3	**Household food: Nutrient intakes**	31
	National averages	31
	Regional, Income Group and Household Composition differences	33
Section 4	**Eating Out: Expenditure, Consumption and Nutrient Intakes**	35
	Expenditure and Consumption	36
	Results by Household Characteristics	38
	Results by Personal Characteristics	42
	Eating Out: Nutrient intakes	45
	Results by Household Characteristics	46
	Results by Personal Characteristics	52
	Household food and eating out: nutrient intakes	52
Section 5	**Analysis of Regional Data**	56
	Introduction	56
	Expenditure	56
	Consumption	58
	Consumption patterns over time	61
	Government Office Regions	64
	Nutrient intakes	65
Appendix A	**Structure of the Survey**	70
	Household food and drink	70
	Food and drink eaten out	78
Appendix B	**Supplementary Tables for the Main Survey**	84
Appendix C	**Supplementary Tables for the Eating out Survey**	114
Appendix D	**Supplementary Tables for Regional Data**	118
Glossary and additional information		128
	Symbols and conventions used	132
	Additional Information	132

Section 1

Introduction and Summary of Results

The annual report on the National Food Survey has provided national data on food expenditure, consumption and nutrient intakes since 1950. This edition presents the data for 1996, and includes comparisons with both one and ten years ago. It would have been possible to have based this year's report on results for the United Kingdom, rather than Great Britain, because the Survey was extended to Northern Ireland in January 1996. However, in order to preserve continuity and to present comparisons with earlier years most data presented are for Great Britain. Nevertheless some United Kingdom and Northern Ireland data are included. Results for Northern Ireland are published by the Department of Agriculture for Northern Ireland and are obtainable from the Northern Ireland National Food Survey Section in Belfast (01232 – 524455).

The results are derived from the responses of a random sample of about 8,000 private households throughout the country. Each of the participating households recorded details of all items of food brought into the home for human consumption during the course of a week. Soft drinks, alcoholic drinks and confectionery brought into the home were also covered. Some information on the numbers of meals eaten outside the home, but not the content or cost of such meals, was recorded for all the households. In addition, a half of the selected households in Great Britain recorded details of all meals, snacks and drinks consumed outside the home. As the data presented in this report are based on a sample, they are subject to sampling error and small changes over time or differences between groups should not necessarily be regarded as statistically significant. Appendix A contains details of the structure and methodology of the Survey, including sampling errors. A glossary of terms is given at the end of the report.

The main household consumption and expenditure data for 1996 are presented in Section 2 and Appendix B of this report. They show averages per person per week for each major type of food.

Aggregate data for Great Britain as a whole are followed by analyses of these data according to various geographical and household characteristics. These provide some insight into patterns of consumption and expenditure in different types of households, but need to be interpreted with some care as an observed difference cannot necessarily be attributed solely to the classification difference under consideration. For example, differences in the level of expenditure between income groups may, in part, reflect differences in the numbers and ages of household members and the number of meals eaten outside the home.

It is important to note that the NFS classifies food in the form in which it is acquired by consumers and that, in the case of household food, food purchased (together with own produced and free food consumed) is used as a proxy for consumption. As a result of the first point, NFS data on the consumption of a particular commodity excludes any of that commodity which is consumed in other forms e.g. sugar consumed as chocolate is "chocolate" in the NFS and pork consumed in pork pies is coded as "meat pies", not as pork.

The summary of nutrient intake data for household food and drink are presented in Section 3 with reference to the Tables in Appendix B. Section 4 and Appendix C present expenditure, consumption and nutrient intake data derived from the Eating Out component of the Survey. Section 5 presents an analysis by Standard Statistical Region with the background data to these being provided in Appendix D. The analysis shows regional results for household expenditure, consumption and nutrient intakes averaged over 1994 – 96 and expressed as deviations from the national average. A comparison of consumption results with averages for 1984 – 86 is also given by region.

Background

An estimated £52 billion was spent on household food (excluding alcoholic drinks) in 1996 (Table 1.1); this was 11.0 per cent of consumers' total expenditure. Since 1950, the relative importance of expenditure on food has declined, reflecting the considerable increase in spending on other items (Figure 1.2).

Table 1.1 Consumers' expenditure in the United Kingdom

	1986 £ b	1986 %	1995 £ b	1995 %	1996 £ b	1996 %
Expenditure on household food	32.6	13.5	49.0	11.0	52.0	11.0
Total consumers' expenditure	241.6	100.0	446.2	100.0	473.5	100.0
Related series:						
Expenditure on alcoholic drinks	16.4	6.8	26.1	5.8	28.0	5.9
Expenditure on catering (meals and accommodation)	16.2	6.7	37.9	8.5	40.7	8.6

Source: Office for National Statistics

Figure 1.2 Household food expenditure as a percentage of total consumers' expenditure

Source: Office for National Statistics, Economic Trends.

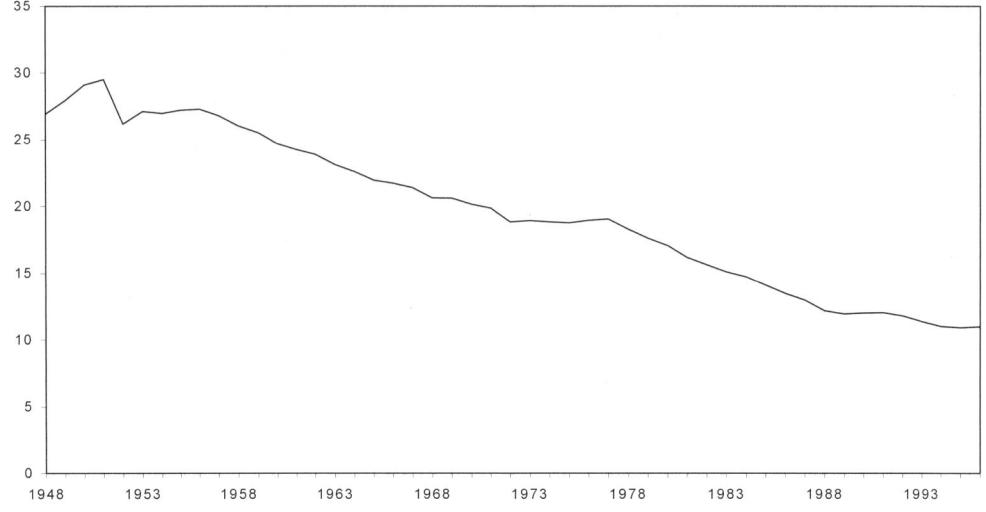

The relatively slow growth in expenditure on household food is, in part, due to the smaller increase in retail food prices as compared to other items, particularly over the period 1978–92, (Figure 1.3). Nevertheless, at constant 1990 prices, expenditure on household food has fallen to 12 per cent of total consumer expenditure in 1996, from 13 per cent in 1986 and 16 per cent in 1976. In 1996 the Retail Price Index for food was 3.3 per cent higher than in 1995 while for all items (including food) the increase was 2.4 per cent.

Figure 1.3 Retail prices for food, and for other items (Jan 1987=100)

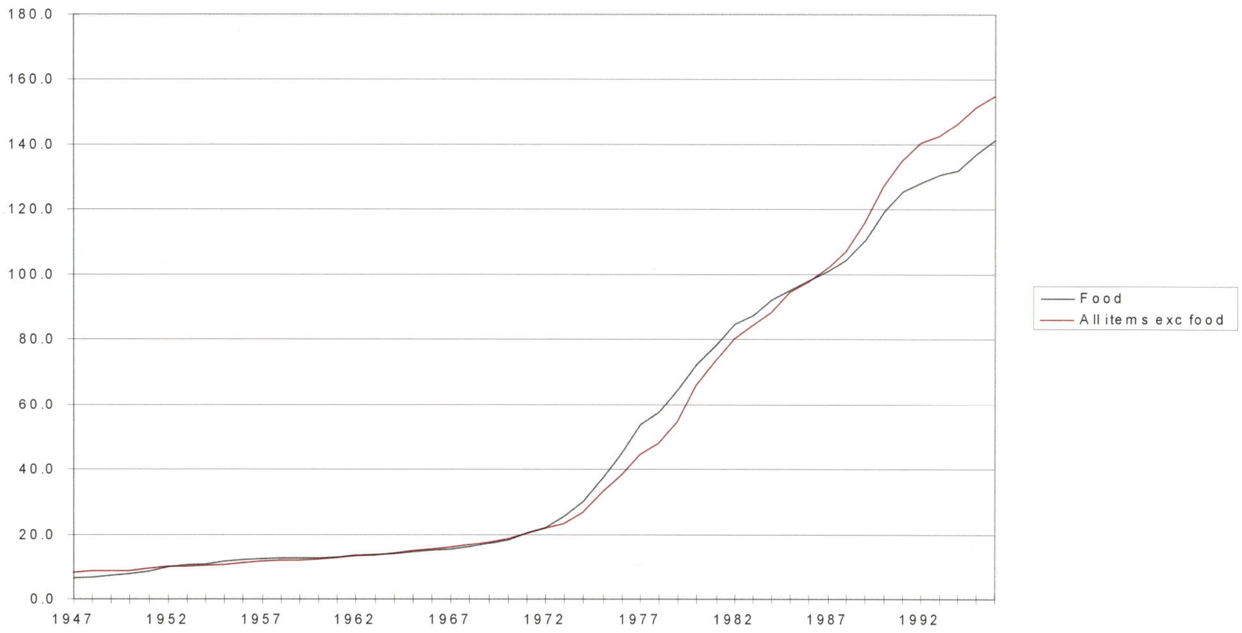

Summary of results – Great Britain, 1996

Expenditure

- In 1996 total expenditure in Great Britain on household food and drink was £16.46 per person per week, 5 per cent higher than in 1995.

- Expenditure on food and drink eaten out was £6.53 per person per week, up 12 per cent.

Consumption

- Household consumption of milk and cream fell by 3 per cent in 1996 due to an estimated 9 per cent fall for whole milk.

- Household consumption of carcase beef and veal fell by 17 per cent in 1996 partly due to a lack of public confidence in its safety following the announcement on 20 March 1996 of a possible link between BSE and CJD. The average price paid by consumers for beef and veal in 1996 was only slightly lower than in 1995.

- There were marked increases in household consumption of mutton and lamb and uncooked poultry to offset the fall in beef, despite price increases.

- There was an 8 per cent fall in the consumption of meat and meat products eaten out in 1996. A fall in consumption of hamburgers, meat pies and meat-based dishes being only partly offset by an increase in consumption of roast or fried chicken and turkey.

- Household consumption of fish increased to its highest level for over twenty years, though consumption of cooked fish fell.

- Household purchases (consumption) of sugar rose for the first time for twenty years, though only back to the 1994 level.

- Household consumption of vegetables other than potatoes rose by 4 per cent in 1996 but it was still 9 per cent lower than ten years ago.

- Consumption of fruit was up by 3 per cent on 1995 and by 17 per cent on 1986.

- Though household bread consumption remained fairly steady in 1996, consumption of other cereals such as biscuits, cakes and pizzas all rose.

Nutrient intakes

- The percentage of food energy derived from fat continued to decline although the fall between 1995 and 1996 was only 0.1 per cent (from 39.8 per cent to 39.7 per cent). There was also a small reduction in the percentage of food energy derived from saturated fatty acids between 1995 and 1996 to 15.4 per cent.

Section 2

Household Food: Expenditure and Consumption

This Section presents results for food brought into the home, (i.e. household food), although there is also a short section on the number of meals eaten outside the home. As in past years, results of the Survey are given for Great Britain. With the inclusion of Northern Ireland in the Survey as from January 1996, some United Kingdom results, particularly on expenditure, are included for comparison in the detailed tables. In 1996 average expenditure on household food in Great Britain rose by 5 per cent to £14.51 per person per week, with higher spending being recorded throughout the year (Table 2.1). The notional value of supplies from gardens, allotments and free sources, at 18 pence per person per week, was also up on the corresponding figure for 1995. Spending on alcoholic and soft drinks and confectionery added a further £1.95 to the average expenditure per person per week. Details of consumption and expenditure by food code are given in Appendix Table B1 and B7 respectively. With a change to a new Survey contractor in 1996 detailed data will have been affected by the inevitable changes in coding practice. For further details see the list of supplementary tables at the start of Appendix B.

Table 2.1 Household food expenditure and total value of food obtained for consumption

per person per week

	Expenditure			Value of garden and allotment produce, etc [a]		Value of consumption [b]		
	1995	1996	Change	1995	1996	1995	1996	Change
Food	£	£	%	£	£	£	£	%
1st Quarter	13.70	14.14	3	0.07	0.11	13.77	14.25	4
2nd Quarter	14.11	14.60	4	0.11	0.10	14.22	14.70	3
3rd Quarter	13.75	14.73	7	0.25	0.32	14.00	15.05	8
4th Quarter	13.62	14.60	7	0.12	0.18	13.74	14.78	8
Yearly average	**13.79**	**14.51**	**5**	**0.14**	**0.18**	**13.93**	**14.69**	**6**
Soft drinks	0.49	0.51	4	...	...	0.49	0.51	4
Alcoholic drinks	1.08	1.14	6	...	...	1.09	1.14	5
Confectionery	0.27	0.30	11	...	...	0.27	0.30	11
Total food and drink (GB)	15.63	16.46	5	0.14	0.18	15.78	16.64	5
Total food and drink (UK)	na	16.46	na	na	0.19	na	16.65	na

(a) valued at average prices paid for comparable purchases.
(b) expenditure on food purchased for consumption in the home, plus the estimated value of garden and allotment produce, etc.

The estimate of total household expenditure on food, soft drinks and confectionery in the United Kingdom, at £15.32 per person per week, was lower than that shown by the Family Expenditure Survey estimate of £42.28 per household per week given an average number of persons per household of 2.44.

Per capita expenditure on convenience foods rose by 5 per cent in 1996, mainly due to a 4 per cent rise in the volume of convenience foods purchased (Figure 2.3). Per capita expenditure on non-seasonal, non-convenience foods rose by an average of 7 per cent almost entirely due to an increase in the average price paid for such food. Further details of the average prices paid for individual food items are given in Appendix Table B2.

Table 2.2 Family Expenditure Survey estimates of expenditure on food in the United Kingdom

	1995	1996	% change
Expenditure on household food [a]	39.93	42.28	6
Average number of persons per household	2.44	2.46	1
Estimated expenditure per person per week	16.36	17.19	5

(a) £ per household per week spent on food including soft drinks, chocolate and sugar confectionery.

Source: Office for National Statistics, The Family Expenditure Survey.

Figure 2.3 Percentage changes in expenditure, prices and quantity of food in 1996, compared with 1995

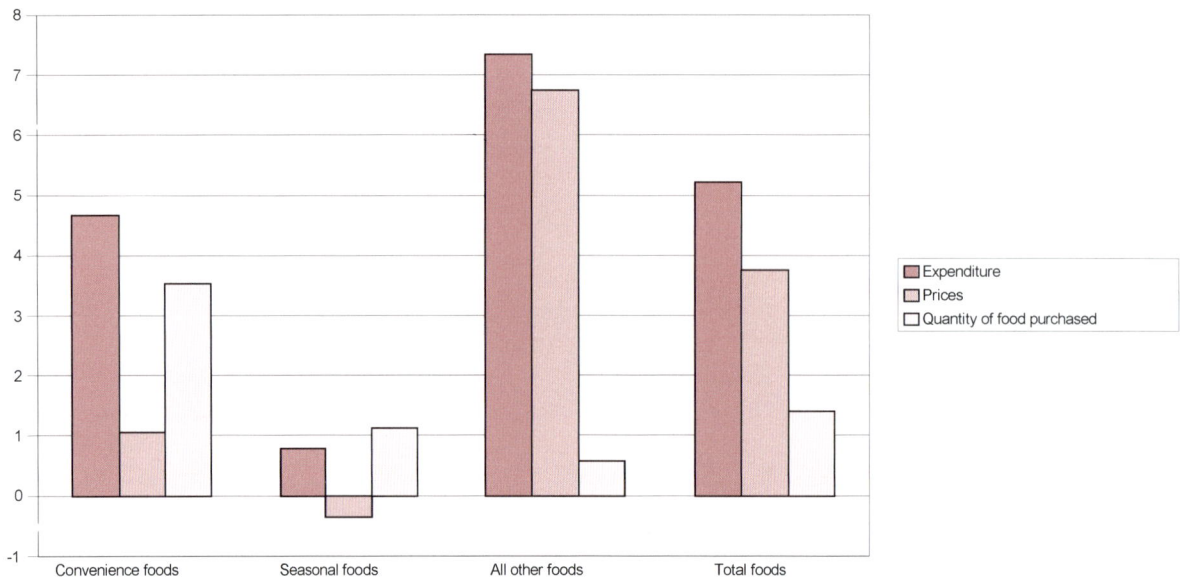

National Averages

This sub-section gives 1996 consumption and expenditure results for Great Britain with comparisons with those for 1986 and 1995 (Tables 2.4 to 2.13 and Table B1). Household spending on all major categories of food, with the exception of milk and cream, rose between 1995 and 1996 (Table 2.4). There were increases of between 10 per cent and 12 per cent on cheese, confectionery and sugar and preserves. The increase for confectionery was almost entirely due to higher consumption whilst in the other two cases higher prices were the main component of the increase. Fish was the only food group to show a fall (of 4 per cent) in the average price paid in 1996 and this was accompanied by a 7 per cent increase in consumption to its highest level for over twenty years. Cereals and alcoholic drink consumption also increased but that of soft drinks declined by 3 per cent as the prices paid rose. There was virtually no change in the consumption of meat and meat products despite a rise in prices paid. Consumption of milk and cream fell by 3 per cent. Further details of changes by individual food types are given in the following paragraphs.

Table 2.4 Consumption and expenditure for main food groups

per person per week

		Consumption			Expenditure		
		1986	1995	1996	1986	1995	1996
		(grams)[a]			(pence)		
Milk and cream	(ml or eq ml)	2360	2170	2106	103.8	141.8	138.8
Cheese		118	108	111	33.9	48.9	53.8
Meat and meat products		1051	945	943	284.6	360.9	384.4
Fish		146	144	154	50.4	72.8	75.0
Eggs	(no)	3.01	1.85	1.87	20.2	17.4	18.4
Fats and oils		297	218	227	36.1	36.6	39.7
Sugar and preserves		284	177	185	17.6	17.2	19.3
Vegetables		2447	2061	2118	127.5	215.2	220.1
Fruit		873	996	1023	70.0	109.4	116.3
Cereals (incl' bread)		1557	1468	1561	159.7	244.6	264.9
Beverages		78	63	64	43.6	44.7	46.3
Miscellaneous		na	na	na	39.0	69.8	74.5
Total food		na	na	na	£9.86	£13.79	£14.51
Soft drinks	(ml)	413	907	884	17.7	49.2	50.8
Alcoholic drinks	(ml)	na	365	386	na	108.5	114.5
Confectionery		na	53	58	na	26.7	29.6
Total all food and drink (GB)		na	na	na	na	£15.63	£16.46
Total all food (UK)		na	na	na	na	na	£14.53
Total all food and drink (UK)		na	na	na	na	na	£16.46

(a) except where otherwise stated

Figure 2.5 Composition of expenditure on household food and drink, 1996

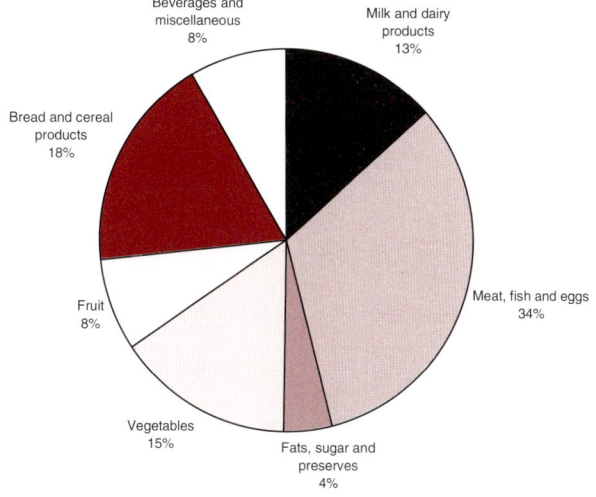

Milk, cream and cheese

Over the ten years from 1986, household consumption of liquid whole milk fell from 3 pints per person per week to around 1.3 pints, a fall of 57 per cent, including an estimated fall of 9 per cent in 1996. In the same period, low-fat milk consumption rose from 0.7 pints to almost 2 pints. Cheese consumption was up 3 per cent on 1995 but down 6 per cent on 1986.

Table 2.6 Consumption and expenditure for milk and cheese

per person per week

		Consumption			Expenditure		
		1986	1995	1996	1986	1995	1996
		(grams)[a]			(pence)		
MILK AND CREAM							
Liquid whole milk, full price	(ml)	1676	778	714[b]	68.6	41.9	37.2[b]
Welfare and school milk	(ml)	52	33	26	...	0.3	0.3
Low fat milks	(ml)	398	1103	1108[b]	15.9	57.3	56.8[b]
Dairy desserts and other milk	(ml or eq ml)	139	114	113	5.8	12.9	13.6
Yoghurt and fromage frais	(ml)	78	127	128	9.6	25.2	26.0
Cream	(ml)	15	14	18	3.9	4.0	5.0
Total milk and cream, (GB)		**2360**	**2170**	**2106**	**103.8**	**141.8**	**138.8**
Total milk and cream, (UK)		**na**	**na**	**2106**	**na**	**na**	**139.0**
CHEESE							
Natural		110	98	99	31.3	44.4	47.9
Processed		8	10	12	2.6	4.6	5.9
Total cheese, (GB)		**118**	**108**	**111**	**33.9**	**48.9**	**53.8**
Total cheese, (UK)		**na**	**na**	**110**	**na**	**na**	**53.4**

(a) except where otherwise stated
(b) these data are estimated because the straight Survey results contained an element of miscoding. No other tables in this report have been adjusted for this

Meat, fish and eggs

Household consumption of carcase meat fell by 3 per cent in 1996, with a 17 per cent reduction in beef and veal partially offset by an increase in mutton and lamb, up 22 per cent. The fall for beef and veal compares with an average annual percentage rate of fall of 7 per cent between 1986 and 1995. There were increases in the purchase of uncooked poultry (up 8 per cent) and pork (up 3 per cent) despite significant increases in price of 18 per cent and 19 per cent respectively. The main reason for these changes in meat consumption and expenditure was the announcement of a possible link between Bovine Spongiform Encephalopathy and Creutzfeldt-Jakob Disease on 20 March 1996.

Although fish consumption was at its highest for over twenty years, purchases of pre-cooked fish fell. Despite a 5 per cent increase in the price paid for eggs, consumption did not fall in 1996. Nevertheless consumption has fallen by 38 per cent since 1986 when it averaged just over 3 eggs per person per week.

Table 2.7 Consumption and expenditure for meat, fish and eggs

		Consumption			Expenditure	per person per week
		1986	1995	1996	1986	1995	1996
		(grams) [a]			(pence)		
MEAT							
Beef and veal		187	121	101	67.4	59.0	49.0
Mutton and lamb		86	54	66	24.1	22.5	28.7
Pork		103	71	73	27.6	25.0	30.4
Total carcase meat		**375**	**247**	**240**	**119.2**	**106.4**	**108.2**
Bacon and ham, uncooked		104	76	77	30.1	32.5	37.7
Poultry, uncooked		196	215	233	37.1	53.7	68.5
Other meat and meat products		376	407	393	98.2	168.3	169.9
Total meat, (GB)		**1051**	**945**	**943**	**165.4**	**360.9**	**384.4**
Total meat, (UK)		na	na	**944**	na	na	**385.6**
FISH							
Fresh		36	30	32	12.1	15.8	16.6
Processed and shell		16	16	18	7.1	11.3	12.4
Prepared including fish products		46	52	53	17.6	27.3	26.0
Frozen, including fish products		46	47	50	13.6	18.5	20.1
Total fish, (GB)		**146**	**144**	**154**	**50.4**	**72.8**	**75.0**
Total fish, (UK)		na	na	**153**	na	na	**74.7**
EGGS, (GB)	(no)	3.01	1.85	1.87	20.2	17.4	18.41
EGGS, (UK)	(no)	na	na	1.88	na	na	18.46

(a) except where otherwise stated

Fats and oils

A 12 per cent fall in the consumption of margarine was accompanied by increases in the consumption of butter (up 8%), low and reduced fat spreads (up 8%) and vegetable and salad oils (up 12%). Overall consumption of oils and fats rose by 4 per cent in 1996. This increase and that for butter were the first for over ten years.

Table 2.8 Consumption and expenditure for fats and oils

	Consumption			Expenditure	per person per week	
	1986	1995	1996	1986	1995	1996
	(grams) [a]			(pence)		
FATS:						
Butter	64	36	39	12.9	10.5	11.9
Margarine	116	41	36	10.8	4.5	3.9
Low fat and reduced fat spreads [b]	31	72	79	4.9	13.2	14.4
Vegetable and salad oils (ml)	39	49	55	3.2	5.6	6.9
Other fats and oils (mainly lard)	48	20	16	4.2	2.9	2.6
Total fats, (GB)	**297**	**218**	**227**	**36.1**	**36.6**	**39.7**
Total fats, (UK)	na	na	**227**	na	na	**39.9**

(a) except where otherwise stated
(b) reduced fat spreads included in other fats and oils in 1986

Sugar and preserves

The average household consumption of sugar and preserves rose by 5 per cent in 1996 due to the first increase in sugar consumption (purchases) for twenty years in spite of a 9 per cent increase in price. Nevertheless consumption of sugar only recovered to its 1994 level.

Table 2.9 Consumption and expenditure for sugar and preserves

	Consumption			Expenditure		*per person per week*
	1986	1995	1996	1986	1995	1996
	(grams)			(pence)		
SUGAR AND PRESERVES:						
Sugar	228	136	144	11.3	9.6	11.1
Honey, preserves, syrup and treacle	57	41	41	6.3	7.6	8.2
Total sugar and preserves, (GB)	284	177	185	17.6	17.2	19.3
Total sugar and preserves, (UK)	na	na	185	na	na	19.4

Vegetables and fruit

Household consumption of fresh potatoes rose only marginally in 1996 despite a 19 per cent fall in price. Consumption was 27 per cent lower than ten years ago. Consumption of fresh green vegetables rose by 4 per cent but was 26 per cent lower than in 1986. Consumption of frozen potato products (including frozen chips) rose by 14 per cent in 1996 with a 6 per cent fall in price. In contrast, consumption of other frozen vegetables fell 7 per cent with a 12 per cent rise in price. There was a 13 per cent fall in the consumption of chips (non-frozen) with a 10 per cent increase in price but this was more than offset by a 21 per cent increase in the consumption of crisps and other non-frozen potato products (excluding instant and canned potatoes). Compared to 1986, consumption of potato products, both frozen and non-frozen, was much higher in 1996 but consumption of other processed vegetables, both frozen and non-frozen, was lower. Consumption of fresh fruit was up 2 per cent in 1996 and fruit juices by 6 per cent. Other fruit products, including canned fruit, however, continued their gradual decline seen since 1986.

Table 2.10 Consumption and expenditure for vegetables and fruit

		Consumption			Expenditure		*per person per week*
		1986	1995	1996	1986	1995	1996
		(grams) [a]			(pence)		
VEGETABLES:							
Fresh potatoes		1100	803	805	21.4	38.4	31.3
Fresh green		315	225	233	16.4	26.6	27.5
Other fresh		477	470	489	34.9	55.9	57.3
Frozen potato products		68	99	113	4.6	12.4	13.3
Other frozen, including vegetable products		110	101	94	10.7	14.6	15.2
Other potato products		57	89	92	16.9	35.3	40.2
Other processed, including vegetable products		321	275	293	22.5	32.0	35.3
Total vegetables, (GB)		2447	2061	2118	127.4	215.2	220.1
Total vegetables, (UK)		na	na	2126	na	na	219.8
FRUIT:							
Fresh		576	672	686	45.5	75.9	79.6
Fruit juices	(ml)	194	244	258	11.2	18.1	20.0
Other fruit products		103	80	79	13.3	15.4	16.7
Total fruit, (GB)		873	996	1,023	70.0	109.4	116.3
Total fruit, (UK)		na	na	1,016	na	na	115.8

(a) except where otherwise stated

Bread, cereals and cereal products

After falling between 1986 and 1991, total household bread consumption remained fairly constant and again showed little change in 1996 (Table 2.11). Within the total, purchases of brown loaves decreased in 1996 while purchases of wholemeal loaves recovered slightly after falling in recent years.

Table 2.11 Consumption and expenditure for bread, cereals and cereal products

	Consumption			Expenditure		per person per week
	1986	1995	1996	1986	1995	1996
	(grams)			(pence)		
BREAD:						
White bread	470	443	441	26.3	27.2	28.9
Brown bread	107	80	71	7.7	7.1	6.3
Wholemeal bread	153	93	99	10.5	7.7	8.1
Other bread (includes rolls and prepared sandwiches)	144	139	142	15.9	26.9	27.7
Total bread, GB	**873**	**756**	**752**	**60.3**	**68.9**	**71.0**
Total bread, UK	**na**	**na**	**757**	**na**	**na**	**71.7**
OTHER CEREALS AND CEREAL PRODUCTS:						
Flour	117	57	70	3.7	2.3	2.7
Cakes and pastries	72	85	87	17.6	27.6	28.9
Buns, scones and tea-cakes	30	36	47	4.6	7.4	9.7
Biscuits	154	135	150	25.7	34.2	39.3
Oatmeal and oat products	16	11	13	2.0	1.2	1.6
Breakfast cereals	124	135	140	19.3	34.1	36.2
Cereal convenience foods	93	134	149	19.5	47.4	49.6
Other cereals	78	117	155	9.1	21.3	25.9
Total cereals including bread, GB	**1557**	**1468**	**1561**	**159.7**	**244.6**	**264.9**
Total cereals, including bread, UK	**na**	**na**	**1566**	**na**	**na**	**266.2**

Consumption of each of the main cereal products, other than bread, rose in 1996 (Table 2.11) and consumption of most of them was much higher than it was ten years ago. However, in the case of flour, particularly, but also biscuits and oatmeal, consumption was lower than ten years earlier.

Beverages and miscellaneous foods

Household consumption of tea and coffee changed little in 1996, (Table 2.12). Consumption of mineral water showed a decrease on the exceptionally high level seen in 1995 but, helped by another warm, sunny summer in 1996 the level was much higher than in all other years. Consumption of ice cream and ice-cream products was also high in both 1995 and 1996.

Table 2.12 Consumption and expenditure for beverages and miscellaneous foods

per person per week

		Consumption			Expenditure		
		1986	1995	1996	1986	1995	1996
		(grams) [a]			(pence)		
BEVERAGES:							
Tea		49	39	38	17.9	18.2	18.1
Coffee		20	16	17	23.3	23.1	24.2
Cocoa and drinking chocolate		5	2	3	1.3	0.8	1.3
Branded food drinks		4	5	5	1.1	2.5	2.7
Total beverages, (GB)		**78**	**63**	**64**	**43.6**	**44.7**	**46.3**
Total beverages, (UK)		**na**	**na**	**64**	**na**	**na**	**46.0**
MISCELLANEOUS:							
Mineral water	(ml)	15	109	104	0.6	4.6	4.4
Soups, canned, dehydrated and powdered		77	67	75	7.3	9.3	10.9
Pickles and sauces		62	80	84	7.9	17.5	19.3
Ice-cream and ice-cream products	(ml)	87	108	107	7.6	15.7	15.7
Other foods [b]		na	na	na	15.7	22.7	24.2
Total miscellaneous, (GB)		**na**	**na**	**na**	**39.0**	**69.8**	**74.5**
Total miscellaneous, (UK)		**na**	**na**	**na**	**na**	**na**	**74.4**

(a) except where otherwise stated
(b) including spreads, salt and other miscellaneous food items

Drinks and confectionery brought home

As with other estimates in this section, estimates for drinks and confectionery shown in Table 2.13 refer only to household consumption and exclude those casual purchases not taken home or not brought to the attention of the main diary-keeper or the interviewer. Although consumption of all soft drinks was 3 per cent lower in 1996, consumption in 1995 was exceptionally high due to the hot summer. Despite the fall from 1995, consumption in 1996 was still much higher than in all other years.

The volume of alcoholic drinks consumed in the home increased by 6 per cent in 1996, with most of the increase coming from lager and beer. Consumption of cider and perry, which during 1995 and 1996 included alcoholic carbonates (Alco-pops), showed an increase of 9 per cent. In 1997 alcoholic carbonates are being coded separately from cider and perry.

Consumption of chocolate and sugar confectionery brought home rose by 9 per cent in 1996, mainly due to an increase for chocolate confectionery.

Table 2.13 Consumption and expenditure for drinks and confectionery brought home

per person per week

	Consumption			Expenditure		
	1986	1995	1996	1986	1995	1996
	(millilitres)			(pence)		
SOFT DRINKS [a]						
Concentrated	98	104	103	6.0	9.1	9.6
Unconcentrated	261	514	490	9.6	25.1	25.5
Low-calorie concentrated	na	40	34	na	3.2	2.7
Low-calorie unconcentrated [b]	54	248	257	2.1	11.9	12.9
All soft drinks, (GB) [c]	**805**	**1482**	**1432**	**17.7**	**49.2**	**50.8**
All soft drinks, (UK) [c]	**na**	**na**	**1443**	**na**	**na**	**51.5**
ALCOHOLIC DRINKS:						
Lager and beer [d]	na	191	200	na	29.4	31.9
Wine	na	110	111	na	43.9	45.3
Other	na	64	74	na	35.2	37.2
Total alcoholic drinks, (GB)	**na**	**365**	**386**	**na**	**108.5**	**114.5**
Total alcoholic drinks, (UK)	**na**	**na**	**380**	**na**	**na**	**112.9**
	(grams)			(pence)		
CONFECTIONERY						
Chocolate confectionery	na	37	41	na	19.5	21.9
Mints and boiled sweets	na	13	14	na	5.8	6.0
Other	na	2	4	na	1.3	1.6
Total confectionery, (GB)	**na**	**53**	**58**	**na**	**26.7**	**29.6**
Total confectionery, (UK)	**na**	**na**	**58**	**na**	**na**	**29.4**

(a) excluding pure fruit juices which are recorded in the Survey under fruit products.
(b) includes low calorie concentrated soft drinks in 1986.
(c) converted to unconcentrated equivalent.
(d) including low alcohol lager and beers.

Meals eaten outside the home

Figures for the number of meals bought and eaten outside of the home are recorded in Table 2.14 and Appendix Table B3. There is evidence to suggest that these data were under recorded in the first quarter of 1996 when a new contractor took over the running of the Survey. The data shown for 1996 are therefore based on the twelve months period April 1996 to March 1997. The average number of meals eaten out per person per week was slightly lower in 1996 than in recent years. Data is also recorded on the source of mid-day meals for children aged 5 to 14 years. The results (Figure 2.15) continue to show a decline in school meals over the last twenty years and more mid-day meals being taken out of household supplies.

Table 2.14 Number of meals out (not from household supply)

per person per week

	1976	1986	1995	1996
Mid-day meals out	1.72	1.73	1.77	1.73[a]
All meals out [b]	2.97	3.37	2.94	2.92

(a) based on April 1996 to March 1997, see text
(b) based on a pattern of three meals consumed a day

Figure 2.15 Average number of mid-day meals per week per child aged 5 to 14 years by source of meal, 1976 to 1996

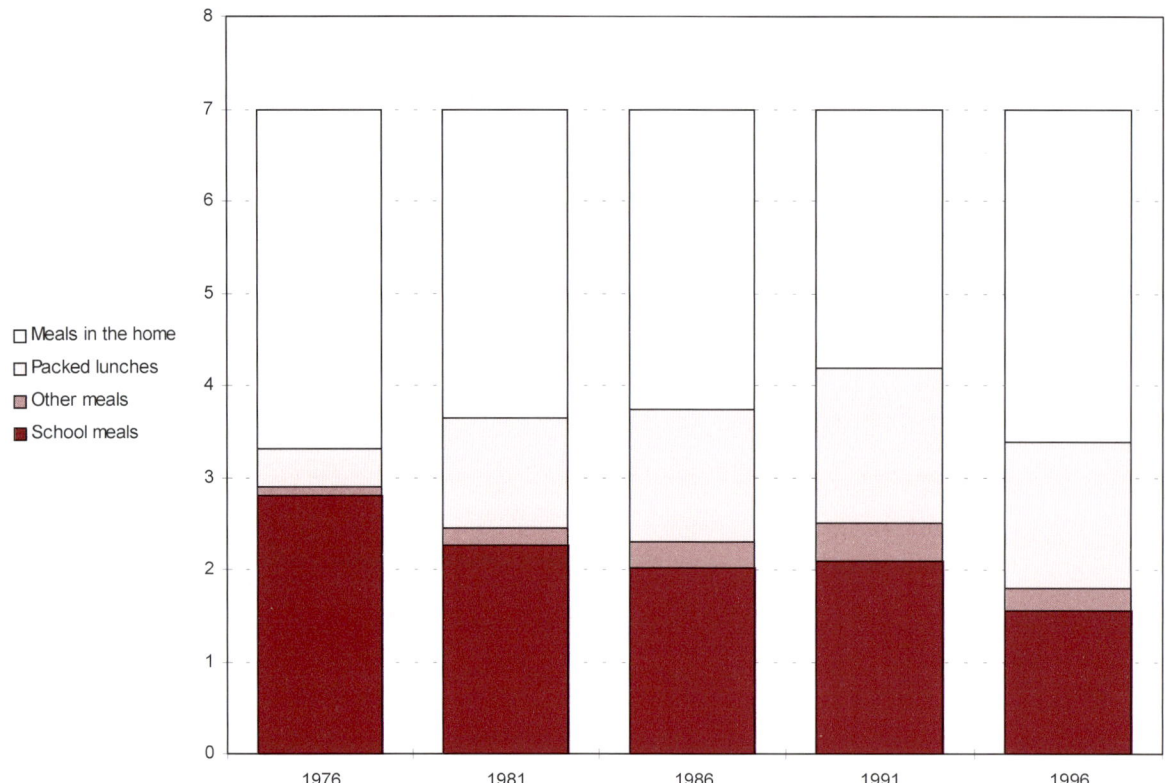

Regional Comparisons

The National Food Survey is designed to be representative of the United Kingdom as a whole, but it also provides regional comparisons. Practical considerations limit the number of separate areas from each region which can be surveyed in any one year (see Appendix A for the structure of the Survey) and, for this reason, comparisons between regions, and, in particular, comparisons between years for the same region, must be interpreted with a degree of caution. Differences in relative prices and in various other factors including the propensity to eat away from the home also affect the comparisons. These are discussed in the special analysis by region given in Section 5.

Regional figures for total weekly expenditure on household food ranged from £13.48 per person in the Yorkshire and Humberside region to £15.21 in the South East / East Anglia region (Table 2.16). Expenditure on drinks and confectionery ranged from £1.51 per person per week in Northern Ireland to £ 2.31 in Scotland.

Some of the most significant regional variations in 1996 (taking account of similar patterns in 1994 and 1995 and the importance of the food in terms of expenditure) include high consumption of carcase meat especially pork, vegetables (fresh potatoes) and beverages (tea) in the West Midlands; fresh fruit in the South East / East Anglia region; alcoholic drinks in the East Midlands and the North West and soft drinks in Scotland.

Low consumption levels (relative to the national average) have been recorded for cheese and sugar and preserves in the North region and vegetables and beverages in Scotland.

Based solely on the one year available (1996), consumption in Northern Ireland was higher than other regions for carcase meat, eggs, fats and oils, vegetables and bread. Consumption was lower for cheese, fish, fruit, all drinks and confectionery (eaten at home).

Apart from Northern Ireland, Scotland recorded the highest consumption of beef and veal in 1996 but the lowest of lamb, pork and uncooked poultry (Figure 2.17). The largest consumer of lamb per person per week was the South East/East Anglia region; pork the East Midlands and Wales and uncooked poultry the North West region. The West Midlands was amongst the largest consumers of each of the four meats in 1996 while the North region was amongst the smallest on each.

Table 2.16 Consumption and expenditure for selected foods, by region, 1996

per person per week

		Regions of England							England	Wales	Scotland	N Ireland
		North	Yorkshire and Humberside	North West	East Midlands	West Midlands	South West	South East/ East Anglia				
CONSUMPTION					(grams)(a)							
Milk and cream	(ml)	2012	2124	2195	2151	2017	2147	2060	2094	2153	2181	2114
Cheese		99	105	107	125	113	116	114	112	107	108	73
Carcase meat		198	221	252	245	266	217	254	243	241	213	289
Other meat and meat products		699	689	780	694	723	669	673	698	729	729	702
Fish		140	161	154	146	154	134	163	155	147	151	131
Eggs	(no)	1.90	2.05	1.82	1.78	1.88	1.91	1.83	1.87	1.80	1.99	2.19
Fats and oils		207	219	200	273	238	230	232	229	226	209	261
Sugar and Preserves		168	190	181	184	210	216	172	184	200	179	189
Vegetables		1994	2110	2037	2196	2269	2185	2152	2141	2153	1899	2422
Of which:												
Fresh potatoes		719	829	852	803	876	877	772	810	862	725	1327
Fresh green vegetables		206	222	193	235	287	246	260	242	221	159	182
Other fresh vegetables		486	456	521	519	490	507	535	498	456	433	400
Processed vegetables		583	603	571	639	616	555	585	591	614	582	513
Fruit		940	856	962	1084	987	1020	1136	1035	1038	900	702
Bread		784	751	800	764	816	714	685	740	798	830	952
Other cereals		750	822	757	875	770	758	884	824	738	709	835
Beverages		58	58	62	60	75	70	66	65	65	58	49
Soft drinks	(ml)	1355	1266	1475	1471	1565	1283	1431	1422	1500	1515	1770
Alcoholic drinks	(ml)	394	354	460	470	386	351	349	384	357	425	144
Confectionery		59	57	57	60	60	59	56	58	72	55	46
EXPENDITURE					(pence)							
Milk and cream		132.1	137.7	147.6	133.4	130.0	137.9	141.5	138.9	140.9	136.6	145.9
Cheese		46.4	47.2	49.8	58.7	55.6	54.7	58.0	54.4	49.8	51.3	37.2
Carcase meat		87.7	99.0	119.1	103.9	117.0	97.7	112.2	108.4	104.8	108.4	145.2
Other meat and meat products		266.0	253.5	292.5	265.6	276.4	247.8	275.4	271.4	283.5	314.3	290.8
Fish		68.9	72.7	74.2	68.4	73.0	65.8	82.1	75.2	68.6	78.1	60.9
Eggs		18.5	18.3	17.0	16.9	17.4	18.3	19.5	18.4	17.0	19.6	20.6
Fats and oils		35.4	34.9	38.0	41.4	41.8	41.3	41.2	39.8	41.8	37.2	51.1
Sugar and preserves		18.7	18.7	17.1	19.4	20.4	24.6	19.0	19.4	20.0	17.8	24.1
Vegetables		213.9	203.3	209.3	220.4	220.5	207.9	238.0	222.1	218.0	203.2	206.3
Fruit		104.1	91.6	104.5	116.4	109.3	118.3	135.8	118.1	114.6	101.3	95.4
Bread		79.8	71.3	79.6	66.2	69.5	64.8	65.9	69.7	72.8	80.9	103.5
Other cereals		194.3	188.6	192.0	200.5	178.2	186.9	204.1	195.2	183.2	189.7	216.4
Beverages		44.7	43.0	46.7	44.4	48.2	50.9	46.4	46.4	46.8	44.3	35.8
Other foods		64.7	67.9	75.5	72.7	66.7	71.1	82.1	74.8	73.8	72.5	68.5
Total food		**£13.75**	**£13.48**	**£14.63**	**£14.28**	**£14.24**	**£13.88**	**£15.21**	**£14.52**	**£14.36**	**£14.55**	**£15.02**
Soft drinks		48.7	41.0	51.8	46.3	51.2	40.6	52.0	48.9	51.8	67.6	78.7
Alcoholic drinks		114.4	89.8	126.6	124.8	109.2	106.5	113.4	112.8	103.4	136.9	48.7
Confectionery		28.2	26.0	30.0	30.7	29.1	28.4	29.7	29.2	39.0	26.8	23.9
Total all food and drink		**£15.67**	**£15.05**	**£16.71**	**£16.30**	**£16.14**	**£15.64**	**£17.16**	**£16.43**	**£16.30**	**£16.87**	**£16.53**

(a) except where otherwise stated

Figure 2.17 Consumption of carcase meat and uncooked poultry by regions, 1996

Grams per person per week

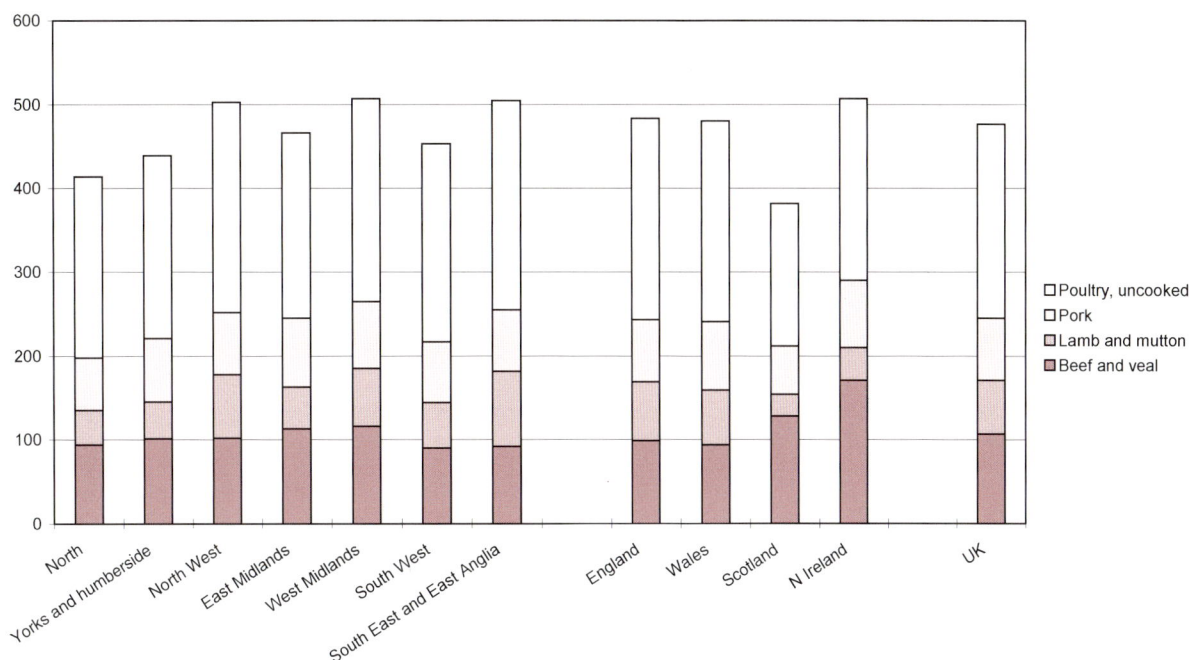

Figure 2.18 Consumption of vegetables by regions, 1996

Grams per person per week

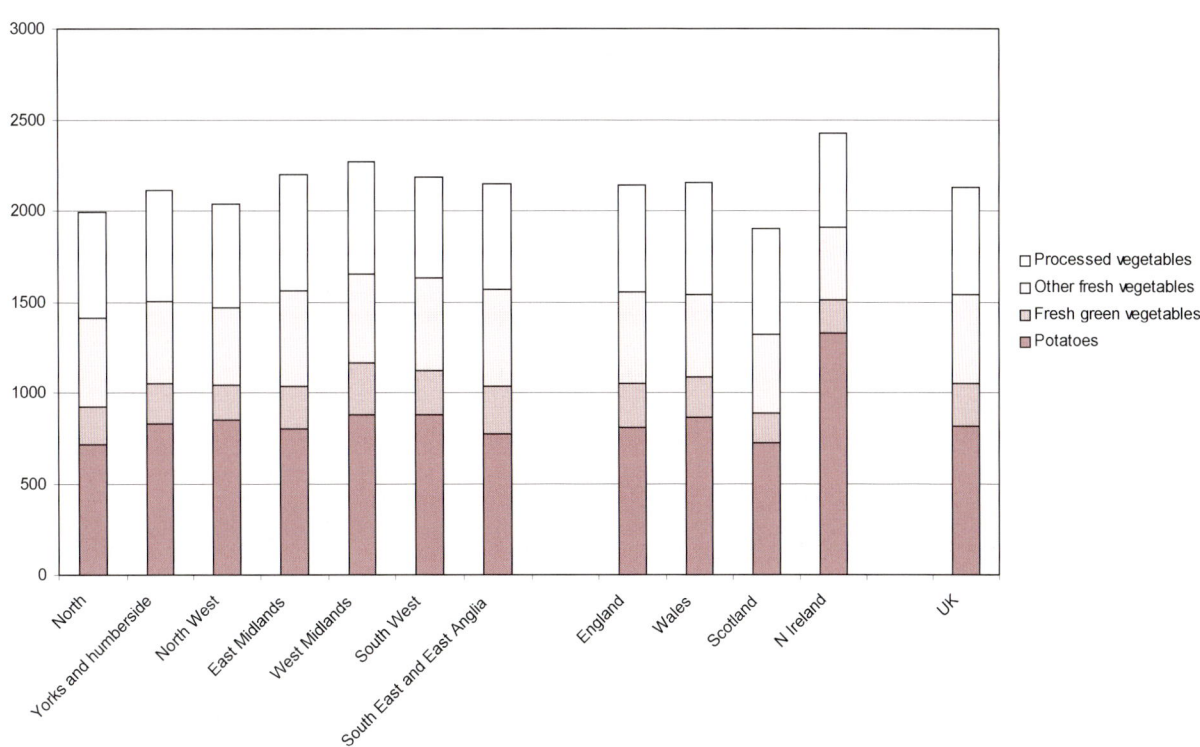

Northern Ireland and Scotland consumed relatively small amounts of each of the four types of vegetable shown in Figure 2.18. The exception to this was the high level of consumption of fresh potatoes in Northern Ireland. The North West region also consumed low levels of vegetables except fresh potatoes. No region was a high consumer on all four types of vegetable but the West Midland region (except other fresh vegetables) and the South West region (except processed vegetables) were high on three out of the four. A more detailed analysis by region in recent years is given in Section 5.

Income Group Comparisons

Average household consumption and expenditure for different head of household (HOH) income groups in 1996 is shown in Table 2.19. The sample distribution of households by income group always differs slightly from the target distribution and from that of previous years. This means that estimates of food consumption and expenditure will not always be entirely comparable with those of earlier years. Some consistent patterns of food purchasing between households with differing levels of income are, however, revealed in the results which are given in more detail by type of food in Appendix Tables B5 and B6. The composition of the survey sample in terms of income groups is shown in Appendix Table A3.

Table 2.19 Consumption and expenditure for selected foods by income group, 1996

grams per person per week [a]

		INCOME GROUP [b]						
		Gross weekly income of head of household						
		Households with one or more earners				Households without an earner		
		A	B	C	D	E1	E2	OAP
CONSUMPTION								
Milk and cream	(ml or eq ml)	1967	1964	2058	2123	2468	2192	2481
Cheese		127	119	111	91	118	90	108
Meat and meat products		887	904	950	958	978	951	1074
Fish		164	136	139	139	213	156	224
Eggs	(no)	1.62	1.56	1.80	1.98	2.22	2.26	2.64
Fats and oils		184	190	223	249	283	238	331
Sugar and preserves		103	130	166	204	264	267	349
Fruit		1348	1070	883	795	1422	781	1208
Vegetables		1999	1948	2075	2171	2630	2198	2396
Of which:								
Fresh potatoes		625	664	818	871	1093	920	967
Fresh green vegetables		253	211	211	193	340	197	364
Other fresh vegetables		588	487	432	429	690	412	585
Processed vegetables		533	586	614	678	507	669	480
Cereals (including bread)		1441	1485	1598	1514	1635	1544	1797
Beverages		56	53	57	64	83	78	112
Other foods		611	450	372	349	468	373	372
Soft drinks	(ml)	979	922	964	888	758	832	504
Alcoholic drinks	(ml)	538	457	379	228	481	221	247
Confectionery		63	62	56	48	66	48	61

(a) except where otherwise stated.
(b) Definition: A £ 595 and over, B £310 and under £595, C £ 150 and under £310, D under £150, E1 £ 150 and over, E2 under £150.

Table 2.19 continued

pence per person per week

	INCOME GROUP (a)						
	Gross weekly income of head of household						
	Households with one or more earner				Households without an earner		
	A	B	C	D	E1	E2	OAP
EXPENDITURE							
Milk and cream	157.2	137.9	133.6	125.8	161.1	117.0	163.3
Cheese	69.8	59.0	50.8	41.1	60.7	39.3	53.9
Meat and meat products	449.6	399.0	370.4	331.7	415.0	323.2	418.1
Fish	99.1	67.3	64.7	59.4	116.6	64.6	108.7
Eggs	18.5	16.3	16.7	17.8	23.3	20.1	26.6
Fats and oils	39.8	36.4	36.6	36.3	53.5	35.8	58.6
Sugar and preserves	14.4	15.0	16.1	18.2	30.3	24.7	36.6
Fruit	183.8	122.8	94.8	78.7	170.5	81.3	136.1
Vegetables	275.2	235.0	209.9	190.7	238.3	185.7	202.9
Cereals (including bread)	309.6	279.0	258.0	223.2	279.5	220.5	276.1
Beverages	47.5	40.1	42.2	40.8	65.1	47.0	70.1
Other foods	97.0	82.5	68.8	60.9	85.1	58.4	67.7
Total food	**£17.62**	**£14.90**	**£13.63**	**£12.24**	**£16.99**	**£12.18**	**£16.18**
Soft drinks	67.8	56.8	52.9	46.0	41.9	41.9	27.4
Alcoholic drinks	203.7	132.9	93.3	64.0	195.2	52.5	84.5
Confectionery	35.4	32.2	28.3	23.9	34.1	23.3	27.6
Total food and drink (GB)	**£20.68**	**£17.12**	**£15.37**	**£13.58**	**£19.70**	**£13.35**	**£17.58**
Total food and drink (UK)	**£20.65**	**£17.10**	**£15.42**	**£13.58**	**£19.72**	**£13.39**	**£17.60**

(a) definition: A £595 and over, B £310 and under £595, C £150 and under £310, D under £150, E1 £150 and over, E2 under £150.

Expenditure on most food groups rose with income, this pattern being particularly marked for cheese, fish, fruit and alcoholic drinks. However spending on sugar and preserves declined with income group while for eggs and fats and oils there was no clear trend.

Pensioner households (OAP), were the largest consumers of eight out of the fifteen food types shown in Table 2.19. However consumption of cheese, "other foods" (including mineral waters, ice cream, soups and sauces), soft drinks and alcoholic drinks was highest in households with the head of household (HOH) in the top income earning bracket (A) and consumption of fresh potatoes, fresh vegetables and fruit was highest in households without an earner but receiving more than £150 per week in income (E1).

Lowest levels of consumption of nine of the food types occurred in the highest two income-earning brackets. The exceptions were cheese, fruit, alcoholic drinks and confectionery, consumption of which was least in the lowest (HOH) income group without an earner (E2); "other foods", in the lowest income earning group (D) and soft drinks in pensioner households.

Figure 2.20 Consumption and expenditure on fruit, by income group, 1996

Consumption (grams per person per week)

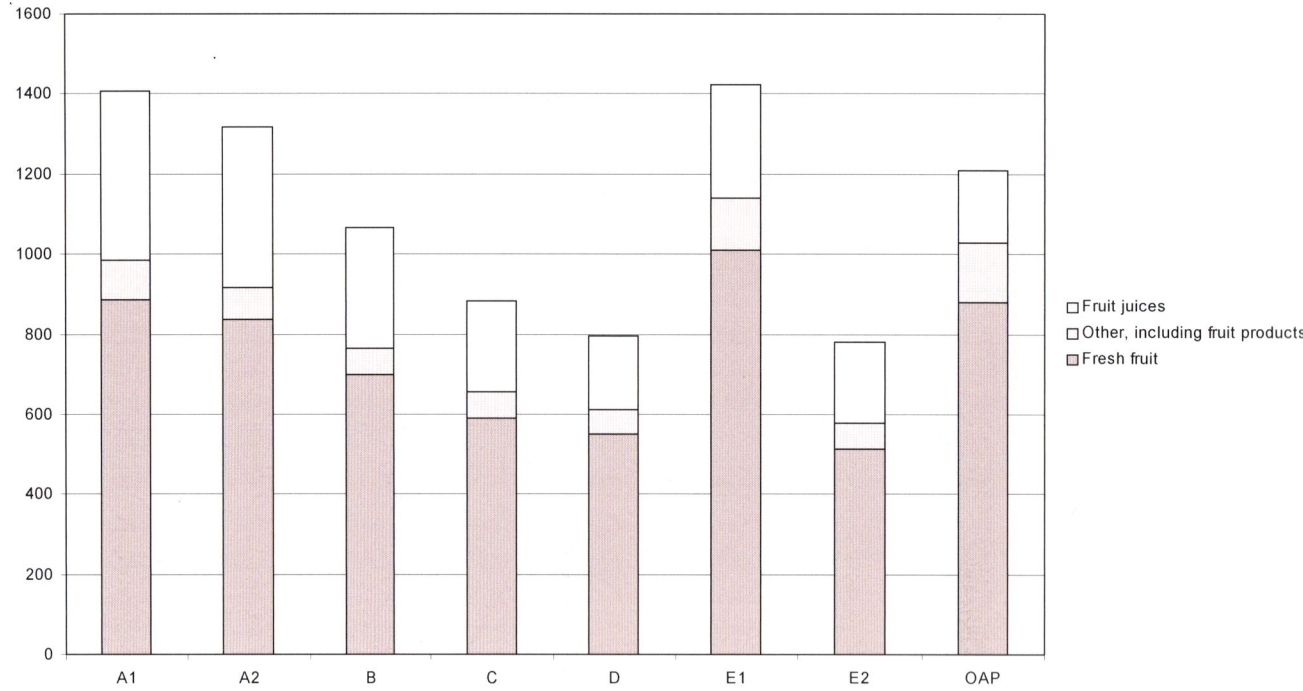

Expenditure (pence per person per week)

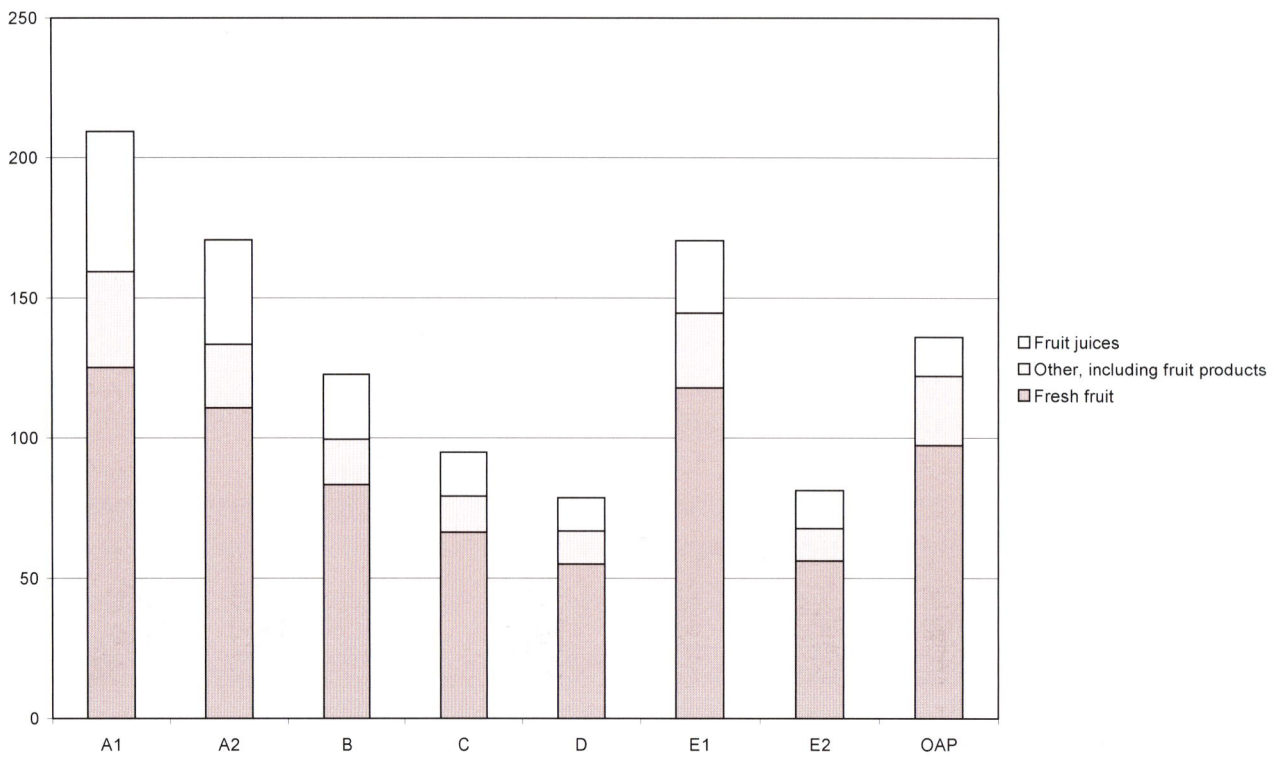

Figure 2.21 Consumption and expenditure on cereals, by income group, 1996

Consumption (grams per person per week)

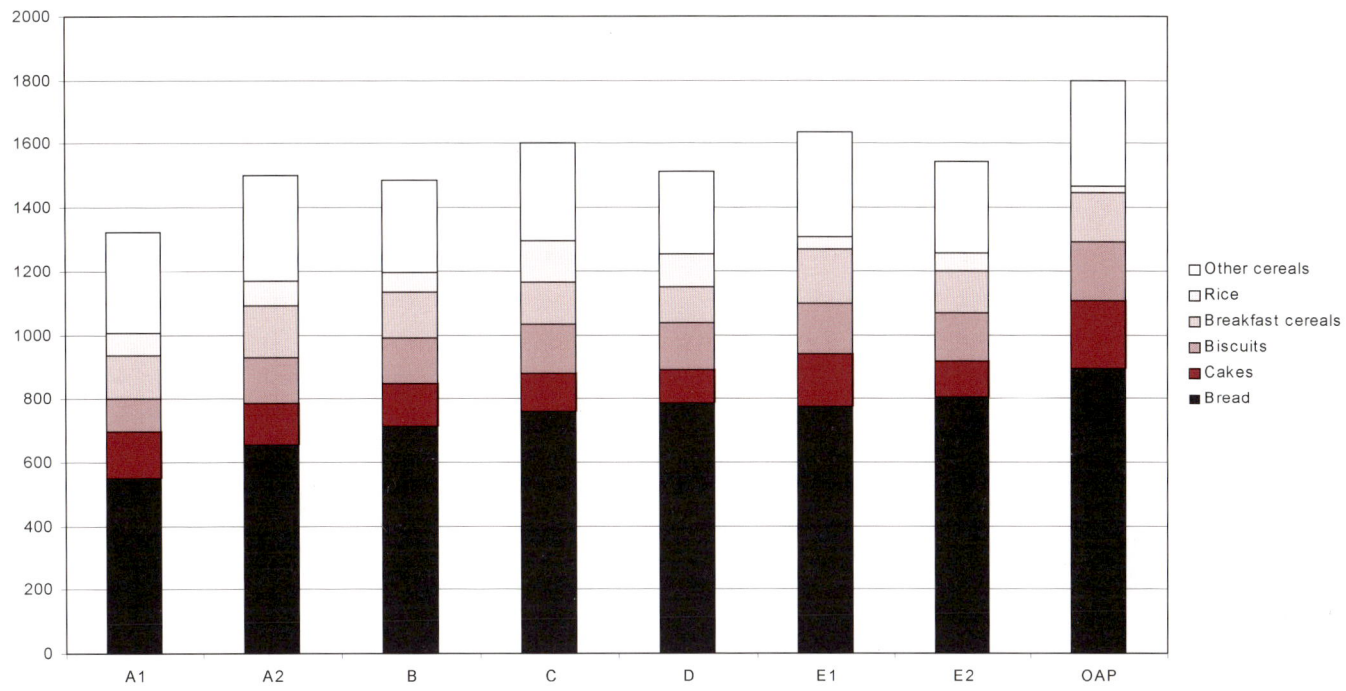

Expenditure (pence per person per week)

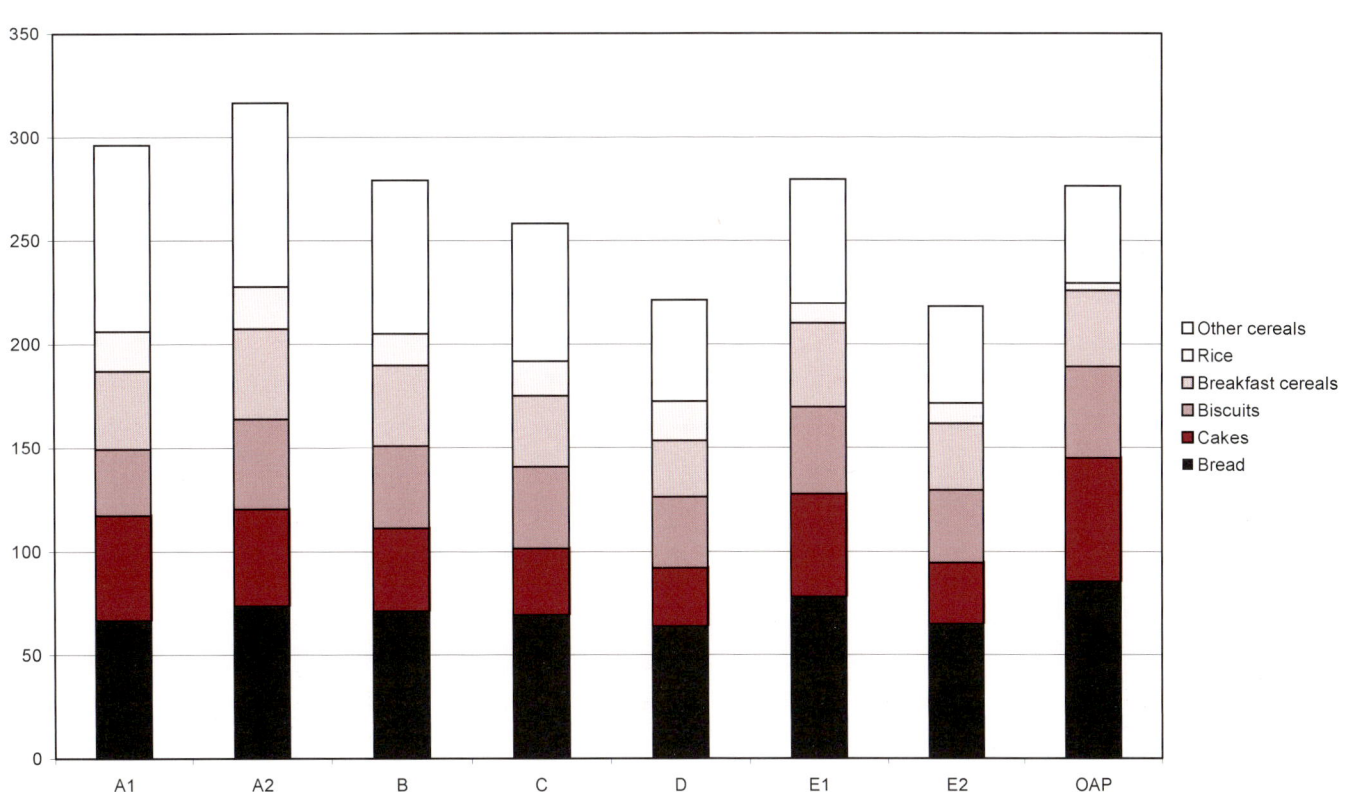

21

Figures 2.20 and 2.21 illustrate the different patterns of consumption and expenditure on selected foods, across income groups. For each of the three fruit categories, consumption generally increased with HOH income. The consumption of fresh fruit was highest for pensioner households and for those households without an earner but receiving more than £150 per week in income group (E1) and secondly for pensioner households (Figure 2.20). In contrast, pensioner households were the lowest consumers of fruit juice.

Pensioner households were the largest consumers of bread, biscuits and cakes and pastries and the smallest of rice (Figure 2.21). For other households, only bread showed a consistent trend with consumption decreasing with (HOH) income. Rice was similar in that the lowest levels of consumption were recorded for those in the top income brackets (A1, A2 and B). Consumption of cakes and pastries and of breakfast cereals generally increased with income, though in both cases, consumption by the highest income group (A1) was lower than by those in groups A2 and B.

Analysis by Household Composition

Table 2.22 Consumption of selected foods by household composition, 1996

grams per person per week [a]

Number of adults		1	1	2	2	2	2	2	3	3 or more	3 or more	4 or more
Number of children		0	1 or more	0	1	2	3	4 or more	0	1 or 2	3 or more	0
Milk and cream	ml or eq ml	2432	2124	2234	2070	2001	1914	1992	2047	2033	1957	1812
Cheese		131	82	137	100	96	86	54	138	103	80	106
Carcase meat		248	146	311	201	183	127	190	332	287	179	277
Other meat and meat products		812	608	805	667	609	535	618	827	647	584	750
Fish		227	112	207	116	103	94	91	189	132	216	145
Eggs	(no)	2.53	1.63	2.19	1.63	1.42	1.35	1.68	2.16	1.84	1.89	1.94
Fats and oils		261	167	291	179	171	162	141	275	250	202	248
Sugar and preserves		269	150	250	113	132	120	136	201	174	201	182
Fresh potatoes		853	768	957	721	659	655	793	991	733	644	795
Fresh green vegetables		312	122	351	184	159	119	94	276	200	153	225
Other fresh vegetables		624	268	657	435	373	310	368	550	448	356	501
Processed vegetables of which:		594	606	608	614	562	545	548	648	598	603	531
crisps and potato snacks		32	57	40	61	68	62	62	41	59	59	42
Fresh fruit		934	447	939	564	557	449	310	758	561	408	617
Fruit juices	(ml)	261	209	291	263	261	167	250	229	279	286	265
Other fruit and fruit products		113	34	198	51	58	42	39	88	53	62	74
Bread		919	673	864	702	639	574	611	869	739	513	723
Other cereals of which:		882	698	856	727	755	730	704	824	1083	707	632
breakfast cereals		160	140	149	123	145	132	144	118	131	144	118
biscuits, cakes, etc		353	245	326	253	270	244	187	302	253	225	231
Tea		56	30	53	31	24	20	24	47	34	19	39
Coffee		25	12	23	18	12	11	8	20	14	8	13
Other beverages		15	6	13	7	5	9	3	8	6	8	3
Other foods		466	335	494	411	401	305	307	474	400	287	307
Total food expenditure		£17.63	£10.59	£17.92	£13.44	£12.48	£10.18	£9.37	£16.98	£13.31	£9.76	£13.94
Soft drinks	(ml)	736	989	775	1040	1048	798	876	903	879	757	853
Alcoholic drinks	(ml)	482	130	545	432	310	268	182	399	249	90	420
Confectionery		59	54	64	57	61	52	52	59	62	44	32
Total food and drink expenditure (GB)		£20.00	£11.71	£20.46	£15.42	£14.18	£11.49	£10.40	£19.06	£14.93	£10.60	£15.90
Total food and drink expenditure (UK)		£20.06	£11.72	£20.48	£15.45	£14.20	£11.54	£10.51	£19.02	£14.90	£11.00	£15.92

(a) except where otherwise stated

The size and composition of a household has a significant effect on household food consumption and expenditure. Table 2.22 shows total expenditure per person per week and consumption for groups of foods classified by the numbers of adults and children in the household. Appendix Table B7 shows expenditure by household composition and detailed food type. Per capita expenditure on food was highest in households with one or two adults and no children, any further increase in household size resulting in lower average spending on food per capita.

Variations between food groups for adult-only households are illustrated in Figure 2.23. As in 1995, expenditure was slightly higher in two adult-only households than in single adult-only households. For milk, fish, sugar and preserves, cereals and beverages expenditure and consumption declined from one to four adults. For carcase meat and soft drinks, expenditure by adult-only households was lowest where there was only one adult.

Figure 2.23 Expenditure on main food groups per person, by number of people in adult only households, 1996

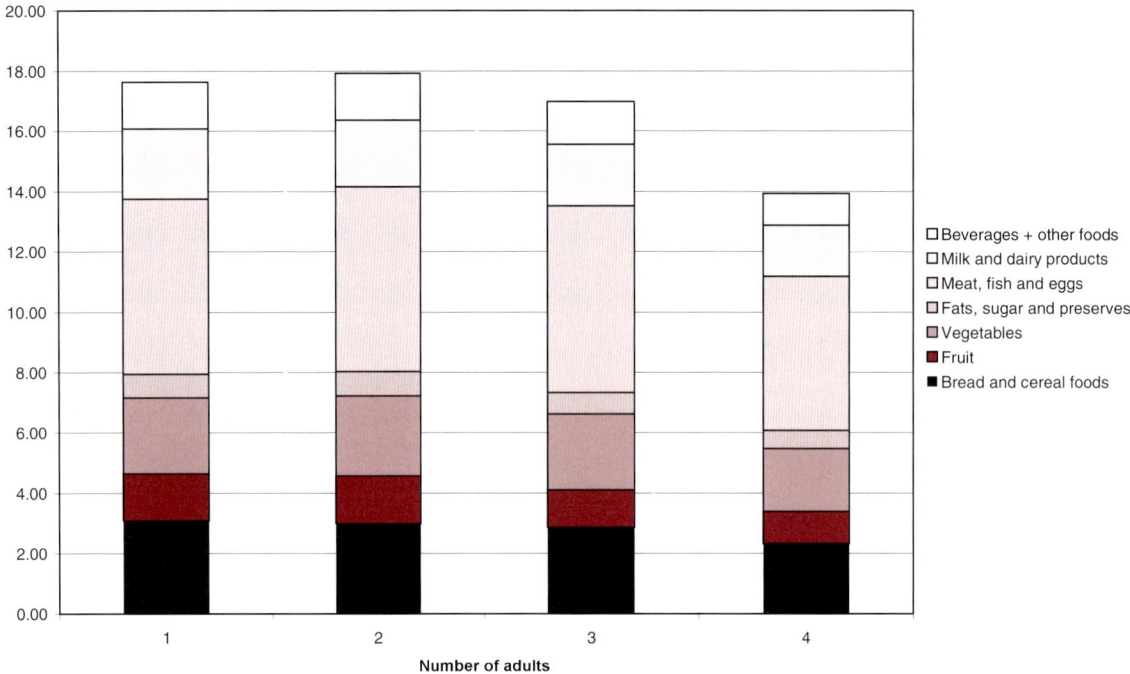

Figure 2.24 Expenditure on main food groups per person, by number of children in two adult households, 1996

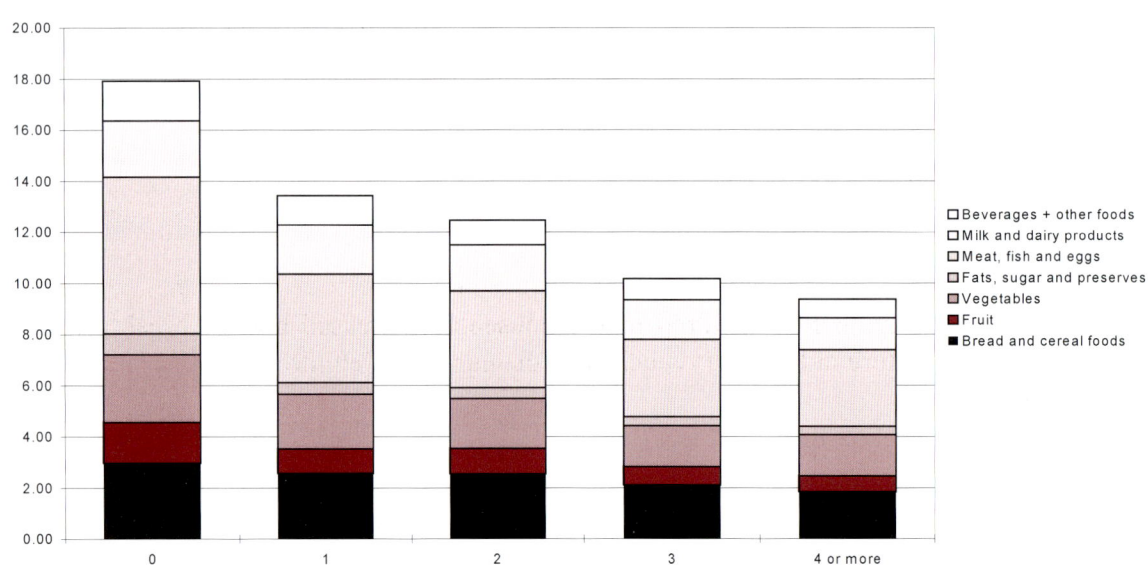

Figure 2.24 illustrates comparisons of expenditure between households with two adults and differing numbers of children. The greatest reduction in expenditure per person occurs between adult-only households and the households with one child, although as in 1995, spending on processed vegetables and soft drinks was higher in two adult households with one child than with no children. Per capita expenditure on most foods declined gradually with the addition of further children to the household.

Figure 2.25 Expenditure on cereals by household composition, 1996

pence per person per week

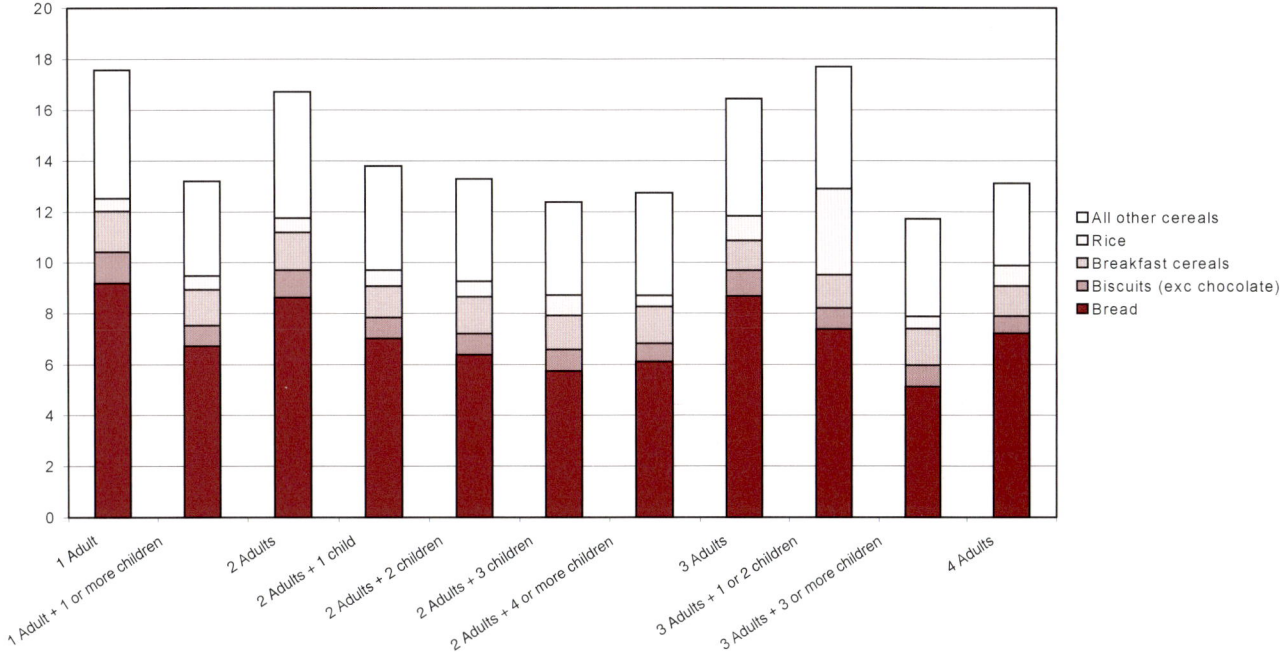

The reduced per capita expenditure observed in households with children may be attributed to various factors, including the lower food requirements of younger children, potential economies of scale, and reduced wastage in larger households. There may also be some effect due to lower, per capita, income being available for spending on each person, especially if the presence of children is associated with a decrease in the number of income-earning adults. As the relationship between household size and per capita expenditure may be influenced by a number of factors, the data do not lend themselves to simple interpretation.

In adult-only households, per capita expenditure on bread, cakes and pastries, biscuits and breakfast cereals decreased as the number of adults increased (Figure 2.25). For bread, cakes and pastries and biscuits, expenditure generally decreased as the number of children in the household increased but for breakfast cereals, expenditure did not vary much with the number of children.

Figure 2.26 Expenditure on alcoholic drinks by household composition, 1996

ml per person per week

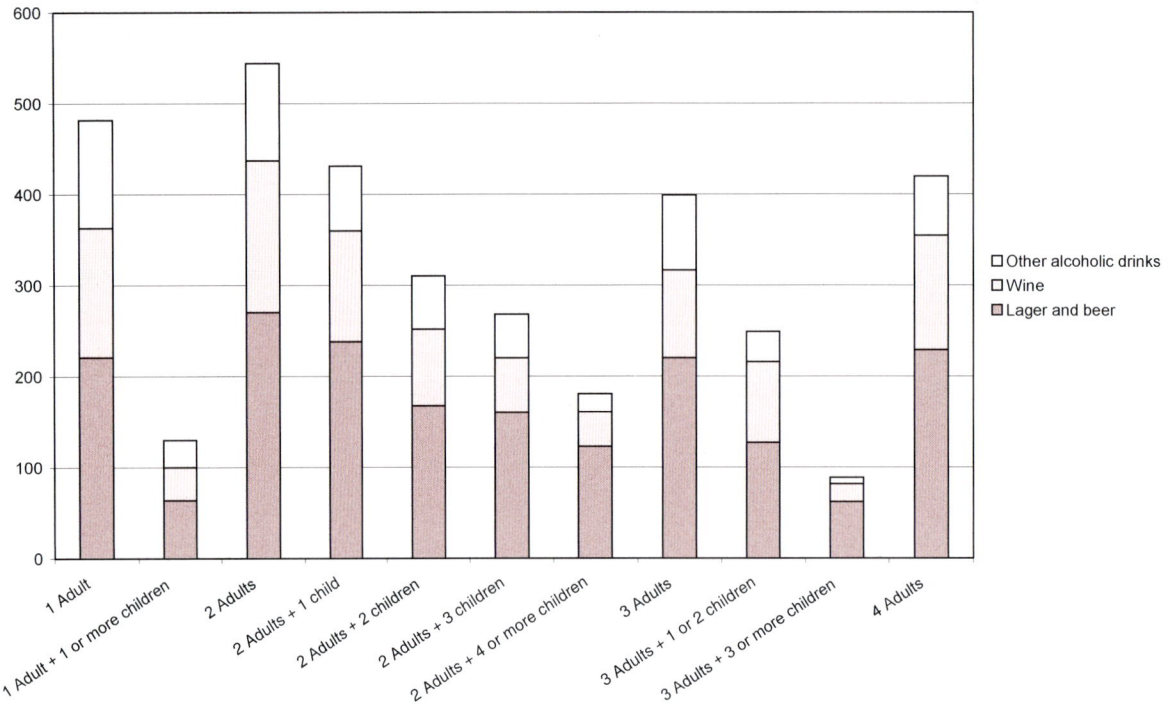

In adult-only households, per capita expenditure on wine was highest where there were two adults. This was also true for beer though, in that case, expenditure was virtually as high in households with four or more adults. Expenditure on beer, on wine and on other alcoholic drinks decreased with an increase in the number of children.

Analysis by Household Composition and Income

Average expenditure on household food showed greater variation per head between households of different composition, particularly those with and without children, than between those in the income groups illustrated in Figure 2.27, (see also Appendix Table B8). The decrease in per capita expenditure with declining income was least pronounced in households with three children. Except for the blip for high income households with 4 children, the reduction in per capita expenditure with increased number of children was more marked in higher income households. The highest average weekly expenditure per person on food and drink was £25.56 for adult-only households in income group A, whereas the lowest was £7.87 in two adult households with four, or more, children and classified to (HOH) income groups D and E2.

Figure 2.27 Household food expenditure per head, by certain household composition groups within income groups, 1996.

pence per person per week

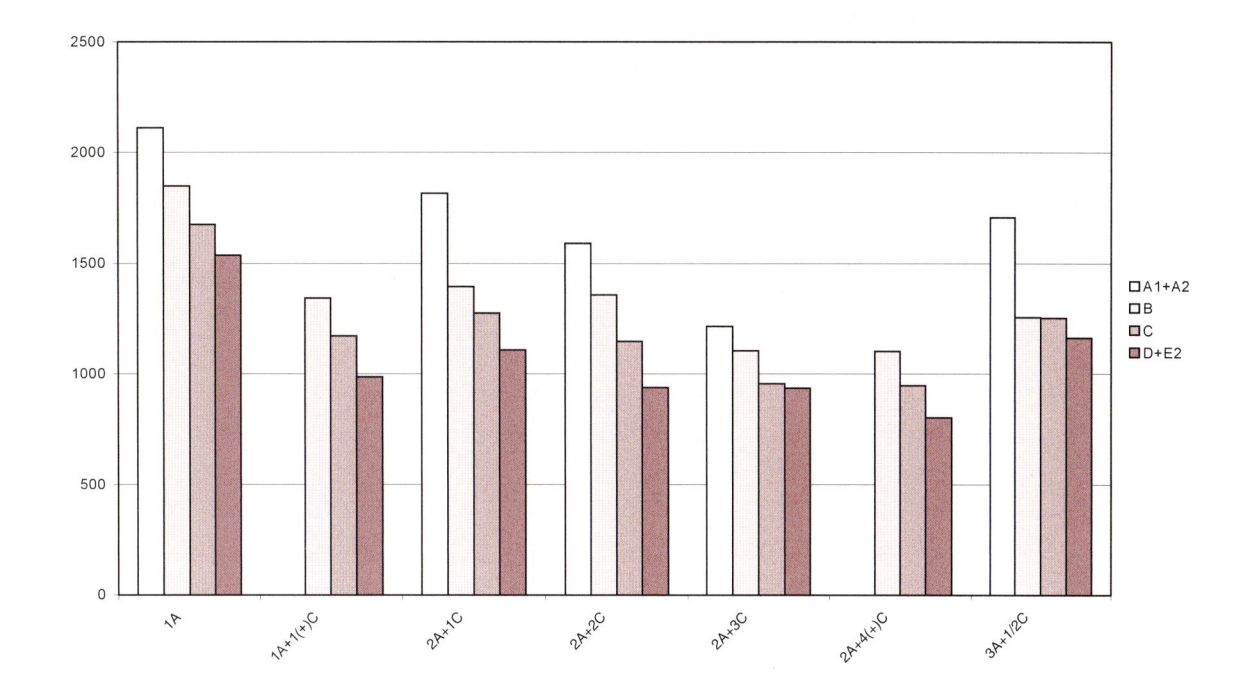

Figure 2.28 Expenditure on selected foods by certain household composition groups within income groups, 1996

Expenditure on butter

pence per person per week

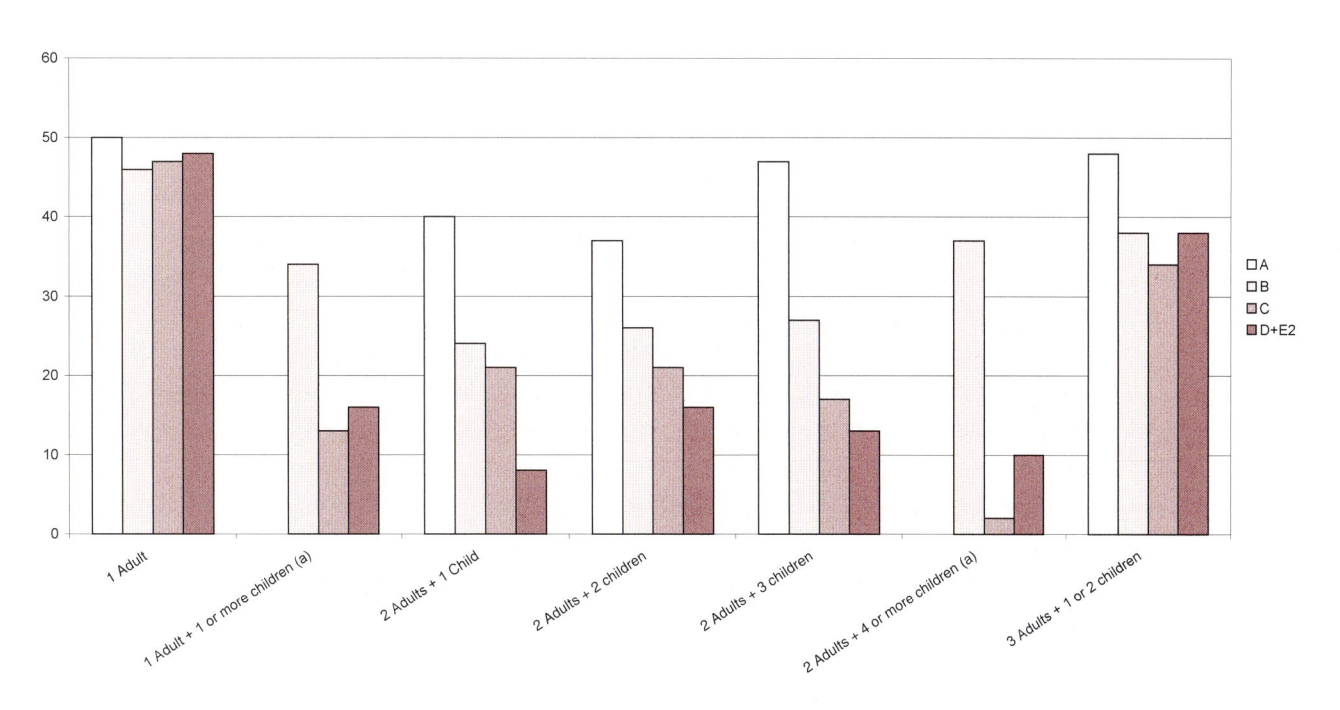

Figure 2.28 continued, Expenditure on low fat spreads
pence per person per week

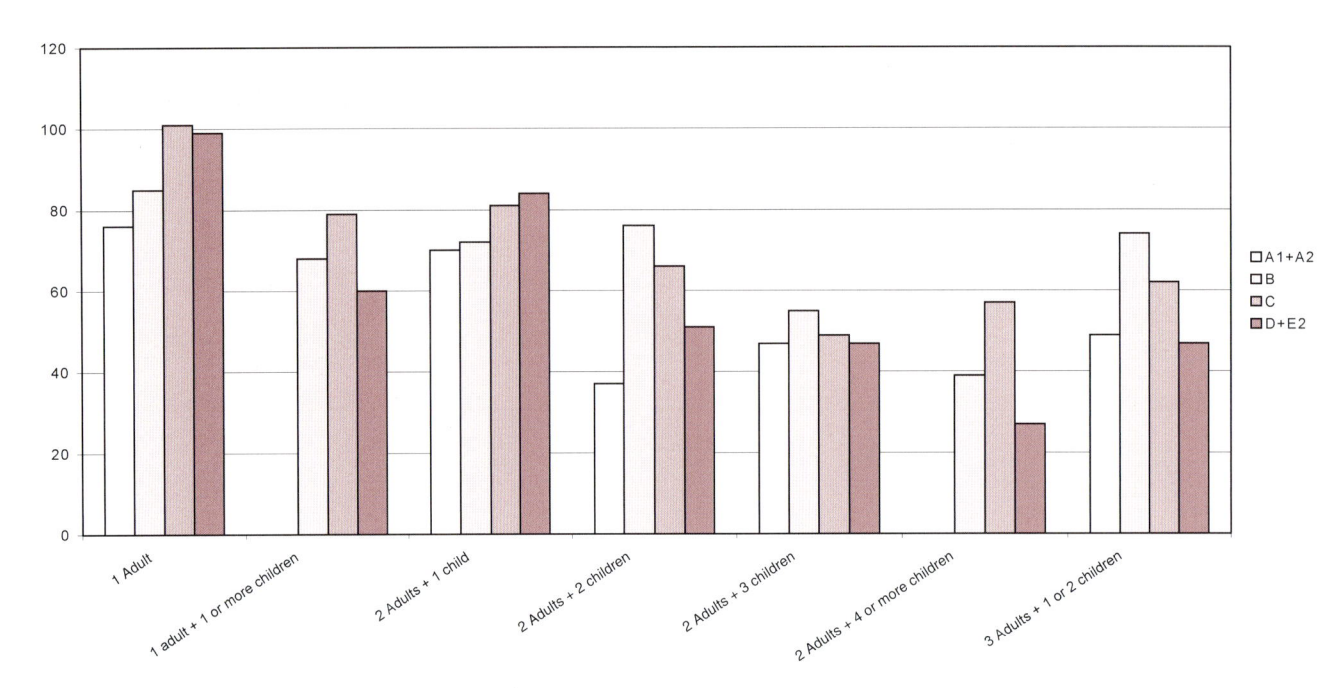

(a) expenditure is not shown for households with one adult and one or more children for income group A and 2 adults and 4 or more children as there are fewer than ten such households in the sample.

In general, adult-only households spent much more (per capita) on butter than households with children irrespective of the income of the head of household (Figure 2.28). In households with children, there was no pattern in expenditure on butter as the number of children increased but there was, in general, a rise in expenditure with the income of the head of household. Per capita expenditure on low and reduced-fat spreads was also highest in adult-only households. In general, expenditure decreased as the number of children increased. In both adult-only households and households with children expenditure on low and reduced-fat spreads tended to be lowest in the highest (HOH) income group.

Analysis by Age of Main Diary Keeper

The main diary-keeper is that person within the household who is mainly responsible for the purchase of food and for the provision of meals. The age of this person is often related to the composition of the household and, to a lesser extent, its income group and level of eating out. The survey results by age of the main diary keeper therefore have to be interpreted with caution.

Consumption of milk and cream, carcase meat, eggs, butter, margarine, cereal products, fresh green vegetables and beverages all rose steadily with the age of the main diary keeper generally to a peak in the 65 to 74 age group but 75 years and over for butter. Consumption of most other foods also rose with age initially but peaked in the 55 to 64 age group. The exceptions were consumption of whole milk, which was lower for the 35 to 54 age group than for most of the other groups; fish, total fats, sugar and preserves, processed vegetables and bread which were lower for the 25 to 34 group than for those under 25 years and soft drinks, alcoholic drinks and confectionery which peaked in the 45 to 54 age group.

Total household food expenditure was £10.48 per person per week where the main diary-keeper was aged under 25 and increased with age up to £18.41 for the age group 55 to 64. Soft and alcoholic drinks, and confectionery added a further £1.47 at age under 25 up to £2.34 per person per week at age group 45 to 54 and £2.29 at age group 55 to 64 where overall expenditure on food and drink was highest at £20.70 per person per week.

Table 2.29 Consumption and expenditure for selected foods by age of main diary keeper, 1996

per person per week

		Under 25	25-34	35-44	45-54	55-64	65-74	75 plus
CONSUMPTION		(grams)[a]						
Milk and cream	(ml or eq ml)	1651	1954	1992	2124	2461	2464	2426
Of which:								
Wholemilk		773	868	728	600	697	961	1157
Low fat milk		656	788	1021	1303	1464	1262	1021
Cheese		89	88	110	133	134	122	98
Carcase meat		135	157	212	287	340	353	296
Other meats and meat products		557	582	677	808	856	787	667
Fish		122	110	127	164	229	232	196
Eggs	(no)	1.34	1.35	1.65	2.15	2.50	2.67	2.30
Fats		159	153	190	261	324	345	290
Of which:								
Butter		17	19	29	45	65	72	74
Margarine		29	29	31	34	49	59	44
Low fat spreads		18	20	23	31	36	29	26
Reduced fat spreads		35	41	47	57	73	71	69
Sugar and preserves		113	112	148	197	273	318	339
Fresh potatoes		498	621	727	943	1,095	1,033	837
Fresh green vegetables		93	132	184	287	376	392	315
Other fresh vegetables		342	367	418	575	690	663	507
Processed vegetables		630	579	597	664	619	474	428
Fruit and fruit products		634	719	925	1,199	1,422	1,378	1,213
Cereals		1300	1311	1541	1686	1790	1852	1627
Of which:								
Bread		618	615	708	852	925	904	747
Breakfast cereals		102	124	144	144	142	167	164
Beverages		36	39	52	70	104	104	102
Soft drinks	(ml)	926	936	976	992	787	572	411
Alcoholic drinks	(ml)	282	367	370	457	449	377	236
Confectionery		40	51	60	64	62	69	54

(a) except where otherwise stated

Table 2.29 *continued*

per person per week

	Under 25	25-34	35-44	45-54	55-64	65-74	75 plus
			Age of main diary-keeper				
EXPENDITURE				(pence)			
Milk and cream	102.0	125.6	130.7	143.2	165.0	163.3	165.0
Of which:							
Wholemilk	33.6	39.9	35.3	31.8	37.4	55.4	68.5
Low fat milk	32.6	38.1	52.1	68.3	76.4	66.3	57.4
Cheese	39.1	41.6	51.7	64.6	68.3	61.7	49.4
Carcase meat	53.4	68.3	88.0	135.6	162.1	163.5	137.8
Other meat and meat products	211.3	233.7	260.8	324.1	331.8	304.7	265.8
Fish	48.1	49.3	58.3	85.7	114.5	119.6	108.5
Eggs	12.2	12.4	15.6	21.6	26.1	27.2	23.8
Fats	23.6	24.9	33.4	45.2	59.5	61.3	57.2
Of which:							
Butter	4.7	5.9	8.8	13.7	19.5	22.1	23.7
Margarine	3.0	2.9	3.3	3.8	5.2	6.6	5.6
Reduced and low fat spreads	9.9	10.8	12.6	16.2	20.0	18.9	18.2
Sugar and preserves	11.5	11.1	15.0	21.1	29.0	33.4	36.9
Fresh potatoes	20.7	24.2	27.8	36.1	43.7	40.2	33.1
Fresh green vegetables	12.2	17.4	23.0	34.5	41.7	41.0	33.0
Other fresh vegetables	41.8	45.2	52.2	69.7	75.4	66.6	52.2
Processed vegetables	106.9	105.3	110.7	114.1	102.6	76.6	66.9
Fruit and fruit products	65.0	79.3	104.7	137.6	165.5	156.4	145.0
Cereals	214.1	234.3	264.1	287.9	292.1	291.3	273.9
Beverages	24.4	29.0	37.3	53.2	74.5	69.4	68.8
Miscellaneous (expenditure only)	61.7	66.8	72.0	82.4	89.5	77.7	67.3
Total Food	**£10.48**	**£11.69**	**£13.45**	**£16.57**	**£18.41**	**£17.54**	**£15.85**
Soft drinks	55.1	52.3	55.9	58.3	45.5	32.2	26.3
Alcoholic drinks	70.4	90.3	97.3	143.3	151.6	145.4	110.7
Confectionery	21.7	25.1	31.5	32.7	31.7	32.9	26.9
Total food and drink (GB)	**£11.95**	**£13.36**	**£15.30**	**£18.91**	**£20.70**	**£19.64**	**£17.48**
Total food and drink (UK)	**£11.97**	**£13.41**	**£15.29**	**£18.86**	**£20.69**	**£19.66**	**£17.50**

Section 3

Household food: Nutrient intakes

National averages

This section of the report summarises the information on the nutritional value of the food brought into homes throughout Great Britain in 1996, and compares results with selected earlier years. In addition, following the inclusion of Northern Ireland in the National Food Survey from 1996, information is presented on nutrient intakes for the UK as a whole. More details of nutrient intakes in 1996 are given in Appendix Tables B9 to B12; Table B9 shows average intakes of a wide range of nutrients, while Tables B10 to B12 show similar information for households in different regions and income groups and with different household compositions. For each category of household, intakes are given not only in absolute amounts but, where possible, they are also compared with the Reference Nutrient Intakes (RNIs) published by the Department of Health in 1991[1]. In addition, each table shows the amounts of selected nutrients provided by soft and alcoholic drinks and confectionery. The contributions made by selected foods to average intakes of a number of nutrients are shown in Appendix Table B13. Information on food and drink consumed out of the home and their contribution to the average intake of energy and nutrients is provided in Section 4. A special analysis giving further information on nutrient intakes for households in different regions in included in Section 5. Contributions to nutrient intakes from pharmaceutical sources in the form of dietary supplements are not recorded in the survey.

Energy

The energy content of the average household diet in Great Britain, excluding soft and alcoholic drinks, and confectionery, was 1,850 kcal per person per day compared with 1,780 kcal in 1995 (Appendix Table B9). This reverses the recent downward trend in energy intake. The energy contribution of soft and alcoholic drinks and confectionery brought home in 1996 raised the average energy intake to 1,960 kcal per person per day compared with 1,880 kcal in 1995. Energy intakes for the UK as a whole (i.e. including Northern Ireland) were the same as those for GB.

Compared with 1995, the largest increases were seen for cereals (+ 44 kcal) followed by vegetables (+11 kcal), fats (+6 kcal), and sugars and preserves (+5 kcal) (Table 3.1).

---

[1] Department of Health, *Dietary Reference Values for Food Energy and Nutrients for the United Kingdom*, Report on Health and Social Subjects No. 41, HMSO, 1991

Table 3.1 Contributions made by groups of foods to GB household energy intake in selected years

	1986	1995	kcal per person per day 1996
Milk and milk products	218	187	187
Cheese	64	57	59
Meat and meat products	327	262	263
Fish	30	28	28
Eggs	34	20	20
Fats	314	217	223
Sugar and preserves	150	92	97
Vegetables	191	187	198
Fruit	68	76	79
Cereals	626	598	642
Other foods	50	53	56
Total food	**2071**	**1778**	**1852**
Soft drinks[a]	na	43	45
Alcoholic drinks[a]	na	27	28
Confectionery[a]	na	34	37
Total food and drink	**na**	**1881**	**1962**

(a) Information on soft and alcoholic drinks and confectionery has only been collected since 1992. Previous estimates were based on supply figures and are not comparable.

Energy content of the household food supply has decreased considerably over the last 10 years with the largest changes in the contribution from fats (-91 kcal in 1996 compared with 1986), meat and meat products (-64 kcal), sugars and preserves (-53 kcal) and milk and milk products (-31 kcal).

Fats, carbohydrate and fibre

The total fat content of the food brought into the home in GB increased from 78 g per person per day in 1995 to 82 g per person per day in 1996. Intake of saturated fatty acids also increased, from 30.8 g per person per day in 1995 to 31.6 g per person per day in 1996. Intakes for the UK as a whole were very similar.

Since there was also an increase in energy intake between 1995 and 1996, the average proportion of food energy obtained from total fat and saturated fatty acids fell slightly, to 39.7 per cent and 15.4 per cent respectively (Table 3.2). This shows further progress towards the targets set out in the White Paper on *The Health of the Nation*[2], which were for the proportion of energy from total fat to be no more than 35 per cent and that of saturated fatty acids to be no more than 11 per cent by the year 2005.

---

[2] Department of Health, *The Health of the Nation*, HMSO, 1992

Table 3.2 Trends in percentage energy from fat and saturated fatty acids

	Fat	Saturated fatty acids
		percentage of food energy [a]
1986	42.6	17.7
1987	42.2	17.4
1988	42.0	17.2
1989	41.9	17.1
1990	41.6	16.6
1991	41.4	16.4
1992	41.7	16.3
1993	41.3	16.1
1994	40.5	15.7
1995	39.8	15.6
1996	39.7	15.4

(a) excluding soft and alcoholic drinks and confectionery

The average carbohydrate content of the household food supply (excluding soft and alcoholic drinks and confectionery) in 1996 was 228 g per person per day (in both GB and the UK), compared with 218 g per person per day in 1995. Soft and alcoholic drinks contributed a further 19 g bringing the average daily intake to 247 g. Intake of fibre, expressed as non-starch polysaccharide, in the average GB (and UK) household diet was 12.4 g per person per day, compared with 11.6 g per person per day in 1995.

Minerals and vitamins

The average intake from household food in 1996 of a range of vitamins and minerals, both with and without the additional contributions made by soft and alcoholic drinks and confectionery, is set out in Appendix Table B9. These are compared with intakes in 1994 and 1995, in Britain, and the Reference Nutrient Intakes (RNIs). The intakes of most minerals and vitamins in 1996 increased over those in 1995, as might be expected with the increase in energy intake.

The average daily intake remained well above the RNI for calcium. Average intakes of iron and zinc were very close to the RNI (97 and 98 per cent respectively) while those of magnesium and potassium were somewhat below the RNI (88 and 83 per cent respectively); for all of these, intakes were closer to the RNI than in 1994 or 1995. The average daily intake of sodium from household food, excluding the contribution from table salt, was 177 per cent of the RNI.

Average intakes of vitamins in 1996 were well above the RNIs set. With the exception of vitamins A and B12, intakes were higher in 1996 than in 1995. Assessed intakes of some vitamins, notably vitamins A and D, were affected by the use of updated nutrient factors for carcase meats in 1996.

Regional, Income Group and Household Composition differences

Nutrient intakes in 1996 in households in different regions and income groups, and with different household compositions, are shown in Appendix Tables B10 to B12. The main sections of these tables do not include the contributions from soft or alcoholic drinks or from confectionery, but their contributions to energy, fat, total carbohydrate and alcohol are shown in section (iv) of each table. As in previous years, the variations in nutrient intakes were generally smaller than the variations in dietary patterns (shown in Appendix Tables B5 to B8) because foods of broadly similar nutritional value tend to be substituted for one another.

For the first time, information on nutrient intakes in Northern Ireland is presented in Table B10. Intakes of food energy, and therefore of several nutrients, was higher in Northern Ireland than in England, Scotland or Wales. The most notable exceptions were intakes of vitamin C, β-carotene and alcohol which were lowest in Northern Ireland. The proportion of food energy derived from fat was highest in Scotland and lowest in Wales. Within England, energy intake was highest in the East Midlands and lowest in the North. The proportion of food energy obtained from fat was also highest in the East Midlands but lowest in the North West.

Differences in nutrient intakes between households of different income groups are shown in Table B11. Amongst the households with earners, energy intake was higher in the two lower income groups (C and D) than in the two higher income groups (A and B). The highest income households, however, derived the greatest proportion of their food energy from fat and saturated fatty acids. There was little clear relationship between the intakes of most minerals and vitamins and income, except for vitamin C where intake was greatest in the highest income groups, in both households with and without an earner. Where intakes were below the RNI, they tended to be low across most, if not all, income groups. However, for iron and zinc the highest income groups, amongst both earners and non-earners, had intakes above the RNI whereas intakes of the other income groups were below the RNI.

As in previous years, differences in nutrient intakes varied more with the composition of the household (Table B12) than between regions or income groups. As expected, households which contained only adults generally had the highest average daily intake of energy per person, reflecting the lower energy requirements of children. However, in many cases, the average intakes expressed as a percentage of the Estimated Average Requirement (EAR) (which takes account of the different requirements of the survey population) were also lower in households with children than in adult only households. With the exception of households with 4 adults, adult only households also tended to have higher intakes of minerals and vitamins, both in absolute terms and when expressed as a percentage of the RNI.

Section 4

Eating Out: Expenditure, Consumption and Nutrient Intakes

Introduction

The Eating Out (EO) part of the National Food Survey (NFS) complements the main part by recording information about household members' food and drink consumption and expenditure which is additional to that brought home and recorded in the main survey. Eating out is defined as consumption of food and drink eaten outside the home which is not obtained from the household's stocks. It therefore covers a range of situations from, for example, food purchased from fast-food outlets at lunchtime through to a formal evening meal in a restaurant. However, food consumed outside the home but taken from household supplies, such as picnics and packed lunches, is covered within the main part of the survey rather than the EO part. Although all food and drink consumed is included in either the main survey or the eating out part, the recording of expenditure on food and drink is restricted to personal expenditure; expenditure for business purposes is excluded. Similarly expenditure on food or drink purchased with other goods or services, e.g. with accommodation, entertainment or school fees, is not included unless it is separately identifiable.

The EO survey is carried out on a sub-sample of the main survey households. Half of the addresses selected in each of the districts covered by the main survey are also included in the EO survey. A description of the structure of the EO survey is given in Appendix A. This shows that the 1996 EO survey was based on 3,471 households (Table A6), compared with 7,921 households in the Main Survey (Table A1). However the results of the EO survey are based on data for individuals, not households, and therefore the effective sample sizes of the two parts of the survey are broadly similar (Tables A 3 and A9).

However, non-sampling errors are larger on the EO survey than the Main Survey. Firstly there is some evidence of under-recording and this may vary over time. This is particularly the case for alcoholic drink consumption which is notoriously difficult about which to obtain reliable information. Secondly 1996 includes some inevitable changes in coding practice which occurred following the employment of new survey contractors. For both these reasons, comparisons of detailed food codes should not be made with earlier years. Table 4.2 does show some data for the individual years and the changes over time should be treated with caution. Difficulties of accuracy and interpretation also mean that detailed EO expenditure data are not given this year.

Expenditure and consumption

National Averages

Expenditure

Table 4.1 shows the main expenditure results for both the Eating Out survey and the Main Survey. The national average expenditure on food and drink eaten outside the home was up 12 per cent in 1996 to £6.53. This compares to an increase on household food and drink of 5 per cent. Expenditure on food and drink eaten out represented 28 per cent of the total expenditure of £22.99. Twelve per cent (£2.84) of this total was spent on alcoholic drinks.

Table 4.1 Eating Out and household expenditure on food and drink

£ per person per week

	1994	1995	1996	% change 1995/96
Total food and drink				
Eaten out	5.74	5.83	6.53	12
Household	14.83	15.63	16.46	5
Total	20.57	21.46	22.99	7
Of which:				
Alcoholic drinks				
Eaten out	1.49	1.52	1.70	12
Household	0.92	1.08	1.14	6
Total	2.41	2.60	2.84	9

Comparison with FES Expenditure Results

Information on household expenditure, including eating out, is also available from the Family Expenditure Survey (FES). However there are some methodological differences between the FES and the EO extension which means that some adjustments have to be made to the normally published data in order to make more meaningful comparisons. In particular the EO extension results in Table 4.2 have been restricted to average expenditure by those aged over 16 years.

It will be seen that the EO extension has consistently produced lower estimates of average expenditure on eating out than the FES, notably for alcoholic drinks. There are several possible factors for the differences in the estimates. Perhaps of greatest importance, the FES requires more active co-operation of all members of a household aged 16 or over in record-keeping and offers a monetary incentive to each diary keeper, which is only paid if all members agree to cooperate. The FES may also include slightly more money spent by adults on children, which the EO extension may record against the children if they actually made the purchase. The two week recording period of the FES may also affect the averages per week.

Table 4.2 Family Expenditure Survey comparisons of expenditure on eating out for persons aged 16 or more, 1996

£ per person (aged 16 years or more) per week

		Jan - Mar	Apr - Jun	Jul - Sep	Oct - Dec	Yearly average
All Food, soft drinks and confectionery	EO	5.07	6.09	5.88	5.75	5.68
	FES	6.13	6.61	7.21	6.72	6.66
Alcoholic drinks	EO	2.07	2.16	2.47	2.12	2.20
	FES [a]	3.52	3.76	3.81	4.28	3.83
Total food and drink	EO	7.14	8.25	8.35	7.87	7.88
	FES	9.65	10.37	11.02	11.00	10.49

(a) includes only alcohol bought at licensed premises
Source: Office for National Statistics, The Family Expenditure Survey

Consumption

Table 4.3 shows average consumption on food and drink eaten outside the home for the three published years of the Eating Out part of the Survey.

There was an 8 per cent fall in the consumption of meat and meat products in 1996 compared with 1994 and 1995. Within this, there was a fall between 1995 and 1996 of around 25 per cent in the consumption of hamburgers, meat pies and meat-based dishes such as casserole, lasagne and chilli con carne and a rise of 31 per cent in consumption of roast or fried chicken and turkey. As a result of these changes, the share of hamburgers, meat pies and meat-based dishes in the eating out consumption of meat and meat products fell to 41 per cent from 54 per cent in 1995 and roast or fried chicken and turkey saw its share increase to 21 per cent from 15 per cent. The main factor in these changes will have been the announcement on 20 March 1996 about the possible link between Bovine Spongiform Encephalopathy (BSE) and Creutzfeldt Jakob Disease (CJD).

Coffee and tea represented 56 per cent and 41 per cent respectively of beverages consumed outside the home in 1996. Nearly two-thirds of soft drinks consumed outside were carbonated drinks and over two-thirds of confectionery was chocolate-based (Appendix Table C1). Over a half of the alcoholic drink consumed outside the home was beer and just over a third was lager.

Table 4.3 Average consumption of food and drink eaten out, 1996

grams per person per week, unless otherwise stated

		1994	1995	1996
Ethnic foods		28	28	32
Meat and meat products		109	108	99
Fish and fish products		(a)	(a)	23
Cheese and egg dishes and pizza		27	26	28
Potatoes and vegetables		(a)	(a)	(a)
Salads		32	30	17
Rice, pasta and noodles		20	18	24
Soup	(ml)	18	16	17
Breakfast cereal		1	1	1
Fruit (fresh and processed)		17	17	18
Yoghurt		6	4	5
Bread		13	14	14
Sandwiches		36	37	35
Rolls		25	26	24
Sandwich/roll extras		9	10	7
Beverages	(ml)	383	389	392
Ice creams, desserts and cakes		57	49	51
Biscuits		6	5	12
Crisps, nuts and snacks		10	9	12
Other foods		34	31	32
Soft drinks including milk	(ml)	310	330	336
Alcoholic drinks	(ml)	539	535	483
Confectionery		21	19	23

(a) Not available on a comparable basis

Results by Household Characteristics

Regional Comparisons

Table 4.4 shows average consumption and expenditure on food and drink eaten out in 1996 by region. Eating Out results are obtained from a subset of those households chosen for the main survey sample. This subset, like the main sample, is designed to be representative of Great Britain as a whole. However, since a limited number of areas are covered within each region during the year, comparisons between regions and between years should be interpreted with caution.

Total per capita expenditure on food and drink eaten out in 1996 was highest in the North West region; expenditure in this region was also higher than the national average in 1994 and 1995. In general the results by region vary a good deal from year to year. Apart from the North West, only the South East / East Anglia region recorded above average expenditure in each of the last three years. Below average expenditure occurred each year in the South West region and in Scotland.

The most significant regional variations in consumption of food and drink eaten out in 1996 (taking account of similar patterns in 1994 and 1995) include high consumption of meat and meat products and bread in the North West region; vegetables (including potatoes) in Wales; soup, rolls and potato snacks in Scotland and alcoholic drinks in the North region.

Table 4.4 Consumption and expenditure on food and drink eaten out by region, 1996

	North	Yorkshire and Humberside	North West	East Midlands	West Midlands	South West	South East/East Anglia	England	Wales	Scotland
CONSUMPTION								*grams per person per week, except where otherwise stated*		
Ethnic meals	43	18	34	25	30	20	39	32	20	43
Meat and meat products	113	76	127	99	83	82	105	100	114	81
Fish and fish products	30	21	26	20	27	12	23	23	22	24
Cheese and egg dishes and pizza	39	22	35	24	28	18	30	29	20	24
Potatoes & vegetables	204	157	191	198	176	136	181	178	217	160
Salads	19	8	22	17	14	14	19	17	19	19
Rice, pasta and noodles	20	17	22	29	22	12	27	23	27	31
Soup (ml)	15	9	24	15	9	9	14	14	14	40
Fruit (fresh and processed)	17	13	25	13	10	13	19	17	23	26
Yoghurt	3	5	6	5	5	4	6	5	8	5
Bread	10	11	19	10	13	10	15	14	17	16
Sandwiches	48	38	46	40	27	22	36	36	33	26
Rolls	22	14	23	40	10	13	22	21	25	46
Beverages (ml)	274	303	368	540	314	292	472	400	493	255
Ice creams, desserts and cakes	55	39	50	55	49	42	55	51	56	50
Biscuits	15	7	11	8	14	12	15	13	10	9
Crisps, nuts and snacks	13	9	11	12	12	9	11	11	12	17
Other foods	48	32	48	39	31	23	42	39	52	42
Soft drinks including milk (ml)	303	235	371	309	300	277	356	324	373	411
Alcoholic drinks (ml)	779	452	619	433	510	406	459	498	587	291
Confectionery	21	17	23	24	29	20	25	24	21	22
EXPENDITURE								*£ per person per week*		
All food and drink	7.16	5.24	7.70	6.63	5.80	5.42	7.07	6.64	6.24	5.95
Of which:										
Alcoholic drinks	2.50	1.60	2.10	1.60	1.60	1.33	1.65	1.72	1.94	1.45

Income Group Comparisons

Table 4.5 shows consumption and expenditure on food and drink eaten out by the income group of the head of the household.

Generally average consumption (per person per week) of food and drink eaten out increased with the income group of the head of household for those households with an earner. Households in the two top highest income earning brackets (A1 or A2) consumed more of every type of food except rolls (highest in B) and crisps (highest in C). Those in households without an earner consumed notably less tea, coffee and sandwiches and rolls but also consumed more alcoholic drinks than households in the lowest earning group for households with an earner. In contrast to the position for household food, pensioner households ate less than other groups of every type of food eaten out, except beverages.

Expenditure on food outside the home generally followed the pattern seen in consumption. Households in the highest earning group, A1, spent three times more on food and drink eaten out than did those in the lowest group with an earner, and twice as much on alcoholic drinks. Pensioner households spent less than any of the other groups on food and drink outside the home.

Analysis by Household Composition

Table 4.6 shows average consumption and expenditure on food and drink eaten out for respondents in households with different compositions. Adult-only households consumed the most sandwiches, bread, soup, fish, biscuits, beverages and alcoholic drinks. Consumption of salads, beverages and alcoholic drinks fell with an increase in the number of children. The only clear increase in consumption with increasing numbers of children occurred for ice-cream, soft drinks and confectionery where consumption increased with the number of children up to three but then fell (for households with four or more children). Consumption of potatoes and vegetables was highest in households with one adult and one adult and a child. There was generally little variation in consumption of meat products and fish across the household categories, although in the latter households with three adults and children consumption was low. As in previous years, consumption of puddings and cakes, biscuits, and crisps and snacks was highest in those households with children. This was also the case with soft and alcoholic drinks, whilst consumption of beverages was highest in adult only households.

As in previous years, per capita expenditure on food eaten out was highest in adult-only households, with food expenditure declining in households with children as the number of children increased. This pattern was especially marked for alcoholic drinks, where single adult households recorded the highest expenditure. Expenditure on soft drinks was much higher in households with children.

Table 4.5 Consumption and expenditure on food and drink eaten out by income group, 1996

		\multicolumn{8}{c}{Income groups}	
		\multicolumn{5}{c}{Gross weekly income of head of household}				
		\multicolumn{5}{c}{Households with one or more earners}	\multicolumn{2}{c}{Households without an earner}		
		£820 and over	£595 and under £820	£310 and under £595	£150 and under £310	Under £150	£150 and over	Under £150		
		A1	A2	B	C	D	E1	E2	OAP	All households
CONSUMPTION		\multicolumn{9}{r}{*grams per person per week, except where otherwise stated*}
Ethnic meals		118	80	35	32	22	11	20	6	32
Meat and meat products		179	159	119	100	86	66	68	34	99
Fish and fish products		43	40	26	19	16	24	20	15	23
Cheese and egg dishes and pizza		63	49	35	24	23	20	23	6	28
Pots. & vegetables		262	261	208	167	161	164	147	101	179
Salads		44	42	22	14	8	17	9	5	17
Rice, pasta and noodles		73	53	28	23	19	8	18	3	24
Soup	(ml)	37	32	22	14	10	13	8	10	17
Fruit (fresh and Processed)		51	44	23	15	12	10	10	8	18
Yoghurt		10	15	5	6	4	3	4	1	5
Bread		31	22	17	15	11	9	6	4	14
Sandwiches		67	76	47	32	28	17	19	9	35
Rolls		19	28	32	30	17	5	11	2	24
Beverages	(ml)	727	510	560	440	221	149	81	103	392
Ice creams, desserts and cakes		93	78	62	44	37	54	39	30	51
Biscuits		14	20	19	10	10	10	6	2	12
Crisps, nuts and snacks		12	13	13	15	10	6	9	-	12
Other foods		68	59	49	35	33	44	27	22	40
Soft drinks including milk	(ml)	484	492	419	367	345	176	210	24	336
Alcoholic drinks	(ml)	876	533	577	507	353	285	458	189	483
Confectionery		39	25	28	27	26	9	17	1	23
EXPENDITURE		\multicolumn{9}{r}{*£ per person per week*}
All food and drink		15.96	9.35	7.99	6.41	4.96	5.00	3.95	2.38	6.53
Of which:										
Alcoholic drinks		2.61	1.75	2.06	1.75	1.26	11.9	1.74	0.63	1.70

Table 4.6 Consumption and expenditure on food and drink eaten out by household composition, 1996

				\multicolumn{7}{c}{Households with}			
No of adults			\multicolumn{2}{c}{1}	\multicolumn{5}{c}{2}	3	\multicolumn{2}{c}{3}	4
No of children			0	1 or more	0	1	2	3	4 or more	0	1 or 2	3 or more	0
CONSUMPTION			\multicolumn{10}{r}{*grams per person per week, except where otherwise stated*}
Ethnic meals			34	31	33	38	21	16	42	41	36	120	43
Meat and meat products			99	110	76	113	104	128	93	104	105	103	116
Fish and fish products			27	20	25	25	21	20	18	21	18	8	22
Cheese and egg dishes and pizza			30	37	23	30	24	35	19	30	27	34	35
Pots. & vegetables			200	240	159	193	169	231	155	172	161	140	153
Salads			19	11	19	17	14	10	5	28	19	37	15
Rice, pasta and noodles			19	32	17	31	26	38	26	19	22	21	27
Soup	(ml)		18	14	21	21	11	12	9	16	14	7	27
Fruit (fresh and processed)			17	25	16	20	16	24	19	21	18	10	22
Yoghurt			4	10	4	5	6	5	5	8	4	12	9
Bread			17	10	15	17	12	11	5	18	13	6	21
Sandwiches			41	34	34	45	27	21	22	53	40	20	47
Rolls			26	32	20	26	25	13	10	35	24	31	32
Beverages	(ml)		427	194	496	428	294	218	91	630	341	223	516
Ice creams, desserts and cakes			51	75	40	50	59	74	51	39	48	40	47
Biscuits			11	13	10	10	13	16	16	7	11	9	31
Crisps, nuts and snacks			9	23	7	11	14	14	12	13	16	16	15
Other foods			50	48	42	40	34	38	30	42	33	22	39
Soft drinks including milk	(ml)		273	470	214	357	371	428	226	386	482	400	471
Alcoholic drinks	(ml)		972	101	568	316	261	179	92	768	510	242	1153
Confectionery			11	41	11	22	33	41	31	15	34	50	22
EXPENDITURE			\multicolumn{10}{r}{*£ per person per week*}
All food			8.34	3.54	7.40	6.64	4.78	4.25	2.49	9.09	7.21	4.39	10.67
Of which:													
Alcoholic drinks			3.57	0.35	1.95	1.18	0.84	0.57	0.27	3.00	1.67	0.76	4.21

Results by Personal Characteristics

Gender

Table 4.7 shows consumption and expenditure on food and drink eaten out in 1996 by the gender of the respondent. As in 1994 and 1995, males generally consumed more of each food category, the exceptions being salads, fruit and yoghurt. Males consumed notably more meat and meat products and potatoes and vegetables than females, and around two thirds more tea and coffee. Males also consumed around five times more alcoholic drinks than females, and more soft drinks, although in this case the difference between the sexes was much less. Consumption of cakes, ice cream, desserts, biscuits and crisps and snacks was similar for both sexes. Per capita expenditure on food and drink consumed by males outside the home was 1.7 times that for females, most notably on alcoholic drinks, where expenditure was four times that for females. Expenditure on food was a third higher for males than for females.

Table 4.7 Consumption and expenditure on food and drink eaten out by sex, 1996

		Male	Female	All persons
CONSUMPTION		\multicolumn{3}{l}{*grams per person per week, except where otherwise stated*}
Ethnic meals		36	30	32
Meat and meat products		129	72	99
Fish and fish products		25	21	23
Cheese and egg dishes and pizza		34	22	28
Pots. & vegetables		205	155	179
Salads		15	19	17
Rice, pasta and noodles		26	22	24
Soup	(ml)	17	16	17
Fruit (fresh and processed)		17	19	18
Yoghurt		5	6	5
Bread		17	11	14
Sandwiches		40	30	35
Rolls		29	19	24
Beverages	(ml)	477	313	392
Ice creams, desserts and cakes		51	51	51
Biscuits		13	11	12
Crisps, nuts and snacks		13	10	12
Other foods		43	37	40
Soft drinks including milk	(ml)	361	312	336
Alcoholic drinks	(ml)	823	168	483
Confectionery		26	20	23
EXPENDITURE				*£ per person per week*
All food		8.36	4.84	6.53
Of which:				
Alcoholic drinks		2.82	0.67	1.70

Age Group

Table 4.8 shows average consumption and expenditure by the age group of the respondent. Average consumption of meat products was highest for respondents between the ages of 5 and 24, being mostly made up of burgers, sausages (including sausage rolls), meat pies (including pasties), and roasted or fried chicken in these age bands. Ethnic food consumption was highest in the 25 to 34 age group. Consumption of potatoes and vegetables peaked in the 5 to 14 age range, with chips accounting for 49 per cent of this category. Consumption of sandwiches and rolls was easily the highest in the 15 to 24 age group and fell slowly before tailing off for respondents over 54 years. Consumption of ice creams, desserts and cakes was highest in the 5 to 14 age band, remaining fairly uniform for ages beyond this group until 54 years and then falling for older groups. As in 1995, consumption of confectionery was highest for those between 5 and 24 years. Consumption of soft drinks rose quickly to a peak in the 15 to 24 age band, before declining steadily with age. Consumption of alcoholic drinks also peaked in this age group, but remained relatively high until falling off in the 65 to 74 years age group. Persons in the 35 to 44 age group consumed the most salad and beverages; those in the 45 to 54 age group the most soup, fish and fruit.

Average expenditure on food eaten out rose with age to a peak in the 25 to 34 age group, before declining steadily. Expenditure on alcoholic drinks was highest in the 15 to 24 year group, generally declining with age thereafter. Expenditure on soft drinks followed a similar pattern. Confectionery expenditure was high between the ages of 5 and 24 years.

Table 4.8 Consumption and expenditure on food and drink eaten out by age, 1996

		under 5	5 - 14	15 - 24	25 - 34	35 - 44	45 - 54	55 - 64	65 - 74	75 and over	All households
CONSUMPTION						grams per person per week, except where otherwise stated					
Ethnic foods		14	23	39	52	45	46	23	9	3	32
Meat and meat products		68	142	141	127	108	89	64	39	32	99
Fish and fish products		14	25	20	22	25	27	25	18	21	23
Cheese and egg dishes and pizza		11	41	45	36	29	28	16	8	5	28
Potatoes and vegetables		110	285	204	189	178	175	139	102	110	179
Salads		5	9	16	19	28	26	20	10	10	17
Rice, pasta and noodles		18	47	23	30	29	22	10	5	3	24
Soup	(ml)	6	6	14	17	21	29	21	11	18	17
Fruit (fresh and processed)		22	19	18	22	21	25	10	7	12	18
Yoghurt		7	8	5	6	6	6	3	1	1	5
Bread		7	7	18	20	19	18	14	7	5	14
Sandwiches		11	14	60	51	50	49	24	15	9	35
Rolls		2	13	41	38	36	32	15	4	3	24
Beverages	(ml)	5	11	303	667	720	643	448	138	107	392
Ice creams, desserts and cakes		38	102	44	45	49	47	37	30	39	51
Biscuits		14	17	17	14	12	12	9	2	6	12
Crisps, nuts and snacks		6	21	31	15	10	5	2	1	1	12
Other foods		19	41	38	51	49	43	37	26	30	40
Soft drinks including milk	(ml)	248	526	794	433	297	210	108	58	25	336
Alcoholic drinks	(ml)	-	3	843	745	632	710	510	298	195	483
Confectionery		12	57	57	24	16	9	3	3	1	23
EXPENDITURE										£ per person per week	
All food		0.50	3.07	12.65	13.55	11.34	10.43	7.65	4.31	3.40	6.53
Of which:											
Alcoholic drinks		-	-	3.07	2.75	2.21	2.48	1.66	1.01	0.63	1.70

Eating Out: Nutrient intakes

National averages

Table 4.9 shows the energy and nutrient intakes from food eaten out, including and excluding soft and alcoholic drinks and confectionery, for 1994 to 1996. Intakes have generally remained quite constant although the proportion of energy derived from fat and saturated fatty acids was lower in 1996 than in previous years. The proportion of energy from carbohydrate, conversely, was higher in 1996 than in

Table 4.9 Nutritional value of food and drink eaten out 1994 to 1996

		\multicolumn{3}{c}{excluding soft and alcoholic drinks and confectionery [b]}	\multicolumn{3}{c}{including soft and alcoholic drinks and confectionery [b]}
		\multicolumn{6}{c}{(i) Intake per person per day}
		1994	1995	1996	1994	1995	1996
Energy	kcal	195	190	200	250	240	255
	MJ	0.8	0.8	0.8	1.0	1.0	1.1
Protein	g	6.6	6.6	6.7	6.9	6.9	7.1
Fat	g	11	11	11	12	11	11
Fatty acids:							
saturated	g	4.2	4.0	4.1	4.6	4.4	4.5
monosaturated	g	4.1	4.0	4.1	4.4	4.2	4.3
polyunsturated	g	1.9	1.9	1.9	1.9	1.9	1.9
Cholesterol	mg	32	32	32	33	33	33
Carbohydrate	g	19	24	21	25	24	28
of which							
total sugars	g	6	5	7	12	12	14
non-milk extrinsic sugars	g	3	3	5	9	9	11
Starch	g	13	13	14	13	13	14
Fibre [a]	g	1.2	1.1	1.2	1.2	1.2	1.2
Alcohol	g	-	-	-	2.9	2.9	2.8
Calcium	mg	57	56	56	73	71	73
Iron	mg	1.0	0.9	1.0	1.1	1.1	1.1
Zinc	mg	0.8	0.8	0.8	0.9	0.9	0.9
Magnesium	mg	22	21	22	31	30	30
Sodium	g	0.28	0.27	0.27	0.29	0.28	0.29
Potassium	g	0.27	0.26	0.27	0.33	0.32	0.32
Thiamin	mg	0.13	0.13	0.14	0.14	0.13	0.14
Riboflavin	mg	0.10	0.10	0.10	0.15	0.14	0.14
Niacin equivalent	mg	2.9	2.9	3.0	3.5	3.5	3.5
Vitamin B6	mg	0.3	0.2	0.2	0.3	0.3	0.3
Vitamin B12	µg	0.4	0.4	0.4	0.5	0.5	0.5
Folate	µg	22	21	21	30	30	28
Vitamin C	mg	6	5	5	8	8	8
Vitamin A:							
retinol	µg	83	79	59	85	80	61
β-carotene	µg	180	173	167	195	188	185
total (retinol equivalent)	µg	113	107	87	117	112	92
Vitamin D	µg	0.20	0.24	0.23	0.21	0.24	0.23
Vitamin E	mg	1.18	1.14	1.19	1.25	1.21	1.26
		\multicolumn{6}{c}{(ii) as a percentage of energy [b]}
Fat		50.3	50.3	47.8	42.3	41.8	40.3
of which:							
Saturated fatty acids		19.2	19.2	18.1	16.6	16.4	15.7
Carbohydrate		36.0	35.7	38.8	38.4	38.2	41.0
Alcohol		-	-	-	8.1	8.4	7.6

(a) as non-starch polysaccharides
(b) in the first set of columns, as a percentage of food and drink excluding contributions from soft and alcoholic drinks and confectionery. In the second set of columns, as a percentage of total energy from eating and drinking out which includes energy from all these sources including alcohol

previous years. Seventy nine per cent of the energy from food and drink eaten out came from food (including beverages) while 10 per cent came from alcoholic drinks, and 6 per cent each from confectionery and from soft drinks. Food groups contributing most to energy intake were potatoes and vegetables; meats; alcoholic drinks; sandwiches and rolls; and puddings and cakes. The same groups, with the exception of alcoholic drinks, were the main contributors to fat intake.

Results by Household Characteristics

Region

As in previous years, the differences in average daily energy intake from food and drink consumed outside the home between England, Wales and Scotland were relatively small in 1996 (Table 4.10). However, larger differences were recorded between the regions of England, with daily intakes ranging from 190 kcal in the South West to 290 kcal in the North. The proportion of energy from fat and saturated fatty acids was higher in Scotland (42.1 per cent and 16.2 per cent respectively) than in either England or Wales. Within England, the proportion of energy from fat and saturated fatty acids was highest in the East Midlands (40.6 per cent and 16.0 per cent respectively). The proportion of energy from fat was lowest in the South West (39.0 per cent) while the proportion from saturated fatty acids was lowest in Yorkshire and Humberside (15.1 per cent). To some extent the differences seen reflect differences in alcohol intake.

Income group

Table 4.11 shows how energy and nutrient intake from food and drink consumed out of the home varies with the income group of the head of household. In households with one or more earners, average intakes of energy and nutrients were greater in the higher income groups. For most, but not all, nutrients, average intakes were higher in households with one or more earners than in households without an earner. Members of OAP households had the lowest average intake of energy and nutrients. Alcohol intake was highest in the highest earning income group (A) but the lowest non-earning income group (E2) derived more of their eating out energy from alcohol than any other group. Those in the highest income groups obtained a greater proportion of energy from fat and saturated fatty acids than those in the lowest income groups, both in households with and without an earner.

Household composition

The average daily intakes of energy and nutrients from food and drink consumed outside the home by members of households of different compositions are shown in Table 4.12. Energy intakes were highest in households with 4 or more adults and no children and lowest in households with 2 adults and 4 or more children. Households with 3 or more adults and 3 or more children obtained the greatest proportion of energy from fat while households with 4 or more adults and no children obtained the lowest proportion of energy from fat. Alcohol intake outside the home and the proportion of energy obtained from alcohol were considerably higher in adult only households than in households containing children.

Table 4.10
Nutritional value of food and drink eaten out by region, 1996

		Regions of England							Scotland	Wales	England
		North	Yorkshire and Humberside	North West	East Midlands	West Midlands	South West	South East/East Anglia			
					(i) Intake per person per day						
Energy	kcal	290	200	285	265	240	190	270	255	275	255
	MJ	1.2	0.8	1.2	1.1	1.0	0.8	1.1	1.1	1.2	1.1
Protein	g	7.8	5.3	8.2	7.4	6.3	5.1	7.6	7.2	7.3	7.1
Fat	g	13	9	13	12	11	8	12	12	12	11
Fatty acids:											
saturated	g	4.9	3.4	4.9	4.7	4.2	3.3	4.7	4.6	4.8	4.4
Monosaturated	g	4.9	3.4	4.8	4.5	4.0	3.1	4.5	4.5	4.6	4.3
Polyunsaturated	g	2.2	1.6	2.2	2.0	1.8	1.3	2.0	2.1	2.0	1.9
Cholesterol	µg	36	24	37	33	30	24	36	33	34	33
Carbohydrate	g	30	22	31	30	26	21	29	28	30	28
Of which:											
Total sugar	g	14	11	15	15	13	11	15	13	15	14
Non-milk extrinsic sugar	g	11	9	12	12	11	9	12	10	13	12
starch	g	16	11	16	15	13	10	14	15	15	14
Fibre [a]	g	1.4	1.0	1.4	1.3	1.2	0.9	1.3	1.3	1.4	1.2
Alcohol	g	4.4	2.5	3.4	2.4	2.8	2.3	2.7	1.8	3.5	2.8
Calcium	mg	85	56	79	77	66	55	77	71	78	72
Iron	mg	1.2	0.8	1.2	1.2	1.0	0.8	1.2	1.1	1.1	1.1
Zinc	mg	0.9	0.6	1.0	0.9	0.8	0.6	0.9	0.8	0.9	0.9
Magnesium	mg	34	24	34	32	28	23	32	28	33	30
Sodium	g	0.32	0.22	0.33	0.30	0.26	0.20	0.30	0.31	0.30	0.28
Potassium	g	0.36	0.26	0.36	0.35	0.30	0.24	0.34	0.31	0.35	0.32
Thiamin	mg	0.16	0.11	0.16	0.15	0.13	0.10	0.15	0.15	0.15	0.14
Riboflavin	mg	0.15	0.10	0.15	0.14	0.12	0.10	0.15	0.12	0.15	0.14
Niacin equivalent	mg	3.9	2.7	4.1	3.7	3.1	2.5	3.8	3.3	3.7	3.5
Vitamin B6	mg	0.3	0.2	0.3	0.3	0.2	0.2	0.3	0.2	0.3	0.3
Vitamin B12	µg	0.5	0.3	0.6	0.5	0.4	0.3	0.5	0.4	0.4	0.5
Folate	µg	35	23	32	29	27	21	29	26	30	28
Vitamin C	mg	9	7	9	8	7	6	8	9	10	8
Vitamin A:											
Retinol	µg	51	42	77	85	53	41	69	51	55	63
β-carotene	µg	218	143	195	187	155	156	196	181	222	183
Total (retinol equivalent)	µg	88	65	109	116	78	67	102	82	92	94
Vitamin D	µg	0.26	0.18	0.28	0.25	0.20	0.16	0.25	0.24	0.24	0.23
Vitamin E	mg	1.48	1.04	1.40	1.31	1.17	0.86	1.30	1.37	1.28	1.24
					(ii) As a percentage of total energy						
Fat		39.7	39.9	39.8	40.6	40.1	39.0	40.5	42.1	39.4	40.2
Of which:											
Saturated fatty acids		15.2	15.1	15.3	16.0	15.7	15.6	15.9	16.2	15.6	15.6
Carbohydrate		38.8	41.0	40.4	41.9	41.3	41.9	41.1	41.6	41.1	41.0
Alcohol		10.7	8.5	8.3	6.4	8.1	8.4	7.0	5.0	8.9	7.7

(a) as non-starch polysaccharides

Table 4.11
Nutritional value of food and drink eaten out by income group, 1996

		Income groups						
		Gross weekly income of head of household						
		Households with one or more earners				Households without an earner		
		£560 and over	£290 and under £560	£140 and under £290	Less than £140	£140 or more	Less than £140	OAP
		A	B	C	D	E1	E2	
		(i) Intake per person per day						
Energy	kcal	400	315	260	210	170	175	80
	MJ	1.7	1.3	1.1	0.9	0.7	0.7	0.3
Protein	g	12.5	8.7	6.9	5.6	4.9	4.8	2.4
Fat	g	18	14	12	9	8	8	4
Fatty acids:								
saturated	g	7.3	5.5	4.6	3.6	2.9	2.7	1.3
monounsaturated	g	6.8	5.3	4.4	3.6	2.9	2.9	1.4
polyunsaturated	g	3.1	2.4	1.9	1.6	1.3	1.4	0.6
Cholesterol	mg	59	41	32	25	23	20	12
Carbohydrate	g	42	35	29	24	18	19	8
Of which:								
total sugars	g	20	17	15	12	9	9	3
non-milk extrinsic sugars	g	16	14	12	10	7	7	3
starch	g	22	17	14	12	10	10	4
Fibre [a]	g	2.0	1.5	1.2	1.0	0.9	0.9	0.5
Alcohol	g	3.9	3.4	2.8	2.0	1.7	2.6	1.0
Calcium	mg	120	90	73	57	48	50	22
Iron	mg	1.9	1.4	1.1	0.9	0.8	0.7	0.4
Zinc	mg	1.5	1.0	0.8	0.7	0.6	0.6	0.3
Magnesium	mg	49	37	31	24	20	21	10
Sodium	g	0.49	0.35	0.29	0.23	0.18	0.19	0.08
Potassium	g	0.51	0.39	0.33	0.26	0.23	0.23	0.11
Thiamin	mg	0.23	0.17	0.14	0.12	0.10	0.10	0.05
Riboflavin	mg	0.22	0.17	0.13	0.10	0.09	0.09	0.05
Niacin equivalent	mg	6.0	4.3	3.5	2.7	2.3	2.3	1.1
Vitamin B6	mg	0.4	0.3	0.3	0.2	0.2	0.2	0.1
Vitamin B12	µg	0.8	0.6	0.4	0.3	0.3	0.3	0.2
Folate	µg	45	34	28	23	20	21	10
Vitamin C	mg	14	10	8	7	6	6	3
Vitamin A:								
retinol	µg	100	83	55	41	45	34	32
β-carotene	µg	339	219	158	146	173	133	119
total (retinol equivalent)	µg	156	120	82	65	74	56	52
Vitamin D	µg	0.43	0.30	0.22	0.16	0.18	0.15	0.08
Vitamin E	mg	2.03	1.53	1.26	1.05	0.88	0.89	0.42
		(ii) As a percentage of total energy						
Fat		41.2	40.3	40.2	39.7	40.7	38.6	41.0
Of which:								
saturated fatty acids		16.3	15.8	15.8	15.2	15.3	14.0	15.2
Carbohydrate		39.5	41.1	41.7	43.0	40.8	40.1	37.7
Alcohol		6.7	7.5	7.5	6.8	6.9	10.4	9.2

(a) as non-starch polysaccharides

Table 4.12
Nutritional value of food and drink by household composition

		No of adults										
		0		1				2		3	3 or more	4 or more
		No of children										
		0	1 or more	0	1	2	3	4 or more	0	0	1 or 2	3 or more	0

		0 adults, 0 ch	0 adults, 1+ ch	1 adult, 0 ch	1 adult, 1 ch	1 adult, 2 ch	1 adult, 3 ch	1 adult, 4+ ch	2 adults, 0 ch	3 adults, 0 ch	3+ adults, 1 or 2 ch	3+ adults, 3 or more ch	4+ adults, 0 ch
		(i) Intake per person per day											
Energy	kcal	275	295	225	265	245	270	200	285	270	275	335	
	MJ	1.2	1.2	0.9	1.1	1.0	1.1	0.8	1.2	1.1	1.1	1.4	
Protein	g	8	8	6	8	7	7	6	8	7	8	9	
Fat	g	12	14	10	12	11	12	10	13	12	13	14	
Fatty acids													
saturated	g	4.5	5.1	4.0	4.8	4.3	4.6	3.7	5.1	4.6	5.7	5.5	
monounsaturated	g	4.3	5.4	3.7	4.7	4.3	4.8	3.7	4.6	4.5	4.9	5.2	
polyunsaturated	g	2.0	2.5	1.7	2.1	1.9	2.1	1.5	2.0	2.0	1.9	2.2	
Cholesterol	g	36	31	32	36	29	30	23	39	33	35	45	
Carbohydrate	g	28	36	23	29	29	33	23	30	31	30	35	
of which:													
total sugars	g	14	17	11	14	15	17	11	15	16	16	18	
non-milk extrinsic sugars	g	11	13	9	11	12	14	9	12	14	13	16	
starch	g	14	19	12	16	14	16	12	15	14	14	16	
Fibre (a)	g	1.3	1.6	1.1	1.3	1.2	1.4	1.1	1.3	1.2	1.3	1.4	
Alcohol	g	5.5	0.6	3.3	1.9	1.5	1.0	0.5	4.4	2.7	1.3	6.6	
Calcium	mg	79	87	63	78	69	76	57	83	73	78	90	
Iron	mg	1.2	1.2	1.0	1.2	1.0	1.1	0.9	1.2	1.1	1.2	1.3	
Zinc	mg	0.9	0.9	0.8	0.9	0.8	0.9	0.7	1.0	0.9	1.0	1.0	
Magnesium	mg	35	31	28	31	27	29	22	36	31	31	41	
Sodium	g	0.30	0.33	0.25	0.32	0.27	0.30	0.24	0.32	0.29	0.31	0.36	
Potassium	g	0.35	0.37	0.29	0.34	0.30	0.35	0.24	0.37	0.33	0.31	0.39	
Thiamin	mg	0.15	0.17	0.12	0.16	0.14	0.16	0.11	0.15	0.14	0.14	0.16	
Riboflavin	mg	0.16	0.13	0.13	0.14	0.12	0.12	0.09	0.16	0.14	0.14	0.19	
Niacin equivalent	mg	4.1	3.4	3.3	3.8	3.1	3.3	2.4	4.2	3.5	3.4	4.6	
Vitamin B6	mg	0.3	0.3	0.2	0.3	0.2	0.3	0.2	0.3	0.3	0.2	0.4	
Vitamin B12	µg	0.6	0.4	0.5	0.5	0.4	0.4	0.3	0.6	0.5	0.4	0.6	
Folate	µg	35	29	27	28	24	27	18	34	29	26	41	
Vitamin C	mg	8	11	7	8	9	11	6	8	8	9	9	
Vitamin A:													
retinol	µg	70	47	67	59	53	44	29	78	84	54	62	
β-carotene	µg	228	188	193	194	151	189	126	210	157	158	200	
total (retinol equivalent)	µg	108	79	99	92	78	75	50	113	110	80	95	
Vitamin D	µg	0.26	0.24	0.24	0.26	0.20	0.20	0.14	0.29	0.21	0.19	0.31	
Vitamin E	mg	1.27	1.65	1.11	1.39	1.21	1.37	1.01	1.34	1.28	1.27	1.39	
		(ii) As a percentage of total energy											
Fat		37.6	42.4	40.2	42.0	40.9	40.9	42.8	39.5	39.6	43.8	37.2	
Of which:													
saturated fatty acids		14.7	15.7	15.9	16.2	15.7	15.3	16.6	16.1	15.4	18.8	14.9	
Carbohydrate		37.6	45.3	38.3	41.1	43.8	45.5	43.9	38.8	42.8	41.3	38.9	
Alcohol		13.9	1.5	10.3	4.9	4.3	2.6	1.9	10.8	6.9	3.4	13.8	

(a) as non-starch polysaccharides

Table 4.13 Nutritional value of food and drink eaten out by age and gender, 1996

		Households with										
		Infants	children				males			females			all
		under 1	1 to 3	4 to 6	7 to 10	11 to 14	15 to 18	19 to 50	51+	11 to 14	15 to 18	19 to 50 not pregnant	19 to 50 pregnant	51+	persons
		(i) Intake per person per day													
Energy	kcal	20	135	220	270	395	380	405	185	370	350	245	175	115	255
	MJ	0.1	0.6	0.9	1.1	1.7	1.6	1.7	0.8	1.6	1.5	1.0	0.7	0.5	1.1
Protein	g	0.7	4.0	6.7	7.8	9.9	9.5	11.1	4.9	8.3	9.1	7.0	5.2	3.7	7.1
Fat	g	1	6	10	12	18	17	18	8	17	16	11	9	6	11
Fatty acids															
saturated	g	0.3	2.3	3.7	4.3	6.5	6.3	7.0	3.0	6.3	6.4	4.5	3.4	2.3	4.5
Monounsaturated	g	0.4	2.4	4.0	4.9	7.3	6.6	6.6	2.9	6.7	6.1	4.1	3.3	2.1	4.3
Polyunsaturated	g	0.2	1.0	1.8	2.2	3.3	2.9	2.8	1.3	2.9	2.7	1.9	1.5	1.0	1.9
Cholesterol	mg	2	15	24	28	34	34	56	27	29	35	33	23	19	33
Carbohydrate	g	3	17	27	35	51	47	41	18	50	43	26	20	12	28
of which:															
total sugars	g	1	9	13	16	27	25	20	9	27	22	13	9	6	14
non-milk extrinsic sugars	g	1	7	9	13	23	22	17	8	24	19	11	7	4	11
starch	g	2	8	14	18	24	22	20	9	22	21	13	11	7	14
Fibre [a]	g	0.2	0.7	1.4	1.7	2.0	1.7	1.7	0.8	1.9	1.6	1.2	0.9	0.7	1.2
Alcohol	g	-	-	-	-	0.1	2.2	7.1	4.4	-	1.1	2.1	0.2	0.7	2.8
Calcium	mg	7	44	72	82	109	104	112	50	93	99	70	61	34	73
Iron	mg	0.1	0.6	1.0	1.2	1.6	1.4	1.7	0.8	1.4	1.4	1.1	0.8	0.6	1.1
Zinc	mg	0.1	0.4	0.8	0.9	1.2	1.2	1.4	0.6	1.0	1.0	0.8	0.7	0.4	0.9
Magnesium	mg	3	14	24	29	39	40	51	25	36	37	29	20	13	30
Sodium	g	0.02	0.16	0.25	0.31	0.42	0.38	0.46	0.20	0.36	0.37	0.27	0.22	0.14	0.29
Potassium	g	0.03	0.17	0.30	0.36	0.46	0.44	0.51	0.24	0.42	0.39	0.31	0.23	0.16	0.32
Thiamin	mg	0.02	0.08	0.14	0.17	0.23	0.20	0.21	0.10	0.20	0.19	0.14	0.11	0.07	0.14
Riboflavin	mg	0.01	0.07	0.11	0.12	0.16	0.16	0.24	0.12	0.13	0.15	0.12	0.10	0.06	0.14
Niacin equivalent	mg	0.3	1.7	2.7	3.1	3.9	4.3	6.0	2.8	3.5	4.1	3.4	2.3	1.7	3.5
Vitamin B6	mg	...	0.1	0.2	0.3	0.3	0.3	0.4	0.2	0.3	0.3	0.2	0.2	0.1	0.3
Vitamin B12	µg	...	0.2	0.3	0.4	0.5	0.5	0.8	0.4	0.4	0.5	0.4	0.3	0.3	0.5
Folate	µg	2	12	22	28	37	36	49	25	30	30	26	19	13	28
Vitamin C	mg	1	7	11	13	15	11	10	5	13	12	8	7	4	8
Vitamin A:															
Retinol	µg	4	28	32	43	55	45	100	56	42	58	67	35	43	61
β-carotene	µg	29	103	200	210	183	193	235	165	161	138	196	114	151	185
Total (retinol equivalent)	µg	9	46	65	78	86	77	140	84	69	81	100	54	68	92
Vitamin D	µg	0.03	0.09	0.14	0.18	0.20	0.21	0.37	0.20	0.21	0.27	0.26	0.15	0.16	0.23
Vitamin E	mg	0.14	0.65	1.16	1.46	2.13	1.89	1.81	0.83	1.99	1.78	1.26	0.95	0.65	1.26
		(ii) As a percentage of total energy													
Fat		42.5	40.7	41.5	40.6	41.5	39.4	39.1	36.9	40.9	41.5	41.6	43.9	43.8	40.3
of which:															
Saturated fatty acids		14.4	15.6	15.0	14.4	14.8	14.8	15.6	14.4	15.2	16.5	16.7	17.1	17.4	15.7
Carbohydrate		45.2	47.3	46.3	47.9	48.4	46.5	37.6	36.1	50.1	45.8	40.8	43.4	39.5	41.0
Alcohol		-	-	-	...	0.1	4.0	12.2	16.3	-	2.3	6.1	0.9	4.1	7.6

(a) as non-starch polysaccharides

51

Results by Personal Characteristics

Age and gender

The differences seen in the consumption of food and drink consumed outside the home by those in different age groups and by males and females are reflected in the average intakes of energy and nutrients shown in Table 4.13. The age and gender groupings are generally those identified as having distinct nutritional requirements in *Dietary Reference Values*[1].

Energy intakes increased with age in children up to 10 years. In males, intakes continued to rise with age, peaking at age 19 to 50 years, while in females energy intakes peaked at 11 to 14 years.

Males had higher intakes of energy and most nutrients from food and drink consumed outside the home in all age groups. Intake of alcohol, in particular, was much lower amongst females with the result that they obtained more of their energy from fat and less from alcohol. Males aged 51 years or over obtained the lowest proportion of energy from fat (and the highest from alcohol) while females in the same age group and pregnant females obtained the highest proportion of energy from fat.

Household food and eating out: nutrient intakes

National averages

Table 4.14 shows the contribution made by food and drink from all sources to intake of energy and a range of nutrients. It thus covers food, alcoholic and soft drinks and confectionery from both household supplies[2] and eating out. Table 4.15 shows the nutrient intakes from food and drink from all sources expressed as a percentage of the Reference Nutrient Intakes (RNI) for 1994 to 1996. For this calculation, wastage of 10 per cent of all nutrients has been deducted from the intakes based on household purchases of food (except alcoholic and soft drinks and confectionery), but no allowance for wastage has been deducted from the recorded eating out intakes.

The energy intake from all sources was 2240 kcal per person per day or 98 per cent of the Estimated Average Requirement (EAR), slightly higher than that in 1994 and 1995. About 11 per cent of energy was obtained from food and drink consumed outside the home. It should be noted that additional energy (and other nutrients) would have been derived from food and drink consumed but under-recorded in the survey, in particular alcoholic drinks.

---

[1] Department of Health, Dietary Reference Values for Food Energy and Nutrients for the United Kingdom. HMSO, 1991.

[2] The energy and nutrients from household food and drink are the averages of the households participating in the Eating Out Extension and differ slightly from those for all households shown in Section 3 (and Appendix Table B9).

The contribution of eating out to total intakes of protein and carbohydrate in 1996 were about 10 per cent, while the contribution to fat intake was about 12 per cent. The contribution of eating out to the total intake of minerals ranged from 8 per cent for calcium and sodium to 11 per cent for magnesium and potassium. Eating Out contributed between 7 per cent (vitamin D) and 12 per cent (vitamin C) of the total intakes of vitamins.

Table 4.14

Nutritional value of food eaten out for Eating out households, 1996

		Household food and drink [a]	Eating Out	Food and drink from all sources	Percent obtained from eating out
		(i) Consumption per person per day			
Energy	kcal	1980	255	2240	11
	MJ	8.3	1.1	9.4	11
Protein	g	66.6	7.1	73.7	10
Fat	g	83.9	11.5	95.4	12
Fatty acids:					
Saturated	g	32.7	4.5	37.2	12
Monounsaturated	g	30.1	4.3	34.5	13
Polyunsaturated	g	15.0	1.9	16.9	11
Cholesterol	mg	236	33	269	12
Carbohydrate		249	28	277	10
of which:					
total sugars	g	111	14	125	11
non-milk extrinsic sugars	g	71	11	82	14
starch	g	138	14	152	9
Fibre [b]	g	12.6	1.2	13.8	9
Alcohol	g	3.8	2.8	6.6	42
Calcium	mg	843	73	916	8
Iron	mg	10.5	1.1	11.6	9
Zinc	mg	8.0	0.9	8.8	10
Magnesium	mg	243	30	273	11
Sodium	g	3.36	0.29	3.64	8
Potassium	g	2.69	0.32	3.01	11
Thiamin	mg	1.47	0.14	1.61	9
Riboflavin	mg	1.65	0.14	1.79	8
Niacin equivalent	mg	27.5	3.5	31.0	11
Vitamin B6	mg	2.1	0.3	2.3	11
Vitamin B12	μg	4.5	0.5	5.0	9
Folate	μg	254	28	282	10
Vitamin C	mg	59	8	68	12
Vitamin A:					
Retinol	μg	582	61	644	10
β-carotene	μg	1753	185	1938	10
Total (retinol equivalent)	μg	874	92	966	10
Vitamin D	μg	3.35	0.23	3.58	7
Vitamin E	mg	10.85	1.26	12.11	10
		(ii) As a percentage of energy			
Fat		38.1	40.3	38.3	
Of which:					
Saturated fatty acids		14.9	15.7	14.9	
Carbohydrate		47.1	41.0	46.4	
Alcohol		1.3	7.6	2.1	

(a) including soft and alcoholic drinks and confectionery but based only on information from households participating in the Eating Out Survey.
(b) as non starch polysaccharide

The average daily intakes of nutrients compared with RNIs were broadly similar for 1994 to 1996 (Table 4.15) with the biggest change seen for vitamin A. Intakes of most nutrients were above the RNI when the contribution from food and drinks consumed outside the home was taken into account. However, intakes of magnesium and potassium were still below the RNI, although higher than when intakes from household food and drink only are compared with RNIs (see Appendix Table B9, which makes allowance for meals eaten outside the home using the net balance).

Table 4.15 Nutritional value of food and drink from all sources as a percentage of RNI [a,b], 1994 to 1996

	1994	1995	1996
Energy [c]	94	92	98
Protein	142	142	149
Calcium	121	118	122
Iron	98	95	102
Zinc	101	98	101
Magnesium	92	90	96
Sodium	176	174	179
Potassium	84	83	88
Thiamin	156	161	175
Riboflavin	142	138	144
Niacin equivalent	191	193	205
Vitamin B6	161	169	176
Vitamin B12	350	333	331
Folate	134	131	138
Vitamin C	165	156	163
Vitamin A (retinol equivalent)	170	164	143

(a) reference Nutrient Intakes from Department of Health, *Dietary Reference Values for Food Energy and Nutrients for the United Kingdom*, HMSO, 1991
(b) based on the intakes and requirements of the population in the Eating Out extension
(c) as a percentage of Estimated Average Requirements

The proportion of energy derived from fat and saturated fatty acids was higher from food eaten out (40.3 per cent and 15.7 per cent respectively) than from household food (38.1 per cent and 14.9 per cent respectively, Table 4.15). The overall proportion of energy from fat contributed by food and drink from all sources decreased from 39.3 per cent in 1994 to 38.6 per cent in 1995 and 38.3 per cent in 1996. The overall proportion of energy from saturated fatty acids decreased from 15.3 per cent in 1994 and 1995 to 14.9 per cent in 1996. During the same period, the overall proportion of energy from carbohydrate increased from 45.6 per cent in 1994 to 45.8 per cent in 1995 and 46.4 per cent in 1996.

Section 5

Analysis of Regional Data

Introduction

This Section provides an analysis of results of the Main Survey on household food by Standard Statistical Region. A regional analysis has been chosen as this year's special topic because this is the last annual report in which the NFS regional results will be based on the SSRs. In next year's report, they will be replaced by the new Government Office Regions that are being used for all other Government statistics. As a precursor to the change, this Section includes some estimates of expenditure on household food in the new Government Office Regions.

As noted in Section 2, while the survey sample is intended to be representative of Great Britain as a whole, for practical reasons, the number of fieldwork areas selected in a given region in any one year is limited (see Appendix Table A2 for 1996). This means that these areas may not be fully representative of that region. As a consequence, it is advantageous to combine data for a number of years in order to obtain more representative results. In this Section, comparisons between regions are made using data averaged over the three years 1994-1996, and trends over time are examined by comparison with the three-year period 1984-1986. Detailed tables showing three-year average expenditure, consumption and nutrient intakes by region are given in Appendix D.

Throughout the Section, the tables and text relate to observed differences between the regional averages of per capita expenditure and consumption. They do not relate to regional contrasts once all other factors such as income, household composition, ownership of a freezer or a microwave or the extent of eating out have been allowed for. However, some indication of the extent of regional variations in these factors is given.

Expenditure

Figure 5.1 shows total per capita expenditure on household food and drink over the period 1994-96, expressed as percentage deviations from the Great Britain average. Percentage deviations were in the range -6 per cent to +5 per cent from the national average. For most regions, average expenditure was below the national average owing to the dominance (in terms of number of households) of the South East/East Anglia region for which expenditure per capita was significantly higher than in all other regions.

Figure 5.1 Expenditure on all household food and drink by region, 1994-96 (deviation from GB average)

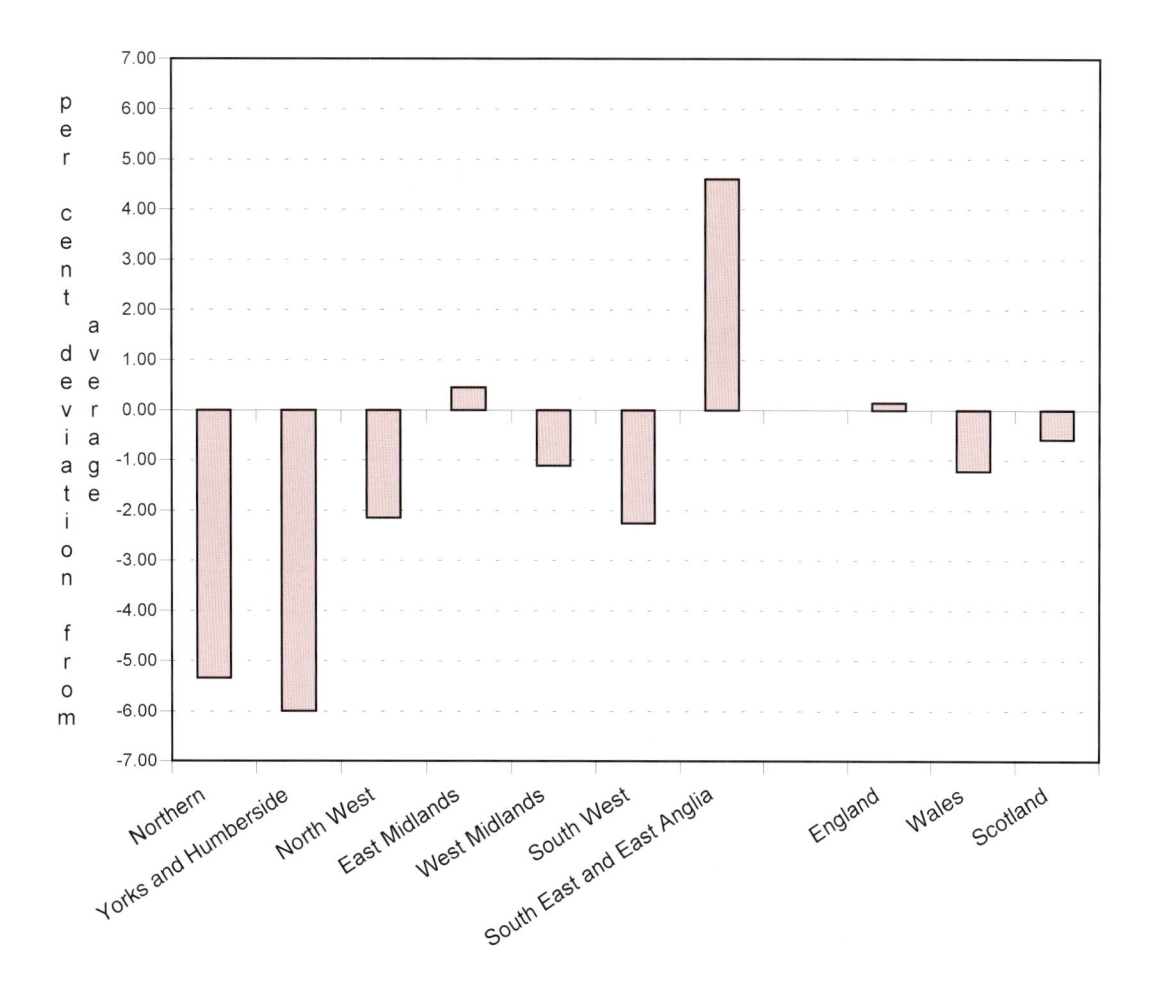

Table 5.2 shows relative average expenditure on different types of household food and drink by region over the period 1994-96, as percentage deviations from the Great Britain average and Appendix Table D1 shows the detailed expenditure data. In the northern regions of England (North, North West and Yorkshire and Humberside) expenditure was generally lower than the national average for most food groups. Expenditure on fats, and sugar and preserves was over 5 per cent lower for all three regions, and that on fruit and vegetables over 8 per cent lower. Expenditure on milk, cream and cheese and beverages was also lower than average in each of these three regions. The North region and Yorkshire and Humberside had markedly lower than average expenditure on soft and alcoholic drinks, whilst in the North West region expenditure on soft drinks was close to the national average and that on alcoholic drinks was above the average. In the South East / East Anglia region, expenditure was higher than average for most food groups, notably dairy products, fruit and vegetables, and beverages.

Table 5.2 Relative expenditure on main food groups by region 1994-96

per cent deviation from Great Britain average

Food Code	North	Yorkshire and Humberside	North West	East Midlands	West Midlands	South West	South East / East Anglia	England	Wales	Scotland
Milk, cream and cheese	-11	-2	-3	4	-1	4	4	1	-2	-6
Meat, fish and eggs	-1	-4	1	-3	...	-8	3	-1	1	5
Fats, sugar and preserves	-6	-5	-6	1	6	11	...	...	9	-6
Fruit and vegetables	-11	-9	-9	...	-1	3	11	1	-1	-13
Cereal products	4	-1	...	3	-4	-5	1	...	-6	4
Beverages and miscellaneous [a]	-9	-6	-4	...	...	4	6	1	-3	-5
Soft drinks	-8	-18	...	-5	6	-22	2	-3	4	30
Alcoholic drinks	-15	-19	7	7	-6	-3	5	...	-8	9
Confectionery	10	-5	-11	10	5	-9	...	-1	19	-4

(a) including mineral water, canned soups, pickles and sauces, ice cream.

Consumption

Table 5.3 shows average household consumption of selected foods in the period 1994 - 96, as percentage deviations from the Great Britain average. Appendix Table D2 shows consumption levels and more details of the type of food consumed (averaged over the three years). The following description indicates, for each region, those foods for which it had either the lowest or highest consumption level in the country averaged over the three-year period.

The North region recorded the lowest consumption levels in the country of low fat spreads, sugar and preserves, fruit and mineral water and the highest consumption of bacon and ham, eggs and processed vegetables. Households in Yorkshire and Humberside had low consumption levels of butter and alcoholic drinks but high levels for whole milk and fish. In contrast, the North West region recorded the highest consumption of alcoholic drinks. They consumed relatively low levels of vegetable oil, wholemeal bread, coffee and confectionery (at home).

The highest recorded levels of consumption of low fat milks, vegetable oil and breakfast cereals were in the East Midlands. The West Midlands consumed the highest levels of pork, poultry, sugar and preserves and tea and the lowest consumption of low fat milk.

The South West recorded the lowest consumption levels of beef, white bread and soft drinks in the country. Consumption of wholemeal and brown bread was high as was that of low fat spreads, fresh vegetables, fruit and coffee. The South East/East Anglia region recorded low consumption of whole milk, beef, bacon and ham and high consumption of lamb, fresh fruit and cereals other than breakfast cereals (including canned pasta, pizzas and other cereal-based convenience foods).

Households in Wales consumed the smallest amount of cereals other than breakfast cereals and the fewest eggs but more butter, white bread and confectionery than consumers in any other region.

Scotland had the lowest consumption levels for a range of foods including meat other than beef, fish, vegetables, fruit, brown bread, breakfast cereals and beverages. In contrast, consumption of beef and soft drinks was easily the highest in the country.

Table 5.3 Relative consumption of selected foods by region 1994-96

per cent deviation from Great Britain average

	North	Yorkshire and Humberside	North West	East Midlands	West Midlands	South West	South East / East Anglia	England	Wales	Scotland
Whole milk	-	8	-2	1	6	2	-7	-1	1	8
Other milk	-5	-1	5	10	-7	...	...	1	4	-6
Beef	14	2	-3	3	5	-9	-9	-3	-1	25
Lamb	-36	-22	17	-24	16	-10	26	5	16	-62
Pork	-4	11	-9	14	23	-1	-3	3	12	-34
Bacon and ham	19	6	10	-4	8	-3	-14	-2	15	-1
Poultry	-3	-5	2	-4	7	4	2	2	6	-18
Fish	2	9	-1	-5	-3	-7	3	1	-4	-11
Eggs	17	8	-1	-3	-1	1	-4	1	-6	-
Butter	-5	-16	-5	-13	-8	11	8	-	16	5
Low fat spreads	-8	-4	-	8	-4	20	-4	-	16	8
Vegetable oils	-20	-4	-24	24	-4	-4	12	-	4	-8
Sugar and preserves	-8	6	1	3	14	7	-7	-	10	-5
Fresh potatoes	5	3	4	4	12	4	-10	...	20	-12
Fresh vegetables	-6	-2	-14	6	4	10	9	3	-1	-25
Processed vegetables	8	6	...	7	3	-7	-2	1	...	-8
Fresh fruit	-16	-9	-10	1	-1	9	11	2	-3	-14
Other fruit and fruit products	-22	-8	-11	7	-3	13	11	2	-2	-15
White bread	5	3	6	6	17	-13	-12	-2	18	6
Brown bread	9	3	10	-4	-6	21	-8	-	5	-12
Wholemeal bread	-2	-1	-7	9	-5	17	3	2	-2	-16
Breakfast cereals	-6	5	-	10	-1	8	-	1	-3	-12
Other cereals	-10	-6	-11	-1	-8	-14	17	1	-16	-
Tea	-3	-3	5	-3	13	-8	-	-	5	-15
Coffee	6	-	-12	-	-6	18	-6	-6	-6	-12
Mineral water	-53	-35	-	-22	-12	28	42	8	-35	-47
Soft drinks	8	-7	2	5	13	-23	-8	-3	14	19
Alcoholic drinks	-3	-11	14	13	-3	-7	-1	1	-4	-3
Confectionery	13	-	-11	11	7	-7	-4	-	15	-4

Demographic factors

Some of the regional differences in household food expenditure and consumption described above will be affected by other factors that may vary between regions. Tables 5.4 to 5.6 therefore indicate differences between regions in respect of some of the characteristics recorded in the Survey on the basis of the 1994-96 regional samples. Owing to differential non-response, these sample estimates may not be unbiased estimates of the population as a whole.

The North Region and Yorkshire and Humberside each had a below average household size and (HOH) income levels. They also spent less on food per capita than other regions as already noted. Average (HOH) income and expenditure on household food were both highest in the South East/East Anglia region. There was little variation between regions in the percentage of households without children.

Table 5.4: NFS Sample 1994-96

Region	North	Yorkshire & Humberside	North West	East Midlands	West Midlands	South West	South East / East Anglia	England	Wales	Scotland	Great Britain
No of households	1411	2212	2921	1930	2246	1845	7663	20228	1416	2217	23861
Average household size	2.49	2.46	2.56	2.57	2.57	2.52	2.54	2.54	2.54	2.46	2.53

percentage of households in region

HOUSEHOLD COMPOSITION [a]

No of adults	No of children											
1	0	25	24	22	19	22	25	23	23	23	27	23
1	1 or more	6	5	6	4	4	4	5	5	6	5	5
2	0	30	33	33	35	35	33	34	34	32	30	33
2	1	10	10	10	10	8	8	8	9	9	9	9
2	2	12	11	11	12	11	11	11	11	11	10	11
2	3	3	3	3	3	4	4	4	4	5	4	4
2	4 or more	1	1	1	1	1	1	1	1	1	1	1
3	0	6	7	7	8	7	6	6	7	6	5	7
3 or more	1 or 2	4	3	4	4	4	5	4	4	4	4	4
3 or more	3 or more	-	-	-	-	1	1	1	1	-	-	1
4 or more	0	2	2	2	2	2	2	2	2	3	3	2

INCOME GROUP [b]

percentage of households in region

A1	1	1	2	1	2	2	4	2	1	1	2
A2	2	3	3	3	4	4	6	4	3	3	4
B	18	23	25	28	26	23	29	26	21	23	25
C	26	29	29	29	27	28	24	27	28	27	27
D	9	8	7	6	6	6	5	6	7	6	6
E1	9	6	7	7	8	12	9	8	9	9	8
E2	19	16	16	13	14	12	13	14	17	17	15
OAP	15	14	12	12	14	14	10	12	15	13	12

(a) see 'Adult' and 'Child' in the Glossary
(b) for definition of income groups see Table A3 of Appendix A and the Glossary

The ownership of a microwave or freezer can have a significant effect on the type and cost of food purchased, however the variations across regions is now relatively small. The percentage of households with a microwave averaged 72 per cent over the period 1994-96, compared with an average of 53 per cent in the period 1989-91. Ownership was highest in Wales, the North region and Yorkshire and Humberside and lowest in the South West region and Scotland. Overall 90 per cent of households in the 1994-96 sample had a freezer but in Scotland and the North region the percentage was 87 per cent and 88 per cent respectively.

Table 5.5 Percentage of households owning a freezer or microwave, 1994-96

percentage of households in region

	Microwave	Freezer
Northern	74	88
Yorkshire and Humberside	74	90
North West	73	89
East Midlands	73	92
West Midlands	72	89
South West	68	91
South East/East Anglia	71	92
England	72	91
Wales	77	91
Scotland	70	87
Great Britain	72	90

Finally Table 5.6 indicates (by means of net balance expressed as percentages) the extent to which individuals in different age ranges were dependent upon household food supplies for their meals in the period 1994-96. For children under 11 years of age and those aged 11 to 18 years, those in the North region consumed a slightly lower than average proportion of their food at home while those in the South West region consumed a larger proportion of the total at home. For those aged over 18 years there was little variation by region.

Table 5.6 Net balances [a] by age of household member and region

	Net balances excluding visitors			
	Age 1-10	Age 11-18	Age 19-50	Age 51+
Northern	81	80	86	92
Yorkshire and Humberside	85	82	85	91
North West	84	81	83	91
East Midlands	85	84	85	92
West Midlands	85	85	86	91
South West	87	86	86	92
South East/East Anglia	86	84	83	90
England	85	83	84	91
Wales	82	80	84	91
Scotland	84	81	83	90
Great Britain	85	83	84	91

(a) see glossary

Consumption patterns over time

Table 5.7 shows the changes in average household consumption for selected foods over the two three-year periods 1984-86 and 1994-96. This sub-section identifies changes in each region which are significantly different from the changes in Great Britain as a whole. For a few foods, the direction of the change over time in the level of consumption is different between regions but in most cases it is just the extent of the change which differs.

Consumption of bacon and ham did not fall as much in the North region as it did nationally over the ten years but consumption of butter and fresh vegetables fell in that region by more than the national average. The increase in consumption of processed vegetables and fresh fruit in Great Britain as a whole was not matched by the increase in the North region. This region was the only region to record a reduction in consumption of cereals other than breakfast cereals (including canned pasta, pizzas and other cereal-based convenience foods) over the ten years and was one of only two (with Wales) to show a reduction in fish consumption.

Yorkshire and Humberside recorded higher than the national increase in consumption of other fruit and fruit products, breakfast cereals and mineral water while the North West region showed a lower than average increase in (primary) poultry consumption.

The upward movement in the consumption of low fat spreads and vegetable oils was largest in the East Midlands. Similarly the downward movement in whole milk, bacon and ham, sugar and preserves and tea were greatest in this region.

Households in the West Midlands increased their intake of fresh fruit and decreased their intake of white bread by more than households in any other region. They were also the only group not to reduce consumption of fresh vegetables. Other notable points for the region were smaller reductions than nationally in consumption of beef, eggs and butter.

Lamb and pork consumption fell more in the South West region than in any other region as did wholemeal bread consumption. Purchases of bacon and ham and of brown bread fell by less than in any other region.

The decline in the consumption of beef, brown bread and coffee was the greatest in the South East/East Anglia region while the region also saw the largest rise in other cereals. Households in this region did not raise their consumption of either low fat spreads or fruit

Wales contributed more than proportionately to the rise in the consumption of poultry, fish and processed vegetables over the ten year period. Consumption of a number of other products such as lamb and bacon and ham fell less steeply in Wales than in Great Britain as a whole. Coffee consumption rose only in Wales.

Households in Scotland recorded sharper falls in the consumption of eggs and fresh potatoes and also showed falls in the use of vegetable oils and fish in contrast to rises in the national averages. They also exhibited an increase in the consumption of wholemeal bread against a national decrease. The increase in the consumption of poultry and the reduction in the consumption of both pork were less marked in Scotland than elsewhere.

Table 5.7 Per cent change in consumption of selected foods by region 1984-86 to 1994-96

	Northern	Yorkshire and Humber-side	North West	East Midlands	West Midlands	South West	South East / East Anglia	England	Wales	Scotland	Great Britain
Whole milk	-54	-53	-59	-61	-56	-57	-59	-58	-58	-55	-57
Other milk	170	172	192	199	186	140	158	169	191	133	167
Beef	-32	-37	-37	-34	-21	-36	-42	-36	-22	-34	-36
Lamb	-45	-31	-36	-48	-43	-50	-28	-36	-26	-48	-36
Pork	-24	-20	-24	-22	-20	-39	-27	-25	-27	-16	-24
Bacon and ham	-10	-15	-20	-23	-20	-10	-17	-17	-10	-16	-16
Poultry	15	26	14	27	18	24	16	19	29	14	19
Fish	-4	5	9	3	7	1	6	5	12	-5	5
Eggs	-43	-38	-38	-46	-36	-40	-39	-39	-43	-47	-40
Butter	-56	-49	-51	-54	-44	-45	-47	-49	-51	-52	-49
Low fat spreads	77	100	108	125	71	58	41	67	93	80	67
Vegetable oils	95	123	70	152	75	40	33	55	77	-97	56
Sugar and preserves	-39	-35	-40	-44	-40	-35	-38	-38	-34	-41	-38
Fresh potatoes	-31	-31	-31	-33	-27	-27	-25	-28	-22	-38	-29
Fresh vegetables	-12	-3	-6	-3	1	-8	-7	-6	-10	-1	-6
Processed vegetables	4	13	13	18	8	4	8	9	20	11	10
Fresh fruit	16	24	27	27	38	21	16	21	26	29	22
Other fruit and fruit products	12	52	27	39	50	34	11	25	32	21	25
White bread	-18	-16	-22	-22	-29	-16	-9	-17	-9	-20	-17
Brown bread	-29	-22	-26	-28	-8	-2	-32	-25	-31	-22	-25
Wholemeal bread	-8	-	-13	-3	-3	-25	-20	-14	-17	4	-13
Breakfast cereals	15	28	13	26	15	17	10	15	3	22	15
Other cereals	-4	9	13	11	14	-	15	11	5	4	10
Tea	-27	-22	-21	-32	-21	-22	-20	-24	-15	-28	-21
Coffee	-5	-11	-17	-15	-11	-5	-24	-16	7	-21	-12
Mineral water	1075	3200	1163	1029	790	2480	550	808	1550	1250	818
Soft drinks [a]	16	8	10	8	10	-17	-4	2	27	33	6
Alcoholic drinks [a]	na	na	na	na	na	na	na	na	na	na	na
Confectionery [a]	na	na	na	na	na	na	na	na	na	na	na

(a) Alcoholic drinks and confectionery were introduced in 1992

Government Office Regions

Table 5.8 Average household expenditure by Government Office regions

pence per person per week

	North East	North West	Merseyside	Eastern	London	South East
Milk and cream	132.1	149.6	142.8	142.5	129.4	148.8
Cheese	46.4	50.7	47.7	57.7	51.6	62.3
Carcase meat	87.8	115.4	128.0	123.3	111.7	106.8
Other meat and meat products	266.0	281.0	320.0	289.0	239.8	291.9
Fish	68.9	72.4	78.6	82.0	86.9	79.0
Eggs	18.5	15.6	20.3	18.0	20.2	19.9
Fats and oils	35.4	37.2	39.9	42.9	38.2	42.2
Sugar and preserves	18.7	18.5	13.7	18.8	18.5	19.4
Vegetables	213.9	208.8	210.5	233.4	234.7	242.6
Fruit	104.1	111.5	87.7	115.4	151.0	136.3
Bread	79.8	76.6	86.9	66.5	64.1	66.8
Other cereals	194.3	193.4	188.6	196.5	208.0	205.5
Beverages	44.7	48.6	42.3	53.3	39.8	47.3
Other foods	64.7	76.7	72.6	81.7	73.2	88.2
Total Food	**£13.75**	**£14.56**	**£14.80**	**£15.21**	**£14.67**	**£15.57**
Soft drinks	48.7	52.7	49.7	49.8	52.8	52.7
Alcoholic drinks	114.4	141.3	91.5	109.3	95.9	127.0
Confectionery	28.2	30.3	29.4	33.0	22.7	32.7
All food and drink	**£15.67**	**£16.80**	**£16.50**	**£17.13**	**£16.39**	**£17.70**

(a) Results are only shown for changed regions. Corresponding data for all SSR's are given in Table 2.16

The new Government Office Regions will be used in next year's report in place of the Standard Statistical Regions. Table 5.8 shows some estimates made for 1996 on the new regional classifications. The relationship between the two sets of areas and the constituent counties and unitary authorities, including those to be set up in April 1998, is shown in Figure 5.9. Statistical regions not shown will be unaffected by the change to Government Office Regions. Estimates of expenditure for the North East and North West GORs are similar to those shown in Table 2.16 for the North and North West SSRs. This reflects the fact that the only changes are that the North SSR loses Cumbria and the North West SSR gains Cumbria and loses Merseyside. The South East/East Anglia region used in this annual report is split into Eastern, London and South Eastern GORs. With a smaller, though better designed sample in 1997, it may be necessary to group together some of the GORs in next year's report.

Table 5.9 Definitions of Standard Statistical regions and Government Office Regions [a]

Standard Statistical Region	County	Government Office Region
North	Northumberland Tyne and Wear Former counties of: Cleveland Durham	North East
	Cumbria	
North West	Greater Manchester Former counties of: Cheshire Lancashire	North West
	Merseyside	Merseyside
East Anglia	Suffolk Norfolk Former county of Cambridgeshire	Eastern
South East	Hertfordshire Former counties of: Bedfordshire Essex	
	Greater London	London
	Oxfordshire Surrey West Sussex Isle of Wight UA Former counties of: Berkshire Buckinghamshire East Sussex Hampshire Kent	South East

(a) excluding those where Standard Statistical Regions and Government Office Regions coincide.

Nutrient Intakes

Average of 1994-96 data

Differences in the regional consumption of foods have been outlined earlier on in this chapter. This section summarises the similarities and differences between household nutrient intakes in the main regions. Nutrient intakes in households in different regions are shown in Table 5.10. Nutrients obtained from alcoholic and soft drinks and confectionery are not taken into account in the main section of this table but their contribution to energy, total fat, carbohydrate and alcohol are shown in section (iv).

The average energy value of foods brought into the home was higher in Wales and England (1850 and 1810 kcal per person per day respectively) than in Scotland (1740 kcal per person per day). Within the seven regions of England, the highest energy intakes were recorded in the East Midlands (1900 kcal per person per day) and the lowest in South East/ East Anglia (1780 kcal per person per day) and the North West (1760 kcal per person per day).

Table Appendix D3 shows the contribution of different foods to intakes of selected nutrients. Cereal and cereal products contributed between 32 per cent and 34 per cent of food energy intakes in all regions. Within this category bread (including white, brown and wholemeal) was the most important source of energy in all regions, followed by cakes, pastries and biscuits. Meat and meat products and fats were the next highest contributors to energy intake in all regions.

Intakes of total fat were highest in the East Midlands (85g per person per day) and lowest in the North West (77g per person per day) and Scotland (78g per person per day). Similarly, intakes of total saturated fatty acids were highest in the East Midlands and lowest in the North West. However, when expressed in terms of energy, these differences become relatively small, the average proportion of food energy contributed by total fat varying only between 39.4 per cent in the North West to 40.5 per cent in the North of England and for saturated fatty acids between 15.3 per cent in the West Midlands to 15.9 per cent in the North (Table 5.10).

As expected, the intakes of micro-nutrients, including folate, vitamin C, β-carotene, iron, potassium and magnesium were lowest in Scotland. With the exception of iron, potassium, magnesium and, in some regions, zinc, the intakes of micro-nutrients across different regions were well above the Reference Nutrient Intake. Despite lower energy intakes, the South East / East Anglia had a higher intake of vitamin C than in other regions. When expressed as nutrient density (per 1000 kcal), intakes of vitamin C were lower in more northerly regions of England than in the South. A similar pattern was also observed for β-carotene and is broadly consistent with regional variations in consumption of fruit and vegetables.

Table 5.10 Nutritional value of household food by region, average of intakes for 1994 - 1996

| | | Regions of England ||||||| England | Wales | Scotland |
		North	Yorkshire and Humber-side	North West	East Midlands	West Midlands	South West	South East/ East Anglia			
		(i) Intake per person per day										
Energy	Kcal	1820	1850	1760	1900	1870	1790	1780	1810	1850	1740
	MJ	7.6	7.8	7.4	8.0	7.9	7.5	7.5	7.6	7.7	7.3
Total protein	g	64.8	64.8	63.3	65.5	65.3	62.3	62.4	63.6	65.4	61.6
Animal protein	g	39.9	40.0	39.5	40.1	40.0	38.3	38.4	39.2	40.5	38.2
Fat	g	82	83	77	85	83	80	79	80	82	78
Fatty acids:											
saturated	g	32.1	32.0	30.2	32.5	31.9	31.4	30.5	31.2	31.9	30.7
monounsaturated	g	30.1	30.4	28.1	31.1	30.3	28.8	28.5	29.3	29.7	28.2
polyunsaturated	g	13.8	14.5	13.3	15.4	14.7	13.9	14.0	14.1	14.3	13.0
Cholesterol	mg	243	240	229	231	233	228	226	231	231	224
Carbohydrate	g	220	225	217	231	231	219	219	222	226	211
of which:											
total sugars	g	86	92	89	96	95	94	90	91	94	85
non-milk extrinsic sugars	g	49	53	51	55	56	54	50	52	54	48
starch	g	133	132	127	135	135	125	129	130	132	126
Fibre [a]	g	11.9	12.0	11.5	12.6	12.4	12.3	11.9	12.0	12.1	10.7
Calcium	mg	790	830	800	860	830	820	800	810	820	790
Iron	mg	10.0	10.1	9.7	10.2	9.9	9.8	9.6	9.8	9.9	9.4
Zinc	mg	8.0	7.9	7.7	8.0	7.8	7.5	7.6	7.7	7.9	7.5
Magnesium	mg	221	224	218	231	227	226	222	223	226	209
Sodium	g	2.71	2.50	2.48	2.58	2.40	2.45	2.39	2.46	3.09	2.52
Potassium	g	2.53	2.55	2.49	2.64	2.61	2.57	2.53	2.55	2.61	2.37
Thiamin	mg	1.36	1.38	1.34	1.42	1.41	1.36	1.33	1.36	1.41	1.28
Riboflavin	mg	1.55	1.63	1.59	1.66	1.59	1.61	1.57	1.59	1.60	1.49
Niacin equivalent	mg	25.8	26.0	25.4	26.2	26.1	25.3	25.2	25.5	26.2	24.4
Vitamin B6	mg	1.9	1.9	1.9	2.0	2.0	1.9	1.9	1.9	2.0	1.8
Vitamin B12	µg	4.6	4.8	4.7	4.5	4.3	4.4	4.5	4.5	4.5	4.4
Folate	µg	233	245	233	251	249	250	243	243	244	218
Vitamin C	mg	49	51	49	56	54	56	57	54	54	46
Vitamin A:											
retinol	µg	650	800	690	680	630	720	690	690	670	630
β-carotene	µg	1600	1700	1660	1760	1690	1730	1700	1690	1740	1400
total (retinol equivalent)	µg	910	1080	960	980	910	1010	970	980	960	870
Vitamin D	µg	2.97	3.16	3.10	3.21	3.23	2.95	2.84	3.01	3.07	2.68
Vitamin E	mg	9.51	10.08	9.38	10.87	10.50	9.79	9.87	9.96	10.14	8.96

Table 5.10 *continued*

		Regions of England							England	Wales	Scotland
		North	Yorkshire and Humber-side	North West	East Midlands	West Midlands	South West	South East/ East Anglia			
		\(ii\) As a percentage of Reference Nutrient Intake [b]									
Energy [c]		87	88	86	90	88	84	86	87	89	84
Protein		142	143	143	144	143	135	140	141	146	138
Calcium		115	120	118	126	119	117	118	119	119	116
Iron		95	97	94	98	95	93	93	94	96	91
Zinc		100	99	98	100	97	93	96	97	100	96
Magnesium		84	85	84	88	85	84	85	85	87	81
Sodium		182	169	170	174	160	162	163	166	210	171
Potassium		80	81	81	83	82	80	81	81	83	76
Thiamin		161	165	163	169	166	159	160	162	169	155
Riboflavin		136	144	142	145	138	139	140	140	141	133
Niacin equivalent		185	187	186	188	186	179	183	184	190	178
Vitamin B6		156	158	157	161	160	155	155	157	164	147
Vitamin B12		331	351	344	327	311	315	330	330	326	324
Folate		124	131	127	134	131	132	131	130	131	118
Vitamin C		126	133	131	145	138	144	149	141	141	122
Vitamin A (retinol equivalent)		147	175	158	157	145	160	158	157	156	142
		\(iii\) As a percentage of food energy									
Fat		40.5	40.3	39.4	40.4	39.8	40.1	39.8	39.9	39.9	40.2
of which:											
Saturated fatty acids		15.9	15.6	15.4	15.4	15.3	15.8	15.4	15.5	15.5	15.9
Carbohydrate		45.2	45.6	46.1	45.7	46.2	45.9	46.1	45.9	45.9	45.6
		\(iv\) Contributions to selected nutrients from soft and alcoholic drinks and confectionery									
Energy	kcal	110	100	100	110	110	100	100	100	110	100
	MJ	0.4	0.4	0.4	0.5	0.5	0.4	0.4	0.4	0.5	0.4
Fat	g	2	1	1	2	1	1	1	1	2	1
Carbohydrate	g	18	17	17	18	19	15	17	17	18	17
Alcohol	g	3.1	2.8	3.7	3.7	3.3	3.3	3.4	3.4	3.2	3.6

(a) as non-starch polysaccharide
(b) Department of Health, *Dietary Reference Values for Food Energy and Nutrients for the United Kingdom*, HMSO, 1991
(c) as a percentage of Estimated Average Requirements

Nutrient Intake Patterns over Time (1984-1996)

Table 5.11 shows that the downward trend in intakes of energy, total fat and saturated fatty acids previously noted[1] continued in all regions between 1984-86 and 1994-96. In all cases the contributions from alcoholic drinks, soft drinks and confectionery are excluded.

In Scotland, energy content of food brought into the home decreased by 14 per cent while in Wales and England intakes fell by 9 per cent and 12 per cent respectively. Within the regions of England, declines in energy intake were greatest in the North and North West (14 and 15 per cent respectively). Total fat intakes also decreased by 18 per cent in Scotland and England and 14 per cent in Wales, while intakes of saturated fatty acids decreased by up to 27 per cent in some regions. The percentage of energy derived from fat and saturated fatty acids decreased slightly in all regions between 1984-86 and 1994-96. This was most marked in the North West.

Table 5.11 Changes in intakes of selected nutrients between 1984-86 and 1994-96

	\multicolumn{7}{c}{Regions of England}			
	North	Yorkshire and Humberside	North West	East Midlands	West Midlands	South West	South East/ East Anglia	England	Wales	Scotland
	\multicolumn{10}{c}{% change}
Energy	-14	-9	-15	-13	-13	-14	-11	-12	-9	-14
Fat	-18	-14	-21	-17	-17	-20	-17	-18	-14	-18
Saturated fatty acids	-24	-20	-27	-25	-24	-26	-24	-24	-22	-24
Vitamin C	-11	2	-3	1	5	-2	-7	-3	-1	-5
β-carotene	-27	-25	-28	-19	-24	-23	-23	-24	-24	-24

β-carotene intakes continued to fall, with the decline in the North West being the most marked (28 per cent). When expressed as nutrient density (per 1000 kcal), the decline was smaller but still apparent. Vitamin C intakes increased only slightly in three regions and decreased in all other regions, in particular the North of England where intakes decreased by 11 per cent. However, when expressed per unit energy (1000 kcal), vitamin C intakes rose everywhere and in the West Midlands by up to 20 per cent.

---

[1] Ministry of Agriculture, Fisheries and Food (1992). *Household Food Consumption and Expenditure 1991*. London :HMSO

Appendix A

Structure of the Survey

Introduction

The National Food Survey is a continuous sampling enquiry into the domestic food consumption and expenditure of private households in the United Kingdom (since the introduction of Northern Ireland into the Survey in January 1996). Each household, which participates, does so voluntarily, and without payment, for one week only. By regularly changing the households surveyed, information is obtained continuously throughout the year, apart from a short break over the Christmas period.

Household food and drink

Structure of the sample for Great Britain

The sample for the National Food Survey is selected so as to be representative of mainland Britain (including Anglesey and the Isle of Wight, but not the Scilly Isles or the islands off the Scottish mainland). A three-stage, stratified, random sampling scheme is used for the selection of addresses. The first stage involves the selection of local authority districts as the primary sampling units. A total of 52 local authority districts are included in the Survey each quarter for sampling purposes. Six or seven of the districts are retired and replaced each quarter, with newly selected districts remaining in the Survey for eight consecutive quarters (re-selection being possible). The local authority districts surveyed at some time during 1996 are listed in Figure A2 of this Appendix. The 52 districts in the Survey in any one quarter are randomly divided into two sets of 26, which are worked alternately for two successive periods of 10 days, there being 32 such periods in the year. In total each of the selected districts is surveyed 30 times during its eight quarters in the Survey, i.e. three or four times each quarter.

The second stage of the selection procedure involves the selection of postal sectors within each of the local authority districts and the third is the selection of 18 delivery points for each of the selected postal sectors. The delivery points are drawn from the Small Users Postcode Address File (PAF) using interval sampling from a random origin.

In 1996, 780 postal sectors were selected at the second stage of sampling and 14,038 addresses at the third stage. When visited, a few of these addresses were found to be institutions or other establishments not eligible for inclusion in the Survey; others were unoccupied or had been demolished. In addition, some addresses were found to contain more than one household. After allowing for these factors, the estimated number of eligible households in the Survey was 12,038. In some households the prospective diary-keeper was interviewed, but refused to give any information; a number of other diary-keepers answered a questionnaire[1], relating to household composition, occupation, etc, but declined to keep a week's record; a further group undertook to keep a record but did not in fact complete it. Finally, some records were lost or rejected at the editing stage. The result was a responding sample of 7,921 individual households, representing 66 per cent of the eligible sample. Details are as follows:-

Table A1 Responding sample to the main part of the Survey in Great Britain[a], 1996

	Households	Households selected (%)
Number of households at the addresses selected in the sample	12038	100
Non-contact	798	7
Interview refused or not practicable	2230	19
Diary-keeper answered a questionnaire but declined to keep a week's record	1089	9
Total non-productive	4117	34
Number of responding households	7921	66

(a) the sample in Northern Ireland consisted of 594 responding households

Table A3 shows how the achieved sample of 7,921 households in Great Britain was distributed according to various characteristics recorded in the Survey. It includes a breakdown of the number of persons in the sample by Standard Statistical Region. Comparison with national population estimates (not shown) suggests that the differential non-response by region is fairly low.

Table A5 shows standard errors for estimates of per capita expenditure and consumption (person per week) by food group.

Information collected

The person, male or female, principally responsible for domestic food arrangements provides information about each household. That person is referred to as the main "diary-keeper". The main diary-keeper keeps a record, with guidance from an interviewer, of all food, intended for human consumption, entering the home each day for seven days. The main Survey therefore excludes any meals out (except those based on food from the household supply, e.g. picnics, packed lunches, etc) and pet food. The Survey also covers soft and alcoholic drinks and chocolate and sugar confectionery brought home, although these are items which are typically likely to be purchased by individual household members for their own consumption without coming to the attention of the main diary-keeper.

The following details are noted for each food item: the description, quantity (in either imperial or metric units) and – in respect of purchases – the cost. Food items obtained free from a farm or other business owned by the household member or from the hedgerow, a garden or allotment is recorded only at the time

---

[1] The questionnaire relates to household composition, occupation, etc

it is used. To avoid the double counting of purchases, gifts of food and drink are excluded if a donating household bought them.

As well as the details about foods entering the household, the diary-keeper also notes which persons (including visitors) are present at each meal together with a description of the type (but not the quantities) of food served. This enables an approximate check to be made between the foods served and those acquired during the week. Records are also kept of the number and nature (whether lunch, dinner, etc.) of the meals obtained outside the home by each member of the household; this is used in the nutritional calculations – see below. The quantity of school milk consumed by children is also recorded.

On a separate questionnaire, details are entered of the characteristics of the family and its members. However names are not collected and the identities of both the persons and the addresses are strictly confidential, only those who were involved respectively with selecting the sample and carrying out the fieldwork know them. They are not even divulged to the Ministry of Agriculture, Fisheries and Food who are responsible for analysing and reporting the Survey results.

As the main part of the Survey records only the quantities of food entering the household, and not the amount actually consumed by individuals, it cannot provide meaningful frequency distributions of households classified according to levels of food eaten or of nutrient intake. However, averaged over sufficient households, the quantities recorded should equate to consumption (in the widest sense, including waste food that is discarded or fed to pets) provided purchasing habits are not disturbed by participation in the Survey and there is no net accumulation or depletion of household food stocks.

Nutritional analysis

The energy value and nutrient content of food obtained for consumption in the home[2] are evaluated using special tables for food composition. The nutrient conversion factors are mainly based on values given in *The Composition of Foods*[3]*)*, and its supplements. The conversion factors are revised each year to reflect changes as a result of any new methods of food production, handling and fortification, and also to take account of changes in the structure of the food categories used in the Survey, i.e. changes in the relative importance of the many products grouped under the heading of "reduced fat spreads". The nutrient factors used make allowance for inedible materials such as the bones in meat and the outer leaves and skins of vegetables. For certain foods, such as potatoes and carrots, allowance is also made for seasonal variations in the wastage and/or nutrient content. Further allowances are made for the expected cooking losses of thiamin and vitamin C; average thiamin retention factors are applied to appropriate food items within each major food group and the (weighted) average loss over the *whole* diet is estimated to be about 20 per cent. The losses of vitamin

---

[2] See Glossary
[3] B Holland, A. A Welch, I D Unwin, D H Buss, A A Paul and D A T Southgate, *McCance and Widdowson's The Composition of Foods* 5th edition, Royal Society of Chemistry and Ministry of Agriculture, Fisheries and Food, Royal Society of Chemistry, 1991

C are set at 75 per cent for green vegetables and 50 per cent for other vegetables. However, no allowance is made for wastage of edible food, except when the adequacy of the diet is being assessed in comparison with recommended intakes (see below). In that context, the assumption is made that, in each type of household, 10 per cent of all foods and hence of all nutrients available for consumption – is either lost through wastage or spoilage in the kitchen or on the plate, or is fed to domestic pets/live-stock[4].

The energy content of the food is calculated from the protein, fat, available carbohydrate (as monosaccharide) and alcohol contents using the respective conversion factors (4, 9, 3.75 and 7 kcal per gram). It is expressed both in kilocalories and megajoules (1,000 kcal = 4.184 MJ). Niacin is expressed as niacin equivalent, which includes one-sixtieth of the tryptophan content of the protein in the food. Vitamin A activity is expressed as micrograms of retinol equivalent, that is the sum of the weights of retinol and one-sixth of the β-carotene. Fatty acids are grouped according to the number of double bonds present, that is into saturated, monounsaturated (both *cis* and *trans*) and polyunsaturated fatty acids. For the diet as a whole, the fatty acids constitute about 95 per cent of the weight of the fat. This proportion varies slightly for individual foods, being lower for dairy fats with their greater content of short-chain acids and a little higher for most other foods.

The nutritional results are tabulated in two main ways for each category of households in the Survey:

a) *Per person (per day)*. This presentation is directly comparable to the per person (per week) presentation in Section 2 of this Report of the amounts of food obtained. However, it has some drawbacks where the interpretation of nutrient intakes is concerned. It does not take into account contributions made by meals consumed outside the home or by foods outside of the diary-keepers' purview (e.g. Confectionery or drinks bought for household consumption without the knowledge of the diary-keeper). Nor is any allowance made for the wastage of edible food. The average per person can also be misleading. For example, average per capita energy intakes in families with small children are invariably less than those for wholly adult households but this does not by itself indicate that the former are less well nourished because, on average, children have a smaller absolute need for energy.

b) *As a proportion of Dietary Reference Values published by the Department of Health*[5]. Some of the above drawbacks are overcome in this presentation. It involves comparing intakes with household needs after the age, sex and possible pregnancy of each member have been taken into account. Allowance is also made for meals eaten outside the home and for the presence of visitors

---

[4] An enquiry into the amounts of potentially edible food which are thrown away or fed to pets in Great Britain recorded an average wastage of about 6 per cent of household food supplies (see R W Wenlock, D H Buss, B J Derry and E J Dixon, *British Journal of Nutrition*, 43, 1980, pp 53-70). However, this was considered likely to be a minimum estimate, and the conventional Survey deduction of 10 per cent was retained thereby preserving continuity with previous years.

[5] Department of Health. *Dietary Reference Values for Food Energy and Nutrients for the United Kingdom*. Report on Health and Social Subjects No 41, HMSO, 1991

by re-defining, in effect, the number of people consuming the household food – *not* by adding or subtracting estimates of the nutrient content of the meals in question. Moreover, for these comparisons, the estimated energy and nutrient contents are reduced throughout by 10 per cent to allow for wastage of edible food. This difference should be borne in mind when comparing these results with the nutritional intakes per person.

Table A2 Local Authority Districts surveyed in 1996

Region [a]	Coverage of regions by county	Local Authority Districts [b] included in the 1996 sample
England:		
North	Cleveland, Cumbria, Durham, Northumberland, Tyne-and-Wear	Blyth Valley, Tynedale *Newcastle-upon-Tyne
Yorkshire and Humberside	Humberside, North Yorkshire, South Yorkshire, West Yorkshire, East Yorkshire	*Sheffield, Leeds, *Calderdale, Ryedale, Kingston-upon-Hull *Wakefield
North West	Cheshire, Lancashire, Greater Manchester, Merseyside	*Stockport, *St Helens, Rossendale, West Lancs *Liverpool, *Bury, South Ribble
East Midlands	Derbyshire, Leicestershire, Lincolnshire, Northamptonshire, Nottinghamshire	Nottingham, Wellingborough, Oadby + Wigston, South Kesteren, Market Harborough
West Midlands	Hereford and Worcester, Shropshire, Staffordshire, Warwickshire, West Midlands	*Coventry, Lichfield, South Stafford, *Birmingham, *Walsall, Nuneaton, Malvern Hills, South Shropshire
South West	Avon, Cornwall, Devon, Dorset, Gloucestershire, Somerset, Wiltshire	Plymouth, Restormel, Stroud, East Devon, Cotswold
East Anglia	Cambridgeshire, Norfolk, Suffolk	Great Yarmouth West Norfolk
South East	Greater London, Bedfordshire, Berkshire, Buckinghamshire, East Sussex, Essex, Hampshire, Hertfordshire, Isle of Wight, Kent, Oxfordshire, West Sussex, Surrey	*Islington, *Brent *Croydon, *Tower Hamlets, *Ealing, *Enfield, *Richmond, Windsor, Epping Forest, Winchester, Chichester, Rushmoor, Thurrock, Canterbury, Cherwell, Newbury
Wales	The whole of Wales	Wrexham Maelor, Cardiff, Arfon
Scotland	The whole of Scotland	*Glasgow, Kirkcaldy, Moray, Stewartry, Renfrew, East Lothian, North-east Fife

(a) these are the Standard Statistical Regions as revised with effect from 1 April 1974.
(b) Local Authority Districts marked * are wholly or partly within Greater London, the Metropolitan districts, or the Central Clydeside conurbation.

Table A3 Composition of the sample responding to the main survey, 1996.

	Households Number	Households %	Persons Number	Persons %	Average number of persons per household	% of households owning a Deep-freezer	% of households owning a Micro-wave
All Households (GB)	7921	100	20002	100	2.53	91	75
Analysis by region							
Wales	502	6.3	1274	6.4	2.54	90	76
Scotland	775	9.8	1885	9.4	2.43	87	73
England	6644	83.9	16843	84.2	2.54	91	75
North	499	6.3	1188	5.9	2.38	88	78
Yorkshire and Humberside	720	9.1	1770	8.8	2.46	90	76
North West	926	11.7	2349	11.7	2.54	90	78
East Midlands	605	7.6	1601	8.0	2.65	93	76
West Midlands	743	9.4	1889	9.4	2.54	90	74
South West	634	8.0	1620	8.1	2.56	94	74
South East/East Anglia	2517	31.8	6426	32.1	2.55	92	74
Northern Ireland[a]	594	n/a	1746	n/a	2.94	85	77
Analysis by income group[b]							
A1	164	2.1	515	2.6	3.14	96	84
A2	312	3.9	996	5.0	3.19	96	87
B	1941	24.5	5784	28.9	2.98	95	86
C	2198	27.7	6286	31.4	2.86	94	82
D	504	6.4	1293	6.5	2.57	88	71
E1	771	9.7	1593	8.0	2.07	93	72
E2	975	12.3	2061	10.3	2.11	83	61
OAP	1056	13.3	1474	7.4	1.40	80	53
Analysis by household composition[c]							
No of Adults / No of children							
1 / 0	1896	23.9	1896	9.5	1.00	78	59
1 / 1 or more	404	5.1	1092	5.5	2.70	90	72
2 / 0	2586	32.6	5172	25.9	2.00	92	75
2 / 1	678	8.6	2034	10.2	3.00	97	87
2 / 2	899	11.3	3596	18.0	4.00	97	86
2 / 3	318	4.0	1590	7.9	5.00	98	86
2 / 4 or more	91	1.1	577	2.9	6.34	97	84
3 / 0	487	6.1	1461	7.3	3.00	95	85
3 or more / 1 or 2	332	4.2	1529	7.6	4.61	98	88
3 or more / 3 or more	38	0.5	249	1.2	6.55	97	82
4 or more / 0	192	2.4	806	4.0	4.20	95	84
Analysis by ownership of dwelling							
Unfurnished, Council	1466	18.5	3516	17.6	2.40	82	61
Unfurnished, other, rented	573	7.2	1400	7.0	2.44	85	68
Furnished, rented	306	3.9	587	2.9	1.92	82	63
Rent free	79	1.0	179	0.9	2.27	97	77
Owns outright	2056	26.0	4095	20.5	1.99	92	70
Owns with mortgage	3441	43.4	10225	51.1	2.97	95	87
Analysis by age of main diary-keeper							
Age under 25	431	5.4	1009	5.0	2.34	86	70
25 - 34	1598	20.2	4832	24.2	3.02	92	80
35 - 44	1593	20.1	54.5	27.0	3.39	94	83
45 - 54	1407	17.8	3701	18.5	2.63	94	82
55 - 64	1181	14.9	1749	12.0	2.04	91	77
65 - 74	1036	13.1	1749	8.7	1.69	87	64
75 and over	659	8.3	869	4.3	1.32	78	46
Age unrecorded	16	0.2	30	0.1	1.88	94	69

(a) Northern Ireland is not included elsewhere in this table. The sample size for Northern Ireland is proportionally bigger than that for Great Britain. This is allowed for when compiling the estimates for the United Kingdom shown in some tables in Section 2 of this report.
(b) for definition of income groups see Table A3 of this Appendix and Glossary.
(c) see 'adult' and 'child' in the Glossary.

Table A4 Distribution of the 1996 sample responding to the main part of the Survey according to income

Income Group	Gross weekly income of head of household [a]	Number of households	In whole sample	*percentage of households In groups A1 to D* realised	target
Households with one or more earner [b]					
A1	£820 or more	164	2.1	3.2	3
A2	£595 but less than £820	312	3.9	6.1	7
B	£310 but less than £595	1941	24.5	37.9	40
C	£150 but less than £310	2198	27.8	42.9	40
D	Less than £150	504	6.4	9.9	10
Total A to D		5119	64.7	100	100
Households without an earner [b]					
E1	£150 or more	771	9.7		
E2	Less than £150	975	12.3		
Pensioner households [c]					
OAP		1056	13.3		
Total all households		7921	100		

(a) or of the principle earner if the head of the household was below £150 (the upper limit for group D).
(b) by convention, the short-term unemployed are classified as 'earners', until they have been out of work for more than a year when unemployment benefit ceases.
(c) see Glossary.

Table A5 Standard errors by food group, 1996

		Expenditure (pence) Mean	Standard error	SE(%)	Consumption (grams unless otherwise stated) Mean	Standard error	SE(%)
Milk and cream	ml	138.8	1.47	1.06	2106	23.30	1.11
Cheese		53.8	1.07	1.98	111	1.76	1.58
Carcase meat		108.2	2.29	2.11	240	n/a	n/a
Beef and veal		49.0	1.45	2.97	101	3.06	3.02
Mutton and lamb		28.7	1.22	4.24	66	5.24	7.98
Pork		30.4	0.85	2.79	73	2.30	3.14
Bacon and ham, uncooked		37.7	0.69	1.83	77	1.73	2.25
Poultry, uncooked		68.5	1.63	2.38	233	4.71	2.02
Other meat and meat products		169.9	3.87	2.28	393	8.67	2.20
Total meat		**384.4**	**5.51**	**1.43**	**943**	**14.60**	**1.55**
Fish		75.1	1.94	2.58	154	3.29	2.14
Eggs (No)		18.4	0.27	1.47	1872	0.03	1.60
Fats and oils		39.7	0.68	1.71	227	5.27	2.33
Sugar and preserves		19.3	0.41	2.12	185	4.22	2.28
Vegetables		220.1	2.30	1.05	2118	27.53	1.30
Fruit		116.3	2.70	2.32	1022	20.75	2.03
Cereals (incl. bread)		264.9	2.37	0.90	1561	21.63	1.39
Beverages		46.3	0.73	1.58	64	0.04	1.90
Other foods		74.5	1.30	1.74	418	11.71	2.80
Total food		**1451**	**13.27**	**0.91**	**n/a**	**n/a**	**n/a**
Soft drinks	ml	50.8	1.15	2.26	884	22.53	2.55
Alcoholic drinks	ml	114.5	4.33	3.78	386	15.59	4.04
Confectionery		29.6	0.96	3.24	58	1.84	3.15
Total food and drink		**1646**	**16.84**	**1.02**	**n/a**	**n/a**	**n/a**

Food and drink eaten out

The eating out (EO) part of the National Food Survey aims to collect information on expenditure and consumption for food and drink eaten outside the home, to supplement the information on household food and drink collected in the main part of the survey. The results complete the assessment of all food and drink consumption by households in Great Britain (and expenditure, although only that by persons and not purchased on business). It is not run in Northern Ireland.

Structure of the sample

The EO part is conducted on a subsample of half of the households selected for the main sample in Great Britain. For the main part (as described above) the 52 local authority districts (LADs) selected in each quarter are split randomly into two sets of 26 and then worked (roughly) alternately for two successive periods of 10 days. The EO Survey is conducted on each of the 26 LADs for only one of the two successive periods (half in the first period of a pair and half in the second). Within the LADs, the sampling of postal sectors and delivery points is the same as for the main part.

The response to the Eating Out part is shown in Table A6. No eating out data is accepted unless the household diary has been completed satisfactorily, in order to cross check certain entries and emphasise the completeness of records taken together. Households where one or more members initially decline to keep an eating out diary are excluded from the EO part, although those households may still keep a household diary. Those households that complete the household diary and eating out diary for each member are said to have responded fully (55 per cent of the eligible sample). Households that complete a main diary and return satisfactory eating out records for some, but not all, members are partial respondents. These records have been included in the analysis, giving a total response rate to the EO part of 59 per cent of eligible households. The composition of the sample is given in Tables A8 and A9. Standard errors are given in Table A10.

Information collected

Participating households are asked to carry out the main part of the survey in the normal way, with the main diary keeper recording household food. Each member of the household over the age of 11, including visitors staying with the household, is additionally given a diary to record all personal consumption of, and expenditure on, snacks, meals, confectionery and drinks eaten outside the home (not from household supplies). The diaries cover both food eaten by the respondent and food paid for by the respondent but consumed by others. The eating out of children under 11 is recorded and separately identified in the main diary keeper's diary.

Table A6 Responding sample to the Eating out part of the survey, 1996

	Households	Households selected (%)
Number of households at the address selected in the sample	5901	100
Number that could not be visited for operational reasons	-	-
Number visited but no contact made	408	7
Main survey requirements		
Interview refused or not practicable	1160	20
Diary-keeper answered a questionnaire but declined to keep a weeks record	560	9
Number of responding households for main survey data	3773	64
Eating Out requirements		
Main survey diary and interview complete: some valid EO diaries	224	4
Main survey diary and interview complete: all valid EO diaries	3247	55
Total responding EO households	3471	59

The following details are recorded in the eating out diary for each food item; the description, the number and size of certain items (where possible), the cost (where the respondent paid), the type of outlet where it was bought, and whether it was consumed on or off the premises. In addition, respondents also note for themselves each day which meals were eaten out, and which eaten at home or at another home, so as to provide a check for the eating out record in the main (household) diary.

The scheme for analysing the types of food eaten out is necessarily much more complex than that for the main part of the survey, since many more foods comprise a number of ingredients and quantities are not collected. There are approximately 1600 individual food codes for eating out, compared with around 230 for household food, many meals and snacks contain items that must be coded separately in order to allow an accurate estimate of consumption and nutrient intakes to be made, for example chicken, gravy, roast potatoes and one or more types of vegetable in a roast chicken dinner. However, it may not be possible to put a cost on every item, so the expenditure may be attributed to a complete dish (course) or to a whole meal or snack code. Where prices are given for individual or component items, these are generally attributed to the item.

For estimating consumption and nutrient intakes, each food code is assigned both a portion size and values for energy and nutrients. Portion sizes were obtained from a variety of sources including catering outlets, MAFFs *Food Portion Size* book, the Dietary and Nutritional Survey of British Adults and package weights. For those foods obtained from a chain outlet or fast food outlet, or other foods with a fairly standard portion size, it is possible to be reasonably confident of the data used. For foods from other restaurants and eating places, the best estimates of portion sizes are made and these are reviewed annually.

The variety of types of foods and drink that are obtained for eating out causes some problems when estimating consumption and nutrient intakes. Estimated portion sizes and nutrient values may vary significantly for similar products. Some foods have a range of codes according to the approximate size of the portion, e.g. a small, standard or large chocolate bar or portion of chips, although others have a single average portion size which is applied in all cases (regardless of the age or gender of the consumer). Interviewers often need to probe for more precise details, such as whether a food was 'low fat' or whether a beverage had sugar added. Such probing is not always possible, or may not provide the detail desired, so some assumption must be made in coding the item. In 1996, 12 per cent of all food and drink items eaten out had some unspecified detail for which an assumption was made.

A number of efforts are made to reduce the possibility of expenditure or consumption being overlooked or omitted by respondents, including the completion of a daily summary grid indicating where main meals and snacks were eaten, if at all. Some respondents record no eating out at all over the survey week and these records are accepted unless there is a reason to suspect under-recording or it appears strongly inconsistent with the meal record kept by the main diary-keeper in the household diary. Table A7 shows the percentage of people in the Eating out part of the Survey for whom no expenditure was recorded by the income group of the head of household. Generally, those in lower income groups were likely to record no expenditure on eating out, particularly for food and soft drinks. 39 per cent of all respondents spent no money on food and drink eaten out.

Table A7 Percentage of people in the EO extension with no EO expenditure in the survey week, by income group, 1996

Income group	Percentage with no EO spending on:				
	Food	Soft drinks	Confectionery	Alcohol	Any food or drink
A1	29	66	75	74	25
A2	35	70	85	79	31
B	37	70	78	78	31
C	41	73	80	82	35
D	49	78	84	86	44
E1	53	87	94	85	50
E2	62	84	87	87	56
OAP	65	97	99	91	62
Total	44	76	83	82	39

The Eating Out extension to the NFS was conducted for two years on a trial basis before results were first published in the 1994 annual report. In that time it underwent a number of methodological changes to improve data quality. The Family Expenditure Survey conducted by the Office for National Statistics provides an alternative source of information on the eating out expenditure of households and this appears to record higher levels of spending, particularly on alcoholic drinks. The results of the National Food Survey Eating out extension are monitored on a quarterly basis and further improvements in data quality and completeness are being sought.

Nutritional analysis

A separate nutrient database has been created for the Eating Out extension to the NFS, based largely on MAFFs Nutrient Databank for the National Diet and Nutrition Survey (NDNS) programme, with additional composite or recipe dishes being created where necessary. Each food code is assigned both a portion size and a total of 44 nutrients, including energy, protein, carbohydrates, fat and fatty acids, alcohol and a range of vitamins and minerals. These values are estimated using *The Composition of Foods* and its supplements, together with info gained from manufacturers and fast food and restaurant chains for specific products. The nutrient values used make allowance for inedible materials such as bones in meat but no allowance has been made for food wastage since there is as yet no reliable information on the proportion of food wasted when eaten out. Both the nutrient information and the portion size assigned to each food are reviewed annually and updated as appropriate.

The nutritional results have been tabulated in the same way as for the main survey and in addition by age and gender since, unlike the main survey, the eating out information was collected by individuals and can be related to age and gender subgroups. The nutritional results from the Eating Out survey have been added to the nutritional results from the main survey (plus soft and alcoholic drinks and confectionery) for households completing the Eating Out part, in order to express the total nutritional results as a proportion of the Dietary reference values. For this analysis the Reference Nutrient Intakes (RNIs) for the individual nutrients and the Estimated Average Requirement (EAR) for energy were weighted for the population in the Eating Out survey. These weighted Reference Values will differ from those used in the analysis of the main survey because of the difference in composition of the two populations. For the comparisons between total intakes and the RNIs, the estimated intakes of energy and nutrients in the component coming from the main survey (excluding soft and alcoholic drinks and confectionery) are reduced by 10 per cent to allow for wastage of edible food.

Table A8 Composition of the sample responding to the Eating Out extension by age and gender, 1996

number of people

Age	Male	Female	Total
Unknown	3	11	14
0-4	269	295	564
5-14	639	594	1233
15-24	477	454	931
25-34	588	683	1271
35-44	558	629	1187
45-54	556	610	1166
55-64	445	436	881
65-74	366	402	768
75+	158	252	410
Total	4059	4366	8425

Table A9 Composition of the sample of households responding to the Eating Out Survey, 1996

		Households [a] Number	%	Persons [b] Number	%	Average number [b] of persons per household
All Households		3471	100	8425	100	2.43
Analysis by region						
Wales		228	6.6	532	6.3	2.33
Scotland		353	10.2	823	9.8	2.33
England		2890	83.3	7070	83.9	
North		199	5.7	457	5.4	2.30
Yorkshire and Humberside		314	9.0	720	8.5	2.29
North West		374	10.8	915	10.9	2.45
East Midlands		263	7.6	665	7.9	2.53
West Midlands		311	9.0	785	9.3	2.52
South West		277	8.0	675	8.0	2.44
East Anglia		127	3.7	327	3.9	2.57
South East		1025	29.5	2526	30.0	2.46
Analysis by income group						
A1		68	2.0	212	2.5	3.12
A2		148	4.3	447	5.3	3.02
B		871	25.1	2448	29.1	2.81
C		992	28.6	2739	32.5	2.76
D		218	6.3	536	6.4	2.46
E1		322	9.3	635	7.5	1.97
E2		395	11.4	775	9.2	1.96
OAP		457	13.2	633	7.5	1.39
Analysis by household composition						
Number of adults	Number of children					
1	0	821	23.7	821	9.7	1.00
1	1 or more	171	4.9	444	5.3	2.60
2	0	1164	33.5	2275	27.0	1.95
2	1	297	8.6	855	10.1	2.88
2	2	383	11.0	1485	17.6	3.88
2	3	143	4.1	681	8.1	4.76
2	4 or more	43	1.2	262	3.1	6.09
3	0	215	6.2	621	7.4	2.89
3 or more	1 or 2	136	3.9	573	6.8	4.21
3 or more	3 or more	20	0.6	117	1.4	5.85
4 or more	0	78	2.2	291	3.5	3.73
Analysis by ownership of dwelling						
Unfurnished, council		577	16.6	1313	15.6	2.28
Unfurnished, other, rented		248	7.1	614	7.3	2.48
Furnished, rented		138	4.0	232	2.8	1.68
Rent free		39	1.1	86	1.0	2.21
Owns outright		911	26.2	1746	20.7	1.92
Owns with mortgage		1558	44.9	4434	52.6	2.85

(a) fully or partially responding households

(b) number of persons for whom satisfactory diaries completed

Table A10 Standard errors for selected EO results, 1996

	Mean	Standard error[a]	SE (%)
Consumption (grams):			
Ethnic foods	32	1.76	5.4
Meat and meat products	99	2.19	2.2
Fish and fish products	23	0.81	3.6
Cheese and egg dishes and pizza	28	0.97	3.5
Potatoes and vegetables	179	3.44	1.9
Salads	17	0.87	5.1
Rice, pasta and noodles	24	1.07	4.5
Soup (ml)	17	0.93	5.6
Baby food	0	0.02	76.5
Breakfast cereal	1	0.12	12.3
Fruit (fresh and processed)	18	0.85	4.7
Yoghurt	5	0.44	8.2
Bread	14	0.51	3.6
Sandwiches	35	1.24	3.5
Rolls	24	1.10	4.6
Sandwich/roll extras	7	0.24	3.3
Miscellaneous foods (e.g. sauces, butter)	17	0.55	3.3
Other additions (e.g. sugar, salt, cream)	15	0.67	4.5
Beverages	392	10.28	2.6
Ice creams, desserts and cakes	51	1.22	2.4
Biscuits	12	0.89	7.4
Crisps, nuts and snacks	12	0.43	3.7
All Food	na	na	na
Soft drinks including milk (ml)	336	7.46	2.2
Alcoholic drinks (ml)	483	19.03	3.9
Confectionery	23	0.85	3.7
Expenditure (£)			
Total food and drink	6.53	0.14	2.1
of which:			
Alcoholic drink	1.70	0.07	4.2

(a) these standard errors generally under-estimate the true standard errors because they do not take account of the complexity of the sample. The design factor for the Main Survey varies from 0.98 for beverages to 1.82 for "other meat and meat products" with a simple average of 1.27.

Appendix B

Supplementary Tables for the Main Survey

List of supplementary tables

		page
B1	Household consumption of individual foods: quarterly and annual national averages, 1996	85
B2	Average prices paid for household foods, 1994 – 1996	93
B3	Meals eaten outside the home, 1996	97
B4	Average number of mid-day meals per week by source, per child aged 5 – 14 years, 1996	98
B5	Household food consumption of main food groups by income group, 1996	99
B6	Household food expenditure on main food groups by income group, 1996	101
B7	Household food expenditure on main food groups by household composition, 1996	103
B8	Household food consumption by household composition groups within income groups: selected food items, 1996	105
B9	Nutritional value of household food: national averages 1994 – 1996	107
B10	Nutritional value of household food by region, 1996	108
B11	Nutritional value of household food by income group, 1996	109
B12	Nutritional value of household food by household composition, 1996	110
B13	Contribution made by selected foods to the nutritional value of household food: national averages, 1996	111

Important note

New Survey contractors were employed from January 1996. This has inevitably led to some changes in coding practice. Readers attempting to compare results at the detailed food code level with those of earlier years should treat the results with caution, especially when the distinctions between food descriptions are potentially ambiguous. Household food items thought to be affected in this way include:-

Broiler chicken and other poultry, Standard and premium white bread loaves, Ice cream and ice cream products and other frozen dairy foods, Ready meals (meat based) and other meat products not specified elsewhere, UK and other butter and Soft and other margarine.

Table B1
Household consumption of individual foods: quarterly and annual national averages, 1996

grams per person per week, unless otherwise stated

	Consumption					Purchases	Percentage of all households purchasing each type of food during survey week
	Jan/ March	April/ June	July/ Sept	Oct/ Dec	Yearly Average	Yearly Average	
MILK AND CREAM							
Liquid wholemilk, full price [a]	835	724	695	742	750	735[b]	42
Welfare milk	19	18	10	10	14	...	...
School milk	10	14	6	16	12	5[b]	1
Low fat milk [a]	1016	1083	1110	1082	1072	1069	60
Condensed milks	17	25	17	26	21	21	5
Infant milks	54	41	20	35	38	33	1
Instant milks	20	9	18	15	16	16	1
Other milks and dairy desserts [a]	32	45	34	39	38	37	14
Yoghurt and fromage frais [a]	131	127	129	123	128	127	39
Cream	14	18	21	18	18	18	14
Total milk and cream	**2149**	**2106**	**2061**	**2106**	**2106**	**2063**	**93**
CHEESE							
Natural [a]	97	97	104	100	99	99	54
Processed	11	13	12	12	12	12	13
Total cheese	**108**	**109**	**116**	**111**	**111**	**111**	**58**
MEAT AND MEAT PRODUCTS							
Carcase meat:							
Beef and veal [a]	111	85	101	108	101	101	30
Mutton and lamb [a]	65	68	73	58	66	65	17
Pork [a]	74	77	72	70	73	73	24
Total carcase meat	**250**	**230**	**245**	**235**	**240**	**239**	**51**
Liver [a]	5	5	5	6	5	5	3
Offal, other liver	2	2	2	2	2	2	1
Bacon and ham, uncooked	76	76	71	85	77	77	39
Bacon and ham, cooked including canned	26	29	37	39	33	33	30
Cooked poultry, not canned	17	18	30	25	23	23	15
Corned meat	13	12	12	10	12	12	10
Other cooked meat, not canned	21	27	19	10	19	19	18
Other canned meats and meat products	27	31	32	35	31	31	13
Broiler chicken, and parts uncooked, Including frozen [a]	118	128	130	134	127	127	27
Other poultry, uncooked	115	103	85	118	106	105	18
Rabbit and other meats	1	1	2	1	1	1	...
Sausages, uncooked, pork	43	51	47	49	47	47	21
Sausages, uncooked, beef	20	14	14	17	16	16	7
Meat pies and sausage rolls, ready to eat [a]	18	21	21	23	21	21	13
Frozen convenience meats and meat products	73	60	60	73	67	67	22
Pate / delicatessen type sausage [a]	9	10	10	9	10	10	10
Other meat products	118	100	113	98	108	107	41
Total other meat and meat products	**701**	**689**	**689**	**734**	**703**	**701**	**86**
Total meat and meat products	**951**	**919**	**934**	**969**	**943**	**940**	**88**
FISH							
White, filleted, fresh	20	19	17	19	19	18	9
White, unfilleted, fresh	2	...	4	1	2	2	...
White, uncooked, frozen	18	21	24	21	21	21	9
Herring, filleted, fresh	...	...	...	1	...	...	...
Herring, unfilleted, fresh	...	...	...	...	...	...	...
Fat, fresh, other than herring	9	14	12	9	11	10	5
White, processed	6	8	10	6	7	7	4
Fat, processed, filleted	2	3	3	2	2	2	2
Fat, processed, unfilleted	1	2	2	2	2	2	2
Shellfish	6	7	7	8	7	7	5
Cooked fish	9	9	13	14	11	11	8
Canned salmon	5	9	9	8	8	8	7
Other canned/bottled fish	23	22	28	21	23	23	17
Fish products, not frozen	11	10	11	11	11	11	9
Frozen convenience fish products	32	27	29	27	29	29	14
Total fish	**145**	**151**	**170**	**150**	**154**	**152**	**57**

Table B1 continued

grams per person per week, unless otherwise stated

	Consumption					Purchases	Percentage of all households purchasing each type of food during survey week
	Jan/March	April/June	July/Sept	Oct/Dec	Yearly Average	Yearly Average	
EGGS	1.88	1.98	1.83	1.80	1.87	1.82	44
FATS:							
Butter [a]	37	39	40	41	39	39	22
Margarine [a]	40	34	34	37	36	36	13
Lard and compound cooking fat	12	9	11	15	11	11	6
Vegetable and salad oils	61	47	60	54	55	55	11
Other fats [a]	83	80	82	93	85	84	34
Total fats	**232**	**208**	**226**	**239**	**227**	**227**	**61**
SUGAR AND PRESERVES							
Sugar	148	122	142	163	144	144	28
Jams, jellies and fruit curds	20	19	18	21	19	18	11
Marmalade	14	14	14	12	14	13	7
Syrup, treacle	4	4	3	4	3	3	1
Honey	5	5	4	5	5	5	2
Total sugar and preserves	**191**	**163**	**180**	**204**	**185**	**184**	**39**
VEGETABLES							
Fresh potatoes [a]	871	705	754	884	805	777	56
Fresh green vegetables:							
Cabbage, fresh	56	53	60	63	58	54	17
Brussels sprouts, fresh	22	2	4	40	17	16	7
Cauliflower, fresh	55	84	75	84	74	72	25
Leafy salad, fresh	36	72	76	38	55	53	31
Peas, fresh	2	4	9	2	4	4	3
Beans, fresh	6	10	44	13	18	10	5
Other fresh green vegetables	10	6	5	5	6	6	3
Total fresh green vegetables	**186**	**231**	**273**	**244**	**233**	**214**	**55**
Other fresh vegetables:							
Carrots, fresh	127	99	92	117	109	103	36
Turnip and swede fresh	40	17	14	44	29	28	10
Other root vegetables, fresh	33	18	14	26	23	21	9
Onions, shallots, leeks, fresh	110	87	90	102	97	92	35
Cucumber, fresh	24	42	44	26	34	33	22
Mushrooms, fresh	38	33	34	37	36	35	28
Tomatoes, fresh	74	107	120	78	94	87	42
Miscellaneous fresh vegetables	59	64	83	63	67	62	26
Total other fresh vegetables	**505**	**467**	**490**	**493**	**489**	**462**	**73**
Processed vegetables:							
Tomatoes, canned/bottled	59	55	37	44	49	49	16
Canned peas	40	33	33	34	35	35	15
Canned beans	134	133	111	121	125	125	34
Canned vegetables other than pulses, potatoes or tomatoes	28	28	26	34	29	29	13
Dried pulses, other than air dried	5	6	3	8	5	5	2
Air dried vegetables	2	3	2	1	2	2	2
Vegetable juices	5	6	6	5	6	6	4
Chips, excluding frozen	24	23	29	27	26	26	15
Instant potato	1	2	1	1	1	1	1
Canned potato	9	9	7	6	8	8	3
Potato products, not frozen [a]	55	57	56	61	57	57	42
Other vegetable products	38	44	48	38	42	42	25
Frozen peas	39	39	29	38	36	36	10
Frozen beans	11	6	8	6	8	8	2
Frozen chips and other frozen convenience potato products	109	104	115	124	113	113	19
All frozen vegetables and vegetable products, nse	57	55	42	46	50	50	13
Total processed vegetables	**615**	**603**	**552**	**593**	**591**	**590**	**80**
Total vegetables	**2177**	**2006**	**2069**	**2214**	**2118**	**2043**	**92**

Table B1 continued

grams per person per week, unless otherwise stated

	Consumption					Purchases	Percentage of all households purchasing each type of food during survey week
	Jan/ March	April/ June	July/ Sept	Oct/ Dec	Yearly Average	Yearly Average	
FRUIT							
Fresh:							
Oranges	83	68	55	44	63	63	14
Other citrus fruit	89	42	41	91	66	66	20
Apples	169	181	164	185	175	167	43
Pears	46	44	27	52	42	41	14
Stoned fruit	13	31	138	19	50	45	13
Grapes	35	31	39	35	35	35	15
Soft fruit, other than grapes	2	30	51	4	21	17	7
Bananas	170	186	202	184	185	185	48
Rhubarb	1	10	4	-	4	1	...
Other fresh fruit	25	39	93	25	45	44	10
Total fresh fruit	**634**	**662**	**813**	**640**	**686**	**663**	**71**
Other fruit and fruit products:							
Canned peaches, pears and pineapple	20	23	21	17	20	20	9
Other canned/bottled fruit	25	23	22	22	23	23	10
Dried fruit/dried fruit products	14	13	12	30	18	18	7
Frozen fruit/fruit products	2	2	3	1	2	2	1
Nuts and nut products	13	13	12	26	16	16	11
Fruit juices	225	271	263	274	258	258	30
Total other fruit and fruit products	**299**	**346**	**333**	**371**	**337**	**336**	**48**
Total fruit	**933**	**1008**	**1146**	**1011**	**1023**	**999**	**79**
CEREALS							
White bread, standard loaves, unsliced	77	67	67	68	70	70	16
White bread, standard loaves, sliced	304	258	233	237	259	258	39
White bread premium loaves	43	94	118	126	95	95	17
White bread softgrain loaves	17	22	17	13	17	17	4
Brown bread	60	68	75	80	71	70	18
Wholemeal bread	109	102	100	87	99	99	22
Other bread [a]	133	136	159	141	142	142	50
Total bread	**744**	**745**	**769**	**752**	**752**	**751**	**90**
Flour	60	72	66	81	70	69	9
Buns, scones and teacakes	56	48	39	43	47	46	26
Crispbread	5	5	5	5	5	5	5
Cakes and pastries	75	87	85	101	87	87	40
Biscuits, other than chocolate biscuits [a]	89	97	93	94	93	93	44
Chocolate biscuits	49	55	47	58	52	52	30
Oatmeal and oatmeal products	16	10	10	13	13	13	4
Breakfast cereals [a]	139	143	143	135	140	140	42
Canned milk puddings	30	28	20	29	27	27	10
Other puddings	8	4	3	11	7	7	4
Rice	68	80	134[c]	55	84	84	18
Cereal based invalid foods (including 'slimming' foods)	-	-	-	-	-	-	...
Infant cereal foods	1	1	1	1	1	1	1
Frozen convenience cereal foods	46	46	49	54	49	49	20
Cereal convenience foods, Including canned, nse	105	108	96	93	100	100	42
Other cereal foods	41	33	36	34	36	36	14
Total cereals	**1528**	**1561**	**1596**	**1560**	**1561**	**1557**	**96**
BEVERAGES:							
Tea	40	35	40	37	38	38	28
Coffee, beans and ground	5	4	4	4	4	4	4
Coffee, instant	13	13	14	13	13	13	21
Coffee, essence	-	-	-	-	-	-	...
Cocoa and drinking chocolate	5	3	2	3	3	3	3
Branded food drinks	6	5	4	5	5	5	4
Total beverages	**69**	**60**	**65**	**63**	**64**	**64**	**46**

Table B1 continued

grams per person per week, unless otherwise stated

	Consumption					Purchases	Percentage of all households purchasing each type of food during survey week
	Jan/ March	April/ June	July/ Sept	Oct/ Dec	Yearly Average	Yearly Average	
MISCELLANEOUS:							
Mineral water	80	100	133	103	104	104	8
Baby food, canned and bottled	7	5	4	3	5	5	1
Soups, canned	90	54	53	88	72	72	21
Soups, dehydrated and powdered	5	3	3	3	3	3	6
Spreads and dressings [a]	17	25	26	20	22	22	13
Pickles and sauces	79	81	82	94	84	84	32
Meat and yeast extracts	6	3	3	4	4	4	8
Table jellies, squares and crystals	3	3	3	3	3	3	3
Ice cream, mousse	60	64	87	54	66	66	10
Ice cream products and other frozen dairy foods [a]	25	50	62	27	41	40	12
Salt	13	12	10	13	12	12	4
Novel protein foods	4	4	4	3	4	4	2
SOFT DRINKS							
Soft drinks, concentrated	93	114	124	85	103	103	16
Soft drinks, ready to drink	438	495	539	490	490	490	37
Low calorie soft drinks, concentrated	32	30	40	35	34	34	5
Low calorie soft drinks ready to drink	205	250	286	288	257	256	19
Total soft drinks	**768**	**889**	**988**	**898**	**884**	**883**	**54**
ALCOHOLIC DRINKS							
Low alcohol beers, lagers and ciders	3	10	3	4	5	5	...
Beers	58	68	72	103	75	75	6
Lagers and continental beers	100	113	136	134	120	120	8
Ciders and perry	25	35	48	34	36	36	4
Wine	97	106	119	124	111	110	16
LA wine, wine and spirit with additions	7	9	9	8	8	8	2
Fortified wines	9	7	12	21	12	12	3
Spirits	10	17	20	22	17	17	5
Liqueurs	1	1	0	2	1	1	...
Total alcoholic drinks	**310**	**365**	**419**	**452**	**386**	**385**	**30**
CONFECTIONERY							
Solid chocolate	13	13	11	15	13	13	14
Chocolate coated/filled bars/sweets	26	27	22	36	28	28	21
Chewing gum	-	1	1	1	1	1	2
Mints and boiled sweets [a]	14	16	14	13	14	14	14
Fudge, toffee, caramels	3	3	3	2	3	3	3
Total confectionery	**57**	**59**	**49**	**68**	**58**	**58**	**37**

(a) these foods are given in greater detail in this table under 'Supplementary classifications'.
(b) it is estimated that 36ml of UHT low fat milk are incorrectly allocated to wholemilk throughout this appendix.

Table B1 continued

grams per person per week, unless otherwise stated

Supplementary classification [c]	Consumption Jan/March	April/June	July/Sept	Oct/Dec	Yearly Average	Purchases Yearly Average	Percentage of all households purchasing each type of food during survey week
MILK AND CREAM							
Liquid wholemilk, full price [a]							
UHT	73	49	39	34	49[b]	46	4
Sterilised	37	34	27	31	32	32	3
Other	725	642	628	677	669	657	38
Total liquid wholemilk, full price	**835**	**724**	**695**	**742**	**750**[b]	**735**	**42**
Low fat milks							
Fully skimmed	144	120	145	140	137	137	11
Semi and other skimmed	872	963	965	943	935	932	54
Total skimmed milks	**1016**	**1083**	**1110**	**1082**	**1072**[b]	**1069**	**60**
Other milks and dairy desserts							
Dairy desserts	21	26	22	23	23	23	12
Other milks	11	19	13	16	15	14	3
Total other milks	**32**	**45**	**34**	**39**	**38**	**37**	**14**
Yoghurt and fromage frais							
Yoghurt	114	111	117	110	113	113	35
Fromage frais	16	16	12	14	15	15	7
Total yoghurt and fromage frais	**131**	**127**	**129**	**123**	**128**	**127**	**39**
CHEESE							
Natural hard:							
Cheddar and Cheddar type	61	59	62	63	61	61	37
Other UK varieties or foreign equivalents	16	15	14	15	15	15	12
Edam and other continental	8	9	12	10	10	10	8
Cottage	7	6	9	5	7	7	6
Other natural soft	5	7	7	7	7	7	7
Total natural cheese	**97**	**97**	**104**	**100**	**99**	**99**	**54**
CARCASE MEAT:							
Beef: joints (including sides) on the bone	9	6	3	9	7	7	1
Joints, boned	13	17	22	20	18	18	4
Steak, less expensive varieties	25	18	20	20	21	21	9
Steak, more expensive varieties	14	15	20	21	17	17	8
Minced	48	26	33	36	36	36	15
Other beef and veal	2	2	2	2	2	2	1
Total beef and veal	**111**	**85**	**101**	**108**	**101**	**101**	**30**
Mutton	5	-	1	1	2	2	...
Lamb: joints (including sides)	31	36	39	34	35	35	6
Chops (including cutlets and fillets)	17	18	20	16	18	17	8
All other	12	13	13	7	11	11	4
Total mutton and lamb	**65**	**68**	**73**	**58**	**66**	**65**	**17**
Pork: (joints including sides)	22	17	18	24	20	20	4
Chops	26	26	24	24	25	25	11
Fillets and steaks	11	13	10	8	11	11	5
All other	15	21	19	13	17	17	6
Total pork	**74**	**77**	**72**	**70**	**73**	**73**	**24**
OTHER MEAT AND MEAT PRODUCTS:							
Liver: Ox	-	-	1	1	-	...	...
Lambs	3	3	2	3	3	3	2
Pigs	2	2	1	1	2	2	1
Other	-	-	1	1	1	1	...
Total liver	**5**	**5**	**5**	**6**	**5**	**5**	**3**

Table B1 continued

grams per person per week, unless otherwise stated

Supplementary classification (c)	Consumption Jan/March	April/June	July/Sept	Oct/Dec	Yearly Average	Purchases Yearly Average	Percentage of all households purchasing each type of food during survey week
OTHER MEATS AND MEAT PRODUCTS							
Bacon and ham, uncooked:							
Joints (including sides and steaks cut from the joint)	17	17	21	30	21	21	8
Rashers, pre-packed	39	34	31	34	34	34	24
Rashers, not pre-packed	20	25	19	21	21	21	13
Total bacon and ham, uncooked	**76**	**76**	**71**	**85**	**77**	**77**	**39**
Cooked poultry, not purchased in cans:							
Cooked poultry, not purchased in cans	13	15	27	21	19	19	13
Takeaway cooked poultry	4	3	4	4	3	3	2
Total cooked poultry, not purchased in cans	**17**	**18**	**30**	**25**	**23**	**23**	**15**
Poultry, uncooked, including frozen							
Chicken other than broilers	85	63	63	46	64	64	9
Turkey	29	38	20	64	38	38	9
All other	1	3	1	9	4	3	1
Total poultry, uncooked, including frozen	**115**	**103**	**85**	**118**	**106**	**105**	**18**
Meat pies and sausage rolls, ready to eat							
Meat pies	11	14	14	15	13	13	9
Sausage rolls, ready to eat	7	8	7	8	8	8	5
Total meat pies and sausage rolls, ready to eat	**18**	**21**	**21**	**23**	**21**	**21**	**13**
Frozen convenience meats or frozen convenience meat products							
Burgers	18	17	15	14	16	16	8
Meat pies, pasties, puddings, others	13	10	10	16	12	12	5
Other frozen convenience meats	42	34	35	43	39	39	15
Total frozen convenience meats or frozen convenience meat products	**73**	**60**	**60**	**73**	**67**	**67**	**22**
Pate and delicatessen-type sausages							
Pate	3	3	3	3	3	3	5
Delicatessen-type sausages	6	7	7	6	6	6	6
Total pate and delicatessen-type sausages	**9**	**10**	**10**	**9**	**10**	**10**	**10**
Other meat products:							
Meat pastes and spreads	2	1	1	1	1	1	3
Meat pies, pasties and puddings	36	26	28	31	31	30	15
Takeaway meat pies, pasties and puddings	2	1	3	1	2	2	2
Ready meals	24	22	19	21	21	21	10
Takeaway ready meals	28	27	33	27	29	29	11
Other meat products, not specified elsewhere	28	23	28	17	24	24	14
Total other meat products	**118**	**100**	**113**	**98**	**108**	**107**	**41**
FISH:							
Fish products, not frozen							
Fish products, not frozen	6	6	7	8	7	7	6
Takeaway fish products	5	3	4	4	4	4	3
Total fish products, not frozen	**11**	**10**	**11**	**11**	**11**	**11**	**9**

Table B1 continued

grams per person per week, unless otherwise stated

Supplementary classification [c]	Jan/March	April/June	July/Sept	Oct/Dec	Yearly Average (Consumption)	Yearly Average (Purchases)	Percentage of all households purchasing each type of food during survey week
FATS:							
Butter; New Zealand	9	15	12	12	12	12	7
Danish	7	6	6	7	7	7	4
UK	12	11	14	13	13	13	8
Other	9	7	8	8	8	8	5
Total butter	**37**	**39**	**40**	**41**	**39**	**39**	**22**
Margarine: Soft	32	26	29	31	30	30	11
Other	8	8	5	5	7	7	3
Total margarine	**40**	**34**	**34**	**37**	**36**	**36**	**13**
Other fats:							
Reduced fat spreads	51	53	50	59	53	53	21
Low-fat spreads	27	22	26	28	26	26	11
Suet and dripping	2	1	1	2	1	1	1
Other fats	4	4	5	5	4	4	3
Total other fats	**83**	**80**	**82**	**93**	**85**	**84**	**34**
VEGETABLES:							
Potatoes							
Previous years crop purchased Jan-Aug	728	456	136	-	333	328	n/a
Current years crop purchased Jan-Aug	143	249	421	-	200	188	n/a
Current years crop purchased Sept-Dec	-	-	197	884	272	261	n/a
Total potatoes	**871**	**705**	**754**	**884**	**805**	**777**	**56**
Beans, canned							
Baked beans in sauce	119	120	99	110	112	112	31
Other canned beans and pulses	15	13	12	12	13	13	6
Total beans canned	**134**	**133**	**111**	**121**	**125**	**125**	**34**
Potato products, not frozen							
Crisps and potato snacks	50	50	50	56	52	51	41
Other potato products, not frozen	6	7	6	5	6	6	4
Total potato products, not frozen	**55**	**57**	**56**	**61**	**57**	**57**	**42**
Other vegetable products:							
Other vegetable products	34	40	42	32	37	37	22
Other vegetables, takeaway	4	3	6	5	5	5	4
Total other vegetable products	**38**	**44**	**48**	**38**	**42**	**42**	**25**
CEREALS:							
Other bread:							
Rolls (excluding starch reduced rolls)	64	70	86	68	72	72	30
Malt bread and fruit bread	5	6	7	8	6	6	4
Vienna bread and French bread	22	27	28	29	26	26	13
Starch reduced bread and rolls	6	5	5	6	6	6	2
Sandwiches	5	4	5	5	5	5	4
Other	31	23	27	25	27	27	13
Total other bread	**133**	**136**	**159**	**141**	**142**	**142**	**50**
Biscuits, other than chocolate							
Sweet biscuits other than chocolate	75	82	79	78	78	78	38
Unsweetened biscuits	13	15	14	16	15	15	14
Total biscuits other than chocolate	**89**	**97**	**93**	**94**	**93**	**93**	**44**

Table B1 continued

grams per person per week, unless otherwise stated

Supplementary classification (c)	Consumption Jan/March	April/June	July/Sept	Oct/Dec	Yearly Average	Purchases Yearly Average	Percentage of all households purchasing each type of food during survey week
CEREALS:							
Breakfast cereals:							
Muesli	10	16	18	11	14	14	4
Other high-fibre breakfast cereals	63	61	58	60	60	60	22
Sweetened breakfast cereals	23	26	25	29	26	26	11
Other breakfast cereals	43	40	42	35	40	40	17
Total breakfast cereals	**139**	**143**	**143**	**135**	**140**	**140**	**42**
Rice:							
Dried rice	55	66	119(d)	40	69	69	11
Cooked rice	14	14	15	15	14	14	8
Total rice	**68**	**80**	**134**	**55**	**84**	**84**	**18**
Frozen convenience cereal foods:							
Cakes and pastries	14	16	15	18	15	15	7
Other	32	30	34	36	33	33	15
Total frozen cereal convenience foods, not specified elsewhere	**46**	**46**	**49**	**54**	**49**	**49**	**20**
Cereal convenience foods (including canned) not specified elsewhere:							
Canned pasta	38	43	34	34	37	37	14
Cakes, puddings and dessert mixes	9	8	7	8	8	8	8
Cereal snacks	7	8	8	12	9	9	10
Pizza	17	17	14	13	15	15	8
Takeaway pizza	5	3	5	5	4	4	2
Other cereal convenience foods	29	28	27	20	26	26	19
Total cereal convenience foods, including canned, nse	**105**	**108**	**96**	**93**	**100**	**100**	**42**
MISCELLANEOUS:							
Spreads and dressings:							
Salad dressings	15	22	24	17	19	19	12
Other spreads and dressings	2	2	2	3	2	2	2
Total spreads and dressings	**17**	**25**	**26**	**20**	**22**	**22**	**13**
Ice-cream products and other frozen dairy foods:							
Ice-cream products (ml)	18	37	46	21	30	30	9
Other frozen dairy foods (ml)	7	13	15	6	10	10	4
Total ice-cream products and other frozen dairy foods	**25**	**50**	**62**	**27**	**41**	**40**	**12**
CONFECTIONERY:							
Mints and boiled sweets:							
Hard pressed mints	2	2	2	1	2	2	3
Boiled sweets	12	14	12	12	13	13	12
Total mints and boiled sweets	**14**	**16**	**14**	**13**	**14**	**14**	**14**

(c) supplementary data for certain foods in greater detail than shown elsewhere in the table; the totals for each main food are repeated for ease of reference

(d) result is inflated by a single large purchase in one surveyed household.

Table B2
Average prices paid[a] for household foods, 1994 – 1996

pence per kg[b]

	Average prices paid 1994	1995	1996
MILK AND CREAM			
Liquid wholemilk, full price	54.6	54.4	52.9
Low fat milks	52.0	52.0	51.5
Infant milks	92.9	92.9	82.2
Instant milks	38.6	40.1	52.6
Other milks	153.6	159.3	234.0
Yoghurt and fromage frais	196.4	199.8	203.9
Cream	250.8	286.2	284.3
CHEESE			
Natural	438.5	452.0	482.0
Processed	471.5	465.5	496.1
MEAT AND MEAT PRODUCTS			
Carcase meat:			
Beef and veal	476.4	487.9	484.8
Mutton and lamb	418.9	414.9	441.0
Pork	332.3	350.3	418.3
Other meat and meat products:			
Liver	244.1	239.8	232.5
Offals, other than liver	245.0	264.6	317.1
Bacon and ham, uncooked	392.3	427.0	493.1
Bacon and ham, cooked, including canned	581.7	587.9	612.4
Cooked poultry, not purchased in cans	541.6	524.1	541.1
Corned meat	277.2	302.1	309.1
Other cooked meat not purchased in cans	613.7	628.0	609.9
Other canned meat/canned meat products	190.5	191.6	195.0
Broiler chicken, uncooked, including frozen	270.8	267.2	313.4
Other poultry, uncooked, including frozen	219.3	216.8	273.6
Rabbit and other meats	403.1	275.7	472.1
Sausages, uncooked, pork	256.5	257.3	270.7
Sausages, uncooked, beef	189.8	203.0	233.9
Meat pies and sausage rolls, ready to eat	321.7	327.9	358.2
Other frozen convenience meats and meat products	349.5	354.5	369.4
Pate and delicatessen type sausages	509.6	518.8	519.4
Other meat products	584.4	589.8	564.5
FISH			
White, filleted, fresh	558.7	557.4	540.0
White, unfilleted, fresh	426.3	416.8	345.7
White, uncooked, frozen	465.2	462.4	466.9
Herring, filleted, fresh	265.0	184.8	346.6
Herring, unfilleted, fresh	221.1	296.6	271.8
Fat, fresh, other than herring	519.0	583.0	573.5
White, processed	536.9	548.9	496.3
Fat, processed, filleted	553.2	603.4	481.4
Fat, processed, unfilleted	302.3	428.3	879.6
Shellfish	882.2	960.4	842.9
Cooked fish	702.2	780.3	751.7
Canned salmon	440.8	494.7	447.8
Other canned/bottled fish	275.9	279.3	278.7
Fish products, not frozen	744.7	725.7	689.5
Frozen convenience fish products	372.8	362.2	363.1
EGGS	9.5	9.6	10.1
FATS			
Butter	260.2	288.0	304.8
Margarine	111.2	109.7	107.8
Low fat and dairy spreads	79.8	83.8	182.6
Vegetable and salad oils	101.0	113.1	123.9
Other fats	187.4	190.7	214.3

Table B2 continued

pence per kg [b]

	Average prices paid		
	1994	1995	1996
SUGAR AND PRESERVES			
Sugar	68.4	70.4	77.2
Jams, jellies and fruit curd	176.7	188.4	201.1
Marmalade	165.2	172.7	188.6
Syrup, treacle	141.5	163.6	161.2
Honey	251.3	283.7	304.2
VEGETABLES:			
Potatoes	36.4	49.0	40.3
Fresh vegetables:			
Cabbages	63.8	72.0	73.8
Brussels sprouts	79.6	99.6	94.2
Cauliflowers	97.4	112.7	105.0
Leafy salad	159.8	171.1	182.8
Peas	264.7	308.4	341.8
Beans	222.5	266.7	249.7
Other green vegetables	233.6	256.9	193.6
Carrots	51.5	54.2	57.1
Turnips and swedes	48.4	56.4	67.6
Other root vegetables	118.1	140.2	119.8
Onions, shallots, leeks	85.7	98.7	86.1
Cucumbers	114.3	139.4	130.3
Mushrooms	269.1	278.1	277.7
Tomatoes	133.8	130.8	141.5
Miscellaneous fresh vegetables	195.6	211.5	203.5
Processed vegetables:			
Tomatoes, canned/bottled	57.1	53.7	52.7
Canned peas	76.2	75.3	81.4
Canned beans	63.0	61.7	63.5
Canned vegetables, other than pulses	133.0	128.2	126.6
Dried pulses, other than air dried	112.6	124.9	136.7
Air-dried vegetables	374.4	336.6	396.7
Vegetable juices	143.4	154.0	176.4
Chips, excluding frozen	330.2	346.2	382.0
Instant potato	280.3	312.7	338.3
Canned potatoes	78.3	82.5	84.1
Potato products, not frozen	489.7	507.9	512.9
Other vegetable products	387.3	388.6	381.5
Frozen peas	102.9	120.4	137.7
Frozen beans	114.4	130.5	163.9
Frozen chips and other convenience potato products	90.9	125.4	117.4
All frozen vegetables/vegetable products, not specified elsewhere	160.9	169.8	180.3
FRUIT			
Fresh:			
Oranges	85.6	94.4	98.5
Other citrus fruit	108.5	114.0	125.1
Apples	100.1	103.4	111.3
Pears	98.4	106.3	106.9
Stone fruit	156.9	194.2	161.7
Grapes	217.7	236.8	221.0
Soft fruit, other than grapes	275.9	309.9	311.0
Bananas	97.1	87.2	91.7
Rhubarb	108.9	109.4	131.7
Other fresh fruit	122.5	105.3	111.8
Other fruit and fruit products:			
Canned peaches, pears and pineapple	94.3	97.4	106.3
Other canned or bottled fruit	138.0	141.2	155.5
Dried fruit and dried fruit products	223.3	235.3	248.0
Frozen fruits and frozen fruit products	386.1	395.8	240.4
Nuts and nut products	384.5	385.1	390.8
Fruit juices	69.1	73.9	77.5

Table B2 continued

pence per kg(b)

	Average prices paid		
	1994	1995	1996
CEREALS			
White bread, standard loaves, unsliced	97.5	98.0	86.2
White bread, standard loaves, sliced	52.5	52.7	57.2
White bread, sliced, premium	73.4	72.1	73.3
White bread, sliced, whole-grain	71.2	69.3	70.6
Brown bread	87.5	89.1	89.0
Wholemeal bread	82.8	81.8	81.5
Other bread	189.3	193.7	195.3
Flour	41.9	40.6	38.8
Buns, scones and teacakes	206.2	208.2	209.3
Cakes and pastries	311.5	324.5	332.1
Crispbread	270.0	283.2	277.4
Biscuits, other than chocolate	197.3	203.1	217.9
Chocolate biscuits	332.6	345.2	340.0
Oatmeal and oat products	116.1	109.0	125.7
Breakfast cereals	250.6	252.5	258.9
Canned milk puddings	105.5	104.2	119.0
Other puddings	363.6	380.2	387.3
Rice	136.5	212.1	171.7
Cereal based invalid foods (including 'slimming' foods)	802.6	1474.6	942.4
Infant cereal foods	847.5	911.5	619.1
Frozen convenience cereal foods	347.0	340.1	347.0
Cereal convenience foods, including canned, not specified elsewhere	348.9	361.3	328.0
Other cereal foods	128.0	127.3	147.8
BEVERAGES			
Tea	479.3	462.5	471.7
Coffee, beans and ground	658.3	819.3	855.8
Coffee, instant	1492.6	1697.5	1577.9
Coffee, essences	479.1	496.4	452.8
Cocoa and drinking chocolate	346.5	344.2	388.6
Branded food drinks	512.2	516.4	509.8
MISCELLANEOUS			
Mineral water	40.5	41.9	42.7
Baby foods, canned/bottled	281.1	303.4	326.9
Soups, canned	112.6	112.3	119.3
Soups, dehydrated and powdered	775.7	741.2	671.4
Spreads and dressings	239.6	244.8	254.9
Pickles and sauces	211.7	218.4	230.9
Meat and yeast extracts	828.1	850.2	792.6
Table jellies, squares and crystals	254.8	274.2	259.4
Ice-cream, mousse	103.3	108.6	104.2
Ice-cream products and other frozen dairy foods	251.9	252.9	217.8
Salt	57.1	57.7	61.0
Novel protein foods	572.8	519.4	473.9
SOFT DRINKS			
Soft drinks, concentrated	89.5	87.0	93.3
Soft drinks, ready to drink	46.5	48.8	52.2
Low-calorie soft drinks, concentrated	90.2	78.0	78.7
Low-calorie soft drinks, ready to drink	49.2	48.1	50.6
ALCOHOLIC DRINKS			
Low alcohol beers, lagers and ciders	120.0	81.7	118.1
Beers	154.1	164.0	169.4
Lagers and continental beers	139.1	149.8	155.1
Ciders and perry	139.6	135.2	137.5
Wine	384.6	400.6	410.7
Low alcohol wine, wines and spirits with additions	289.7	343.2	268.1
Fortified wines	520.5	512.9	520.5
Spirits	1338.0	1372.2	1330.9
Liqueurs	1253.0	1427.2	1030.9

Table B2 continued

pence per kg(b)

	Average prices paid		
	1994	1995	1996
CONFECTIONERY			
Solid chocolate	515.2	537.2	570.5
Chocolate coated/filled bars and sweets	533.6	530.0	527.2
Chewing gum	802.8	970.4	779.3
Mints and boiled sweets	418.6	433.6	421.4
Fudge, toffee and caramels	417.2	441.4	433.2

(a) it should be noted that since the results for household consumption presented in this Report include both purchases and 'free' food, average prices paid cannot in general be derived by dividing the expenditure on a particular food by average consumption.

(b) pence per kg, except for the following; per litre of milk, yoghurt, cream, vegetable and salad oils, vegetable juices, coffee essence, ice-cream, ice-cream products and other frozen dairy food, soft drinks, alcoholic drinks; per equivalent litre of condensed, dried and instant milk; per egg.

Table B3
Meals eaten outside the home, April 1996 to March 1997(a)

per person per week

	Meals not from the household supply		Net balance (b)	
	Mid-day meals	All meals out (c)	Persons	Visitors
All households (GB)	1.73	2.92	0.86	0.05
Analysis by region				
North	1.89	3.01	0.86	0.05
Yorkshire and Humberside	1.66	2.72	0.87	0.04
North West	1.89	3.16	0.85	0.05
East Midlands	1.67	2.75	0.87	0.04
West Midlands	1.58	2.63	0.87	0.04
South West	1.37	2.47	0.87	0.05
South East/East Anglia	1.78	3.05	0.85	0.05
England	1.72	2.90	0.86	0.05
Scotland	1.77	3.04	0.85	0.05
Wales	1.86	3.05	0.85	0.05
Northern Ireland	1.71	2.69	0.87	0.05
Analysis by income group				
A1	2.82	5.05	0.75	0.07
A2	2.37	4.00	0.80	0.05
B	2.07	3.51	0.83	0.04
C	1.70	2.86	0.86	0.04
D	1.54	2.46	0.88	0.05
E1	1.24	2.06	0.90	0.06
E2	1.37	2.30	0.88	0.05
OAPs (all)	0.83	1.42	0.93	0.05
Analysis by household composition				
Number of adults / Number of children				
1 / 0	1.62	3.03	0.85	0.08
1 / 1 or more	2.54	4.16	0.80	0.06
2 / 0	1.39	2.48	0.88	0.06
2 / 1	1.92	3.23	0.84	0.04
2 / 2	1.83	2.96	0.86	0.03
2 / 3	1.85	2.85	0.86	0.02
2 / 4 or more	1.73	2.44	0.89	0.03
3 / 0	1.71	2.92	0.86	0.05
3 or more / 1 or 2	1.90	3.10	0.85	0.03
3 or more / 3 or more	2.06	3.11	0.85	0.04
4 or more / 0	1.69	3.02	0.85	0.04
Analysis by age of main diary-keeper				
Under 25	2.14	3.81	0.81	0.05
25 – 34	1.97	3.40	0.83	0.04
35 – 44	2.06	3.30	0.84	0.04
45 – 54	1.76	2.97	0.85	0.05
55 – 64	1.28	2.27	0.89	0.07
65 – 74	0.87	1.56	0.92	0.05
75 and over	0.91	1.47	0.93	0.03
Analysis by house tenure				
Unfurnished; council	1.58	2.50	0.88	0.04
Other rented	1.67	2.87	0.86	0.05
Furnished; rented	2.23	4.24	0.79	0.05
Rent free	1.50	2.76	0.86	0.08
Owned outright	1.20	2.14	0.89	0.06
Owned with mortgage	1.98	3.31	0.84	0.04
Analysis by ownership of deep freezer/microwave				
Microwave only	2.08	3.64	0.82	0.04
Freezer only	1.49	2.51	0.88	0.05
Household with a deep freezer and microwave	1.78	2.99	0.85	0.05
Households owning neither	1.60	2.73	0.86	0.05

(a) data for quarter 1, 1996, is known to have been under-recorded and therefore the twelve month period April 1996 to March 1997 has been used in this table
(b) see Glossary
(c) based on a pattern of three meals per day

Table B4

Average number of mid-day meals per week, by source, per child aged 5 – 14 years, 1996

per person per week

	Meals not from the household supply		Meals from the household supply	
	School meals	other meals out	Packed meals	Other
All households (GB)	1.55	0.24	1.60	3.61
Analysis by region				
North	2.73	0.10	1.02	3.15
Yorkshire and Humberside	1.76	0.20	1.53	3.51
North West	1.54	0.17	1.83	3.46
East Midlands	1.33	0.33	2.10	3.24
West Midlands	1.60	0.31	1.36	3.73
South West	1.03	0.22	1.70	4.05
South East/East Anglia	1.42	0.21	1.76	3.61
England	1.53	0.22	1.68	3.57
Scotland	1.33	0.38	1.05	4.24
Wales	2.06	0.26	1.37	3.31
Northern Ireland	1.98	0.02	1.27	3.73
Analysis by income group				
A1	2.08	0.27	1.35	3.30
A2	1.54	0.23	2.05	3.18
B	1.18	0.29	1.96	3.57
C	1.24	0.23	1.72	3.81
D	1.94	0.24	1.29	3.53
E1	2.77	0.21	0.57	3.45
E2	2.56	0.11	0.72	3.61
OAPs (all)	(a)	(a)	(a)	(a)
Analysis by household composition				
Number of adults	Number of children			
1	1 or more	2.53	0.21	0.92	3.34
2	1	1.39	0.26	1.70	3.65
2	2	1.27	0.26	1.86	3.61
2	3	1.44	0.26	1.66	3.64
2	4 or more	1.79	0.13	1.48	3.60
3 or more	1 or 2	1.62	0.27	1.42	3.69
3 or more	3 or more	0.99	0.03	1.34	4.64
Analysis by age of main diary-keeper				
Under 25	1.85	0.15	0.89	4.11
25 – 34	1.63	0.20	1.53	3.64
35 – 44	1.50	0.25	1.70	3.55
45 – 54	1.57	0.33	1.60	3.83
55 – 64	1.19	0.32	0.92	4.57
65 – 74	(a)	(a)	(a)	(a)
75 and over	(a)	(a)	(a)	(a)
Analysis by house tenure				
Unfurnished; council	2.32	0.17	0.85	3.66
Other rented	1.56	0.11	1.69	3.64
Furnished; rented	1.28	0.17	0.86	4.69
Rent free	0.89	0.30	2.26	3.55
Owned outright	1.72	0.31	1.39	3.58
Owned with mortgage	1.29	0.27	1.88	3.56
Analysis by ownership of deep freezer				
Household with a deep freezer	1.54	0.24	1.61	3.61
Households not owning a deep freezer	1.94	0.38	1.32	3.36

(a) estimates are not shown as these household groups contain samples of fewer than 20 children aged 5 to 14 years.

Table B5
Household food consumption of main food groups by income group, 1996

grams per person per week, except where otherwise stated

		\u00a3820 and over	\u00a3595 and under \u00a3820	\u00a3595 and over	\u00a3310 and under \u00a3595	\u00a3150 and under \u00a3310	Under \u00a3150	\u00a3150 and over	Under \u00a3150	OAP
		A1	A2	All A	B	C	D	E1	E2	
MILK AND CREAM										
Liquid wholemilk, full price	ml	404	573	515	611	714	886	874	1023	1058
Welfare and school milk	ml	9	16	14	13	11	43	32	116	1
Low fat milks	ml	962	1165	1096	1072	1088	956	1301	847	1150
Yoghurt and Fromage frais	ml	194	186	189	147	123	102	130	71	106
Other milks and dairy desserts	ml	190	84	119	102	108	124	104	126	145
Cream	ml	48	26	34	19	14	12	26	9	22
Total milk and cream		**1807**	**2050**	**1967**	**1964**	**2058**	**2023**	**2467**	**2192**	**2482**
CHEESE										
Natural		121	112	115	107	97	80	107	81	97
Processed		13	11	12	12	13	10	10	9	11
Total cheese		**135**	**123**	**127**	**119**	**111**	**91**	**118**	**90**	**108**
MEAT:										
Beef and veal		87	98	94	89	104	109	114	106	118
Mutton and lamb		77	78	78	50	66	63	83	63	100
Pork		56	68	64	71	75	61	76	64	101
Total carcase meat		**221**	**243**	**236**	**211**	**246**	**233**	**273**	**233**	**320**
Bacon and ham, uncooked		67	65	66	69	75	80	95	64	124
Poultry, uncooked		217	255	242	233	229	244	235	223	238
Other meats and meat products		288	372	343	391	400	401	375	431	392
Total meat and meat products		**793**	**935**	**887**	**904**	**950**	**958**	**978**	**951**	**1074**
FISH:										
Fresh		54	35	42	24	22	24	72	35	53
Processed and shell		44	18	27	18	16	10	28	14	29
Prepared, including fish products		57	52	54	53	54	48	54	54	59
Frozen, including fish products		39	42	42	40	47	58	59	52	83
Total fish and fish products		**195**	**149**	**164**	**136**	**139**	**139**	**213**	**156**	**224**
EGGS:	no	1.77	1.55	1.62	1.56	1.80	1.98	2.22	2.26	2.64
Eggs purchased	no	1.69	1.47	1.55	1.52	1.73	1.90	2.20	2.21	2.61
FATS:										
Butter		55	39	45	34	32	29	70	31	65
Margarine		16	17	17	27	34	52	36	49	69
Low fat and dairy spreads		50	60	57	76	81	79	84	115	107
Vegetable and salad oils	ml	42	64	57	40	61	69	72	64	52
Other fats		9	10	9	14	16	21	21	20	37
Total fats		**171**	**190**	**184**	**190**	**223**	**249**	**283**	**238**	**331**
SUGAR AND PRESERVES:										
Sugar		64	69	67	95	133	173	198	224	265
Honey, preserves, syrup and treacle		44	30	36	35	33	71	66	43	84
Total sugar and preserves		**109**	**99**	**103**	**130**	**166**	**204**	**264**	**267**	**349**
VEGETABLES										
Fresh potatoes		651	611	625	664	818	871	1093	920	967
Fresh green		259	251	253	211	211	193	340	197	364
Other fresh		650	556	588	487	432	429	690	412	585
Frozen, including vegetable products		178	163	168	205	210	239	187	238	195
Other processed, including vegetable products		342	376	365	381	404	439	320	431	285
Total vegetables		**2080**	**1957**	**1999**	**1948**	**2075**	**2171**	**2630**	**2198**	**2396**

Table B5 continued

grams per person per week, except where otherwise stated

		Income group — Gross weekly income of head of household							
		Households with one or more earners					Households without an earner		
		£820 and over	£595 and under £820	£595 and over	£310 and under £595	£150 and under £310	Under £150	£150 and over	Under £150	OAP
		A1	A2	All A	B	C	D	E1	E2	
FRUIT:										
Fresh		886	836	853	699	591	549	1009	514	880
Other, including fruit products		98	81	86	64	66	64	130	64	148
Fruit juices	ml	423	401	409	304	226	182	283	203	180
Total fruit		**1407**	**1318**	**1348**	**1070**	**883**	**795**	**1422**	**781**	**1208**
CEREALS:										
White bread, standard loaves		143	198	179	276	359	417	293	431	369
Softgrain and premium loaves		80	122	108	115	107	114	111	117	114
Brown bread		83	71	75	63	67	68	82	68	110
Wholegrain bread		80	93	88	102	84	79	141	79	169
Other breads		164	171	169	156	142	108	148	109	130
Total bread		550	654	619	712	759	786	775	804	892
Flour		68	65	66	48	73	48	106	63	128
Cakes		146	131	136	134	120	104	165	112	216
Biscuits		105	145	132	144	152	145	160	152	184
Oatmeal and oat products		14	9	11	11	8	11	20	14	28
Breakfast cereals		137	159	152	143	132	114	170	130	154
Other cereals		304	338	325	294	356	306	239	270	196
Total cereals		**1324**	**1501**	**1441**	**1485**	**1598**	**1514**	**1635**	**1544**	**1797**
BEVERAGES:										
Tea		21	29	26	30	34	40	45	48	77
Coffee		29	19	23	16	16	15	23	16	20
Cocoa and drinking chocolate		3	2	2	2	6	4	4	6	5
Branded food drinks		6	3	6	4	4	5	10	7	10
Total beverages		**59**	**55**	**56**	**53**	**57**	**64**	**83**	**78**	**112**
MISCELLANEOUS:										
Soups, canned, dehydrated and powdered		70	70	70	64	70	67	97	87	112
Mineral water	ml	349	267	295	127	69	61	124	60	43
Ice-cream and other frozen dairy food		106	105	106	110	99	101	122	101	117
Other foods		137	131	133	145	131	116	121	118	99
Total miscellaneous		**671**	**578**	**611**	**450**	**372**	**349**	**468**	**373**	**372**
SOFT DRINKS:										
Concentrated	ml	81	150	126	112	102	107	84	109	66
Ready to drink	ml	348	540	475	461	545	562	468	520	301
Low calorie, volume as purchased	ml	340	397	378	349	318	219	206	204	137
Total soft drinks	ml	**769**	**1087**	**979**	**922**	**964**	**888**	**758**	**832**	**504**
ALCOHOLIC DRINKS:										
Lager and beer	ml	190	254	233	235	224	113	179	135	129
Wine	ml	244	221	224	156	91	65	193	45	45
Others	ml	62	85	81	66	64	50	109	41	63
Total alcoholic drinks	ml	**495**	**560**	**538**	**457**	**379**	**228**	**481**	**221**	**247**
CONFECTIONERY:										
Chocolate confectionery		48	48	49	45	41	31	42	32	33
Mints and boiled sweets		15	10	12	14	13	14	18	12	23
Other		1	2	2	3	3	2	6	4	5
Total confectionery		**65**	**62**	**63**	**62**	**56**	**48**	**66**	**48**	**61**

Table B6
Household expenditure on main food groups by income group, 1996

pence per person per week

	\multicolumn{5}{c}{Households with one or more earners}		Households without an earner		
	£820 and over	£595 and under £820	£595 and over	£310 and under £595	£150 and under £310	Under £150	£150 and over	Under £150	OAP
	A1	A2	All A	B	C	D	E1	E2	
MILK AND CREAM									
Liquid wholemilk, full price	21.0	30.3	27.1	30.9	36.5	44.1	48.7	50.7	61.0
Welfare and school milk	0.2	0.4	0.4	0.4	0.2	0.3	0.1	0.2	-
Low fat milks	54.3	62.7	59.8	56.0	47.9	47.0	67.1	41.4	61.3
Yoghurt and fromage frais	43.2	38.9	40.4	31.0	24.9	19.0	25.7	13.2	61.3
Other milks and dairy desserts	24.8	16.5	19.3	14.5	13.3	11.9	12.0	9.1	14.7
Cream	15.8	7.4	10.2	5.2	3.9	3.4	7.5	2.4	5.9
Total milk and cream	**159.3**	**156.2**	**157.2**	**137.9**	**133.6**	**125.8**	**161.1**	**117.0**	**163.3**
CHEESE									
Natural	68.0	60.4	63.0	52.7	44.5	36.2	55.7	33.0	48.2
Processed	7.8	6.6	6.8	6.3	6.3	4.9	5.0	4.2	5.6
Total cheese	**75.8**	**66.7**	**69.8**	**59.0**	**50.8**	**41.1**	**60.7**	**39.3**	**53.9**
MEAT:									
Beef and veal	55.0	53.5	54.0	46.3	48.5	46.1	57.7	43.1	58.0
Mutton and lamb	46.5	37.6	40.6	24.6	25.1	24.0	41.2	25.7	43.1
Pork	27.4	30.3	29.3	31.0	30.0	23.3	32.8	25.9	41.3
Total carcase meat	**128.9**	**121.4**	**123.9**	**101.9**	**103.6**	**93.4**	**131.7**	**94.8**	**142.5**
Bacon and ham, uncooked	40.0	36.2	37.5	35.5	36.5	34.9	47.6	27.9	57.6
Poultry, uncooked	95.6	92.5	93.5	74.8	63.8	58.0	73.2	53.7	63.4
Other meats and meat products	178.4	203.1	197.7	186.8	166.5	145.4	162.6	146.8	154.6
Total meat and meat products	**442.9**	**453.1**	**449.6**	**398.9**	**370.4**	**331.7**	**415.0**	**323.2**	**418.1**
FISH:									
Fresh	35.1	20.5	25.5	12.4	11.3	10.3	40.8	15.1	28.3
Processed and shell	40.1	16.6	24.6	5.4	9.7	5.9	22.2	6.9	13.8
Prepared, including fish products	34.8	26.7	29.5	25.8	25.5	23.8	27.1	24.1	29.1
Frozen, including fish products	19.5	19.6	19.6	16.7	18.2	19.4	26.4	18.6	37.4
Total fish and fish products	**129.5**	**83.4**	**99.1**	**67.3**	**64.7**	**59.4**	**116.6**	**64.6**	**108.7**
EGGS:									
Eggs purchased	20.8	17.4	18.5	16.3	16.7	17.8	23.3	20.1	26.6
FATS:									
Butter	17.3	12.9	14.4	36.4	9.8	8.4	21.0	35.8	20.1
Margarine	2.1	2.0	2.0	3.0	3.7	5.1	3.8	4.8	7.8
Low fat and dairy spreads	10.2	12.5	11.7	14.0	14.6	13.5	15.4	12.8	19.7
Vegetable and salad oils	11.1	8.8	9.6	6.7	6.2	6.3	10.0	6.0	6.1
Other fats	1.8	2.2	2.1	2.1	2.3	3.0	3.4	2.7	4.9
Total fats	**42.4**	**38.4**	**39.8**	**36.4**	**36.6**	**36.3**	**53.5**	**35.8**	**58.6**
SUGAR AND PRESERVES:									
Sugar	5.6	6.2	6.0	7.7	10.0	12.8	16.0	16.5	19.9
Honey, preserves, syrup and treacle	11.0	7.1	8.4	7.2	6.1	5.5	14.3	8.1	16.6
Total sugar and preserves	**16.6**	**13.2**	**14.4**	**15.0**	**16.1**	**18.2**	**30.3**	**24.7**	**36.6**
VEGETABLES:									
Fresh potatoes	35.4	28.7	31.0	29.3	39.8	30.5	38.6	32.5	37.6
Fresh green vegetables	53.0	38.3	43.3	28.3	22.4	18.5	40.2	19.7	34.7
Other fresh vegetables	104.9	79.0	87.8	62.2	49.5	43.7	77.4	42.2	56.9
Frozen, including vegetable products	29.5	27.5	28.2	29.4	29.2	28.5	25.0	26.5	28.9
Other processed, including vegetable products	80.3	87.3	84.9	85.9	79.1	69.4	62.0	64.9	44.8
Total vegetables	**303.2**	**260.8**	**275.2**	**235.0**	**209.9**	**190.6**	**238.3**	**185.8**	**202.9**

Table B6 continued

pence per person per week

	Income group Gross weekly income of head of household								
	Households with one or more earners						Households without an earner		
	£820 and over	£595 and under £820	£595 and over	£310 and under £595	£150 and under £310	Under £150	£150 and over	Under £150	OAP
	A1	A2	All A	B	C	D	E1	E2	
FRUIT:									
Fresh	125.3	110.8	115.7	83.4	66.3	55.1	117.9	56.2	97.4
Other, including fruit products	34.1	22.7	26.6	16.2	13.0	11.7	26.7	11.5	24.7
Fruit juices	50.0	37.1	41.5	23.1	15.6	11.9	25.8	13.6	14.0
Total fruit	**209.4**	**170.6**	**183.8**	**122.8**	**94.8**	**78.7**	**170.5**	**81.3**	**136.1**
CEREALS:									
White bread, standard loaves	10.4	13.2	12.3	17.8	22.1	24.4	19.2	25.0	27.8
Softgrain and premium loaves	6.8	9.0	8.2	8.4	7.6	8.2	8.7	8.3	8.9
Brown bread	7.7	6.6	7.0	5.6	5.5	6.0	8.4	5.7	10.7
Wholegrain bread	7.7	7.9	7.8	8.2	6.5	6.2	11.9	6.4	14.8
Other breads	34.0	36.9	35.9	31.2	27.5	19.0	29.8	19.5	23.0
Total bread	**66.6**	**73.6**	**71.2**	**71.1**	**69.2**	**63.8**	**78.0**	**64.8**	**85.3**
Flour	3.0	2.7	2.8	1.9	2.6	1.9	4.3	2.4	5.2
Cakes	50.6	46.8	48.1	40.0	32.3	28.2	49.6	29.7	59.6
Biscuits	32.1	43.4	39.6	39.9	39.3	34.3	42.2	35.0	44.3
Oatmeal and oat products	2.5	1.8	2.0	1.4	1.0	1.2	2.3	2.1	3.0
Breakfast cereals	37.6	43.6	41.6	38.8	34.4	27.2	40.4	32.3	36.9
Other cereals	103.7	104.6	104.3	85.9	79.1	66.7	62.7	54.3	41.8
Total cereals	**296.0**	**316.5**	**309.6**	**279.0**	**258.0**	**223.2**	**279.4**	**220.5**	**276.1**
BEVERAGES:									
Tea	10.7	16.2	14.3	14.7	15.8	17.4	23.3	20.9	35.7
Coffee	33.6	27.2	29.4	22.2	23.4	19.6	35.0	21.2	27.4
Cocoa and drinking chocolate	1.4	0.7	0.9	1.0	1.0	1.5	1.7	2.0	2.0
Branded food drinks	3.1	2.8	2.9	2.2	2.0	2.3	5.1	2.9	4.9
Total beverages	**48.8**	**46.8**	**47.5**	**40.1**	**42.2**	**40.8**	**65.1**	**47.0**	**70.1**
MISCELLANEOUS:									
Soups, canned, dehydrated and powdered	13.6	11.3	12.1	9.3	9.9	8.3	15.6	11.2	16.5
Mineral water	16.1	11.2	12.9	5.6	2.8	2.1	5.2	2.2	2.4
Ice-cream and other frozen dairy foods	20.2	18.7	19.2	18.0	14.4	12.9	18.0	11.1	14.5
Other foods	58.4	50.0	52.8	49.6	41.6	37.6	46.1	33.9	34.3
Total miscellaneous	**108.3**	**91.2**	**97.0**	**82.5**	**68.8**	**60.9**	**84.9**	**58.4**	**51.2**
SOFT DRINKS:									
Concentrated	9.0	16.7	14.1	10.8	9.2	9.6	7.8	8.6	6.3
Ready to drink	22.2	35.2	30.8	26.4	27.3	25.6	23.2	23.5	14.8
Low calorie, volume as purchased	20.3	24.4	23.0	19.7	16.4	10.8	10.9	9.8	6.3
Total soft drinks	**51.6**	**76.2**	**67.8**	**56.8**	**52.9**	**46.0**	**41.9**	**41.9**	**27.4**
ALCOHOLIC DRINKS:									
Lager and beer	37.0	46.3	43.1	39.2	34.9	19.1	26.6	18.2	15.9
Wine	137.6	96.3	108.9	58.4	31.5	23.0	77.6	14.8	17.0
Others	42.9	52.3	51.6	35.3	26.9	21.9	91.0	19.5	51.6
Total alcoholic drinks	**220.6**	**194.9**	**203.7**	**132.9**	**93.3**	**64.0**	**195.2**	**52.5**	**84.5**
CONFECTIONERY:									
Chocolate confectionery	28.5	28.7	28.6	24.6	21.5	16.8	23.9	16.4	16.9
Mints and boiled sweets	7.1	4.7	5.5	6.1	5.4	5.9	7.5	5.0	8.6
Other	0.9	1.4	1.2	1.6	1.4	1.0	2.8	1.9	2.1
Total confectionery	**36.5**	**34.8**	**35.4**	**32.2**	**28.3**	**23.9**	**34.2**	**23.3**	**27.6**

Table B7
Household food expenditure on main food groups by household composition, 1996

pence per person per week

	\multicolumn{10}{c}{Households with}	
Number of adults	1		2					3	3 or more		4 or more	All households
Number of children	0	1 or more	0	1	2	3	4 or more	0	1 or 2	3 or more	0	
MILK AND CREAM												
Liquid wholemilk, full price	52.3	43.2	35.8	34.3	37.7	37.7	30.2	35.0	41.1	55.0	30.2	38.9
Welfare and school milk	0.0	0.5	0.0	0.4	0.6	0.8	0.0	0.0	...	0.1	0.0	0.3
Low fat milks	64.3	42.4	68.5	50.5	46.6	40.7	55.9	64.1	53.2	28.1	55.9	55.1
Yoghurt and fromage frais	28.0	23.1	27.7	31.4	30.9	22.7	12.2	21.3	19.8	13.8	18.9	26.0
Other milks and dairy desserts	16.1	8.5	12.7	23.7	15.4	12.1	5.6	8.0	12.2	9.9	9.1	13.6
Cream	6.3	1.8	7.6	4.2	3.4	2.5	6.1	6.4	3.8	4.2	6.1	5.0
Total milk and cream	**167.0**	**119.5**	**152.3**	**144.4**	**137.7**	**116.4**	**100.2**	**134.7**	**130.1**	**111.0**	**120.2**	**138.8**
CHEESE												
Natural	59.4	30.9	62.0	43.1	38.6	33.8	46.7	62.0	41.6	30.7	46.7	47.9
Processed	5.8	5.2	6.7	5.1	6.3	5.3	4.2	5.9	6.3	5.0	4.2	5.9
Total cheese	**65.2**	**36.1**	**68.7**	**48.2**	**44.9**	**39.1**	**24.0**	**67.8**	**47.9**	**35.7**	**50.8**	**53.8**
MEAT:												
Beef and veal	50.7	23.1	68.7	39.3	35.1	23.2	28.3	74.9	49.2	18.3	67.9	49.0
Mutton and lamb	35.4	17.9	39.6	19.7	20.3	12.8	26.7	32.6	34.2	25.9	34.3	28.7
Pork	28.6	16.4	41.6	26.7	25.3	19.3	18.6	47.3	25.1	20.8	27.6	30.4
Total carcase meat	**114.7**	**57.4**	**149.9**	**85.6**	**80.8**	**55.3**	**73.6**	**154.8**	**108.6**	**64.9**	**129.8**	**108.2**
Bacon and ham, uncooked	47.9	22.0	52.3	29.2	26.3	21.6	20.4	54.0	33.0	16.1	45.1	37.8
Poultry, uncooked	68.1	51.9	84.9	67.6	57.1	43.3	45.0	88.1	67.0	52.4	79.7	68.5
Other meats and meat products	210.4	132.0	193.8	202.8	151.6	130.9	113.4	205.6	147.0	98.9	165.1	169.9
Total meat and meat products	**441.1**	**263.3**	**480.6**	**356.0**	**315.8**	**251.1**	**252.4**	**502.4**	**355.5**	**232.3**	**419.7**	**384.4**
FISH:												
Fresh	26.4	11.0	29.8	8.9	7.9	4.0	3.7	18.9	9.3	19.4	13.3	16.6
Processed and shell	16.5	4.0	1.8	7.6	8.3	5.1	2.8	18.0	16.1	8.9	12.2	12.4
Prepared, including fish products	38.9	15.9	35.0	20.8	18.6	13.0	12.9	36.8	19.9	15.3	28.6	26.0
Frozen, including fish products	31.8	14.3	25.1	17.0	14.2	15.2	14.7	21.4	17.7	18.3	18.4	20.1
Total fish and fish products	**113.6**	**45.2**	**108.0**	**54.4**	**48.9**	**39.3**	**34.1**	**95.2**	**63.0**	**61.9**	**72.5**	**75.0**
EGGS: (purchased)	**26.1**	**14.4**	**23.0**	**15.2**	**13.4**	**11.5**	**14.2**	**23.0**	**17.4**	**15.0**	**18.6**	**18.4**
FATS:												
Butter	17.2	4.7	17.9	7.0	7.5	6.5	7.6	15.2	11.2	6.4	13.5	11.9
Margarine	5.1	3.2	4.8	2.9	3.1	3.1	3.0	4.5	3.6	7.6	3.0	3.9
Low fat and dairy spreads	17.4	10.5	18.8	14.3	11.6	8.3	7.3	16.7	12.1	6.1	16.3	14.4
Vegetable and salad oils	6.7	3.9	9.4	5.0	5.2	4.0	1.7	11.0	7.9	6.9	7.4	6.9
Other fats	3.4	1.6	4.1	1.8	1.6	1.6	1.0	3.4	2.5	0.5	1.7	2.6
Total fats	**49.8**	**23.8**	**54.9**	**31.1**	**29.0**	**23.6**	**20.6**	**50.8**	**37.3**	**27.5**	**41.8**	**39.7**
SUGAR AND PRESERVES:												
Sugar	16.1	9.8	14.4	6.6	8.1	7.3	8.6	13.1	10.8	13.0	10.6	11.1
Honey, preserves, syrup and treacle	12.9	4.0	12.7	6.1	5.9	4.4	3.7	6.8	5.8	6.2	7.8	8.2
Total sugar and preserves	**29.0**	**13.9**	**27.1**	**12.7**	**14.0**	**11.6**	**12.3**	**19.9**	**16.6**	**19.2**	**18.4**	**19.3**
VEGETABLES:												
Fresh potatoes	36.0	27.5	39.2	28.5	27.7	19.7	25.0	41.0	27.6	19.7	31.5	31.3
Fresh green	39.4	13.2	40.4	23.0	19.5	14.5	11.0	31.7	23.2	17.4	24.0	27.5
Other fresh	72.6	31.6	78.0	51.5	45.3	34.9	30.2	67.5	47.9	44.2	59.1	57.3
Frozen, including vegetable products	28.6	22.1	32.1	28.0	27.4	23.6	28.7	32.2	27.6	19.7	26.6	28.5
Other processed, including vegetable products	75.1	74.8	75.3	82.8	78.2	67.9	66.0	79.0	78.0	54.3	65.9	75.5
Total vegetables	**251.7**	**169.2**	**265.0**	**213.8**	**195.1**	**160.7**	**160.9**	**251.3**	**204.4**	**155.4**	**207.2**	**220.1**

Table B7 continued

pence per person per week

Number of adults	1		2					3	3 or more		4 or more	All households
Number of children	0	1 or more	0	1	2	3	4 or more	0	1 or 2	3 or more	0	
FRUIT:												
Fresh	110.8	49.5	109.6	64.8	65.5	49.8	34.5	86.9	64.4	39.7	74.3	79.6
Other, including fruit products	22.8	6.0	25.6	10.7	13.5	9.0	8.7	19.4	11.7	11.8	15.1	16.7
Fruit juices	22.2	14.4	23.9	20.6	19.3	12.5	17.5	18.3	20.5	16.4	18.0	20.0
Total fruit	**155.8**	**69.9**	**159.1**	**96.2**	**98.3**	**71.3**	**60.7**	**124.7**	**96.6**	**67.9**	**107.4**	**116.3**
CEREALS:												
White bread, standard loaves	17.7	20.3	23.0	18.1	18.1	16.3	19.4	25.6	21.4	13.5	18.3	20.8
Softgrain and premium loaves	9.2	8.0	9.3	8.2	6.6	6.6	3.9	9.3	7.9	5.9	10.5	8.2
Brown bread	12.2	2.9	8.8	3.9	3.4	3.0	2.7	8.8	4.5	3.4	8.5	6.3
Wholegrain bread	14.4	3.7	11.9	6.7	5.0	3.2	3.6	9.7	6.1	3.7	6.3	8.1
Other breads	35.2	17.2	34.5	27.5	23.7	16.0	17.1	32.5	28.1	11.0	24.8	27.7
Total bread	**95.6**	**52.3**	**87.5**	**64.4**	**56.9**	**45.2**	**46.7**	**85.9**	**68.0**	**37.5**	**68.4**	**71.0**
Flour	2.5	0.6	4.0	1.0	1.2	1.7	3.7	3.7	5.2	6.7	2.1	2.7
Cakes	51.4	27.2	49.1	34.0	35.2	23.0	20.7	42.6	34.2	20.1	33.0	38.6
Biscuits	43.9	34.0	41.8	37.4	41.5	39.0	26.6	39.5	37.2	29.4	31.5	39.3
Oatmeal and oat products	2.6	1.6	2.5	0.7	1.1	0.8	1.3	1.4	1.1	1.0	0.7	1.6
Breakfast cereals	38.8	36.9	37.1	32.5	39.9	36.1	35.3	30.8	34.2	34.3	30.4	36.2
Other cereals	73.4	67.2	76.0	87.0	79.6	65.0	51.3	81.6	81.2	53.6	65.9	75.6
Total cereals	**308.3**	**219.6**	**298.0**	**257.1**	**255.5**	**210.7**	**185.5**	**285.6**	**261.0**	**182.4**	**232.0**	**264.9**
BEVERAGES:												
Tea	27.8	12.6	25.7	15.0	11.0	9.0	9.6	22.3	14.3	7.8	19.2	18.0
Coffee	35.0	17.0	33.6	21.4	17.2	14.7	12.6	28.8	19.0	8.2	20.6	24.2
Cocoa and drinking chocolate	1.9	1.4	1.6	1.1	1.1	1.4	1.0	1.2	0.7	1.5	0.5	1.3
Branded food drinks	4.9	1.2	4.4	2.0	1.1	1.7	0.2	3.4	2.0	1.8	1.4	2.7
Total beverages	**69.6**	**32.2**	**65.3**	**39.5**	**30.4**	**26.8**	**23.4**	**55.6**	**36.0**	**19.2**	**41.7**	**46.2**
MISCELLANEOUS:												
Soups, canned, dehydrated and powdered	19.2	7.3	14.7	9.6	7.4	6.7	5.1	11.8	7.9	4.1	8.1	10.9
Mineral water ml	5.6	2.3	5.7	3.9	3.9	2.0	1.4	5.5	5.9	3.5	2.2	4.4
Ice-cream and other frozen dairy foods	14.3	14.6	16.9	14.8	16.5	14.7	17.3	17.9	13.8	14.3	11.8	15.7
Other foods	46.5	28.0	52.9	47.2	39.8	32.2	25.0	52.2	37.8	20.2	41.4	43.5
Total miscellaneous	**85.6**	**52.2**	**90.2**	**65.8**	**67.7**	**55.6**	**48.8**	**87.4**	**65.4**	**48.2**	**63.5**	**74.5**
SOFT DRINKS:												
Concentrated	7.7	11.2	7.2	11.0	12.1	12.0	11.6	9.0	10.4	15.3	5.6	9.6
Ready to drink	24.4	24.8	22.8	30.8	26.4	21.8	22.9	29.0	27.1	26.7	29.9	25.6
Low calorie, volume as purchased	12.8	16.0	15.4	17.6	19.3	12.0	7.5	17.9	14.5	7.5	15.0	15.6
Total soft drinks	**44.9**	**51.9**	**45.4**	**59.5**	**57.9**	**45.8**	**42.0**	**55.8**	**51.9**	**49.5**	**50.5**	**50.8**
ALCOHOLIC DRINKS:												
Lager and beer	36.4	10.6	42.8	36.5	27.5	23.4	17.3	35.0	19.9	3.6	42.7	32.0
Wine	60.2	11.5	68.4	47.2	33.6	22.2	15.6	40.0	40.9	7.6	53.0	45.4
Others	65.6	9.6	65.6	26.4	20.6	13.6	5.7	43.3	17.3	2.4	32.6	37.2
Total alcoholic drinks	**162.2**	**31.7**	**176.9**	**110.0**	**81.7**	**59.1**	**38.6**	**118.3**	**78.2**	**13.6**	**128.3**	**114.5**
CONFECTIONERY:												
Chocolate confectionery	20.6	20.6	22.3	22.4	23.1	19.7	16.8	25.8	25.0	17.0	13.9	21.9
Mints and boiled sweets	6.4	5.7	7.2	5.2	6.6	5.7	4.0	5.8	5.3	3.1	2.1	6.0
Other	2.6	1.4	2.1	1.3	1.3	0.8	1.2	1.6	1.3	1.6	1.3	1.6
Total confectionery	**29.7**	**27.8**	**31.6**	**28.9**	**31.2**	**26.2**	**22.0**	**33.2**	**31.6**	**21.6**	**17.4**	**29.6**

Table B8
Household food consumption by household composition groups, within income groups: selected food items, 1996

grams per person per week [a]

Income group A

Households [b] with

	Adults only	2 adults and 1 child	2 adults and 2 children	2 adults and 3 children	3 or more adults 1 or more children
Milk and cream ml or eq ml	1850	2071	2177	1647	1994
Cheese	151	106	103	108	150
Carcase meat	297	227	184	122	262
Other meats and meat products	788	735	540	499	630
Fish	250	108	140	43	166
Eggs no	1.96	1.69	1.19	1.41	1.48
Fats	197	218	144	229	176
Sugar and preserves	126	71	87	50	154
Potatoes	793	650	498	597	517
Fresh green vegetables	323	272	182	168	268
Other fresh vegetables	721	624	490	453	556
Processed vegetables	538	561	491	563	527
Fresh fruit	1099	813	762	682	612
Other fruit and fruit products	496	575	466	234	503
Bread	725	569	514	454	771
Other cereals	777	826	790	948	871
Tea	30	32	24	19	25
Coffee	32	33	14	8	21
Cocoa and drinking chocolate	3	8	1	0	1
Branded food drinks	6	10	3	11	5
FOOD EXPENDITURE	**£21.43**	**£18.00**	**£15.72**	**£11.97**	**£16.95**
Soft drinks	976	984	1054	822	1051
Alcoholic drinks	901	388	330	426	400
Confectionery	47	60	56	75	100
FOOD AND DRINK EXPENDITURE	**£25.56**	**£20.62**	**£18.08**	**£14.15**	**£20.35**

grams per person per week [a]

Income group B

Households [b] with

	Adults only	1 adult 1 or more children	2 adults and 1 child	2 adults and 2 children	2 adults and 3 children	2 adults and 4 or more children	3 or more adults 1 or more children
Milk and cream	1956	1716	2011	2015	1841	2239	1900
Cheese	148	126	104	109	95	72	97
Carcase meat	285	173	198	180	125	60	180
Other meats and meat products	836	666	651	631	505	613	616
Fish	183	105	119	102	108	132	112
Eggs	1.85	1.46	1.68	1.24	1.20	1.29	1.69
Fats	224	190	163	171	149	116	220
Sugar and preserves	155	98	85	131	85	100	156
Potatoes	790	659	635	547	539	515	729
Fresh green vegetables	285	160	188	178	135	85	184
Other fresh vegetables	642	378	446	426	339	273	381
Processed vegetables	646	583	580	572	472	537	547
Fresh fruit	899	659	629	616	525	305	591
Other fruit and fruit products	447	463	315	344	259	311	358
Bread	804	653	713	660	594	628	676
Other cereals	787	862	712	803	728	730	764
Tea	44	21	29	22	16	12	25
Coffee	22	17	17	11	12	7	13
Cocoa and drinking chocolate	3	4	2	3	1	4	1
Branded food drinks	8	4	1	3	1	1	1
FOOD EXPENDITURE	**£18.48**	**£13.68**	**£13.98**	**£13.46**	**£10.88**	**£10.59**	**£12.66**
Soft drinks	886	1217	984	1002	788	1074	793
Alcoholic drinks	641	300	504	355	254	378	276
Confectionery	63	62	55	66	56	92	60
FOOD AND DRINK EXPENDITURE	**£21.40**	**£15.68**	**£16.25**	**£15.35**	**£12.27**	**£12.39**	**£14.19**

Table B8 continued

grams per person per week [a]

	Income group C						
			Households [b] with				
	Adults only	1 adult	2 adults and				3 or more adults
		1 or more children	1 child	2 children	3 children	4 or more children	1 or more children
Milk and cream	2110	2162	2116	1914	2051	1968	2036
Cheese	140	93	93	86	93	50	96
Carcase meat	284	163	207	191	122	185	354
Other meats and meat products	802	645	652	627	535	678	663
Fish	184	167	107	96	82	58	134
Eggs	2.10	1.36	1.32	1.55	1.31	1.52	2.10
Fats	276	133	164	180	130	134	274
Sugar and preserves	203	120	122	126	135	138	179
Potatoes	935	541	778	800	602	793	705
Fresh green vegetables	286	187	178	142	98	125	186
Other fresh vegetables	552	361	359	300	267	279	450
Processed vegetables	665	606	611	571	534	525	580
Fresh fruit	775	481	480	476	397	266	471
Other fruit and fruit products	353	296	274	271	194	116	238
Bread	870	606	730	667	576	659	724
Other cereals	812	788	745	707	760	628	1374
Tea	44	29	28	24	19	32	33
Coffee	23	11	14	11	9	9	12
Cocoa and drinking chocolate	3	0	2	3	2	2	3
Branded food drinks	5	2	4	2	1	0	4
FOOD EXPENDITURE	£16.55	£11.87	£12.50	£11.37	£9.47	£9.37	£12.22
Soft drinks	878	981	1079	1189	822	887	914
Alcoholic drinks	483	176	469	319	341	160	151
Confectionery	55	72	59	62	51	39	53
FOOD AND DRINK EXPENDITURE	£18.70	£13.32	£14.32	£12.95	£10.78	£10.20	£13.31

grams per person per week [a]

	Income group D and E2						
			Households [b] with				
	Adults only	1 adult	2 adults and				3 or more adults
		1 or more children	1 child	2 children	3 children	4 or more children	1 or more children
Milk and cream	2265	2133	1990	2046	1941	1976	2372
Cheese	116	70	95	74	47	28	74
Carcase meat	300	149	205	170	139	255	265
Other meats and meat products	841	592	679	562	644	752	671
Fish	188	97	123	90	113	107	260
Eggs	2.46	1.82	2.27	1.96	1.75	2.17	1.55
Fats	303	179	226	164	210	119	275
Sugar and preserves	306	172	166	193	224	137	276
Potatoes	964	819	763	775	970	816	1104
Fresh green vegetables	297	98	135	126	94	22	168
Other fresh vegetables	583	222	445	284	218	128	442
Processed vegetables	692	610	728	577	719	534	894
Fresh fruit	693	401	363	404	246	267	628
Other fruit and fruit products	296	193	239	222	140	402	375
Bread	963	715	697	615	534	593	695
Other cereals	827	661	605	711	602	481	797
Tea	59	34	38	25	28	30	55
Coffee	19	10	13	14	16	4	16
Cocoa and drinking chocolate	5	6	3	2	17	2	7
Branded food drinks	9	2	0	2	16	0	7
FOOD EXPENDITURE	£15.23	£9.68	£10.66	£9.31	£8.93	£7.41	£11.54
Soft drinks	807	981	1039	864	647	898	741
Alcoholic drinks	345	95	244	141	97	22	111
Confectionery	52	48	55	48	34	12	38
FOOD AND DRINK EXPENDITURE	£16.87	£10.59	£11.97	£10.23	£9.51	£7.87	£12.49

Table B9
Nutritional value of household food: national averages 1994 - 1996

		1994	1995	1996 GB	1996 GB[a]	1996 UK	1996 UK[a]
		\multicolumn{6}{c}{(i) Intake per person per day}					
Energy	(kcal)	1790	1780	1850	1960	1850	1960
	(MJ)	7.5	7.5	7.8	8.2	7.8	8.3
Total protein	(g)	62.5	63.0	65.0	65.5	65.1	65.6
Animal protein	(g)	38.6	39.1	39.8	40.2	39.8	40.2
Fat	(g)	80	78	82	83	82	83
Fatty acids:							
saturated	(g)	31.1	30.8	31.6	32.5	31.7	32.5
monounsaturated	(g)	29.6	28.7	29.3	29.9	29.4	29.9
polyunsaturated	(g)	13.9	13.4	14.8	14.9	14.8	14.9
Cholesterol	(mg)	231	226	233	234	233	234
Carbohydrate [b]	(g)	217	218	228	247	228	247
of which:							
total sugars	(g)	91	90	92	110	92	110
non-milk extrinsic sugars	(g)	52	51	53	70	53	71
starch	(g)	126	128	136	136	136	137
Fibre [c]	(g)	11.7	11.6	12.4	12.5	12.4	12.5
Alcohol	(g)	-	-	-	3.6	-	3.6
Calcium	(mg)	810	810	820	840	820	837
Iron	(mg)	9.7	9.5	10.1	10.3	10.1	10.3
Zinc	(mg)	7.8	7.6	7.8	7.8	7.8	7.8
Magnesium	(mg)	220	218	229	239	229	239
Sodium	(g)	2.50	2.51	2.62	2.64	2.62	2.65
Potassium	(g)	2.49	2.51	2.60	2.66	2.60	2.67
Thiamin	(mg)	1.28	1.34	1.44	1.45	1.45	1.45
Riboflavin	(mg)	1.59	1.57	1.60	1.64	1.60	1.64
Niacin equivalent	(mg)	24.7	25.3	26.5	27.1	26.5	27.1
Vitamin B6	(mg)	1.8	1.9	2.0	2.0	2.0	2.1
Vitamin B12	(µg)	4.7	4.5	4.3	4.4	4.3	4.4
Folate	(µg)	238	237	248	252	248	252
Vitamin C	(mg)	53	52	55	59	54	59
Vitamin A:							
retinol	(µg)	740	740	575	577	574	576
β-carotene	(µg)	1680	1640	1680	1733	1674	1728
total (retinol equivalent)	(µg)	1020	1010	855	865	853	864
Vitamin D [d]	(µg)	2.64	2.96	3.35	3.35	3.35	3.35
Vitamin E	(mg)	9.46	9.50	10.68	10.80	10.68	10.79
		\multicolumn{6}{c}{(ii) As a percentage of Reference Nutrient Intake [e]}					
Energy (f)		86	85	89	94	89	94
Protein		139	140	145	146	145	146
Calcium		118	118	120	122	120	122
Iron		93	92	97	100	98	100
Zinc		98	96	98	99	98	99
Magnesium		84	83	88	91	88	91
Sodium		169	170	177	179	178	180
Potassium		79	80	83	85	83	85
Thiamin		153	161	173	174	173	174
Riboflavin		140	139	141	145	141	145
Niacin equivalent		178	183	192	196	192	196
Vitamin B6		149	198	162	169	163	170
Vitamin B12		343	328	317	323	317	323
Folate		128	127	133	135	133	135
Vitamin C		139	136	143	155	142	154
Vitamin A (retinol equivalent)		165	164	139	140	138	140
		\multicolumn{6}{c}{(iii) As a percentage of food energy}					
Fat		40.5	39.8	39.7	38.2	39.7	38.2
of which:							
saturated fatty acids		15.7	15.6	15.4	14.9	15.4	14.9
Carbohydrate		45.6	46.0	46.2	47.2	46.2	47.2

a) columns include soft and alcoholic drinks and confectionery
b) available carbohydrate, calculated as monosaccharide
c) as non-starch polysaccharide
d) contributions from pharmaceutical sources of this (or any other) vitamin are not recorded by the Survey
e) Department of Health, *Dietary Reference Values for Food Energy and Nutrients for the United Kingdom*, HMSO, 1991. Before comparison with the Reference Nutrient Intakes ten percent has first been deducted from each absolute intake given above to allow for wastage, and an allowance has also been made for meals not taken from the domestic food supply.
f) as a percentage of Estimated Average Requirement.

Table B10
Nutritional value of household food by region, 1996

		\multicolumn{7}{c}{Regions of England}				
		North	Yorkshire and Humber-side	North West	East Midlands	West Midlands	South West	South East/ East Anglia	England	Wales	Scotland	N Ireland
		\multicolumn{11}{c}{(i) Intake per person per day}
Energy	(kcal)	1760	1830	1810	1960	1890	1840	1870	1860	1860	1810	1960
	(MJ)	7.4	7.7	7.6	8.2	7.9	7.7	7.8	7.8	7.8	7.6	8.2
Total protein	(g)	61.9	64.3	66.7	66.7	66.4	63.1	64.9	65.0	65.2	64.7	67.5
Animal protein	(g)	37.5	39.4	42.0	40.0	40.4	38.5	39.3	39.7	40.1	40.1	40.1
Fat	(g)	78	80	78	89	83	82	82	82	82	80	87
Fatty acids:												
saturated	(g)	30.2	31.3	30.9	32.4	32.1	32.0	31.7	31.6	32.0	31.7	35.0
monounsaturated	(g)	28.1	29.0	28.0	32.5	29.8	29.3	29.4	29.4	29.1	29.0	30.5
polyunsaturated	(g)	13.9	14.1	13.5	17.9	14.9	14.6	15.1	14.9	14.8	13.8	15.0
Cholesterol	(mg)	223	238	235	228	236	231	234	233	231	232	255
Carbohydrate	(g)	215	225	223	238	233	227	231	229	230	220	242
of which:												
total sugars	(g)	86	91	92	95	95	97	92	92	96	89	90
non-milk extrinsic sugars	(g)	49	53	53	53	55	57	52	53	56	50	51
starch	(g)	129	135	132	143	138	129	140	137	134	131	153
Fibre [a]	(g)	12.1	12.1	12.1	13.4	12.8	12.4	12.6	12.5	12.3	11.6	13.1
Calcium	(mg)	820	814	819	867	827	828	812	820	814	825	800
Iron	(mg)	10.1	10.0	10.1	10.6	10.2	10.1	10.1	10.1	10.0	10.0	10.7
Zinc	(mg)	7.8	7.6	7.9	8.0	7.8	7.5	7.8	7.8	7.8	7.8	8.0
Magnesium	(mg)	229	222	228	237	230	228	233	230	229	223	230
Sodium	(g)	2.56	2.60	2.72	2.66	2.67	2.58	2.52	2.59	2.69	2.77	2.84
Potassium	(g)	2.60	2.53	2.62	2.68	2.65	2.60	2.63	2.61	2.64	2.53	2.62
Thiamin	(mg)	1.44	1.42	1.45	1.52	1.47	1.43	1.44	1.44	1.47	1.41	1.58
Riboflavin	(mg)	1.48	1.58	1.64	1.65	1.59	1.62	1.60	1.60	1.60	1.58	1.62
Niacin equivalent	(mg)	24.8	26.1	27.3	27.1	26.9	26.1	26.5	26.5	26.6	26.0	27.4
Vitamin B6	(mg)	1.8	1.9	2.0	2.0	2.0	2.0	2.0	2.0	2.0	1.9	2.2
Vitamin B12	(µg)	4.1	4.4	4.8	4.4	4.1	4.1	4.3	4.3	4.2	4.4	4.1
Folate	(µg)	230	243	244	257	255	256	253	250	243	234	259
Vitamin C	(µg)	53	49	52	58	54	53	59	55	54	49	45
Vitamin A												
retinol	(µg)	512	581	574	606	570	585	593	581	542	543	538
β-carotene	(µg)	1670	1600	1610	1800	1730	1710	1720	1700	1760	1480	1450
total (retinol equivalent)	(µg)	790	848	843	906	858	869	880	864	835	790	779
Vitamin D	(µg)	3.22	3.36	3.45	3.56	3.56	3.34	3.26	3.37	3.44	3.14	3.40
Vitamin E	(mg)	10.08	10.02	9.88	12.9	11.1	10.5	10.8	10.8	10.9	9.9	10.5
		\multicolumn{11}{c}{(ii) As a percentage of Reference Nutrient Intake [b]}
Energy [c]		83	87	88	94	89	86	90	89	91	87	93
Protein		136	142	149	150	145	137	145	145	149	144	150
Calcium		114	118	121	128	119	118	119	120	122	121	115
Iron		94	96	98	102	97	96	98	97	98	97	102
Zinc		95	96	101	101	97	92	99	98	100	98	99
Magnesium		83	85	88	91	86	85	90	88	90	85	88
Sodium		172	175	186	182	178	171	172	176	187	187	192
Potassium		77	80	84	86	83	81	84	83	87	80	84
Thiamin		162	169	175	182	174	169	174	173	179	170	187
Riboflavin		130	139	146	147	139	140	142	141	145	139	142
Niacin equivalent		179	188	199	196	192	184	193	192	196	189	195
Vitamin B6		149	158	165	168	163	159	164	162	168	156	184
Vitamin B12		298	321	350	327	295	295	318	317	311	319	299
Folate		120	130	132	139	135	135	137	133	134	126	138
Vitamin C		136	128	136	153	139	135	155	143	145	128	116
Vitamin A (retinol equivalent)		127	137	137	147	137	137	143	139	138	128	125
		\multicolumn{11}{c}{(iii) As a percentage of food energy}
Fat		39.9	39.6	38.9	40.9	39.5	40.0	39.6	39.7	39.6	40.1	39.9
of which:												
saturated fatty acids		15.5	15.4	15.4	14.8	15.3	15.6	15.3	15.3	15.5	15.8	16.1
Carbohydrate		46.0	46.3	46.3	45.5	46.4	46.3	46.5	46.3	46.3	45.6	46.4
		\multicolumn{11}{c}{(iv) Contribution to selected nutrients from soft and alcoholic drinks and confectionery}
Energy	(kcal)	100	100	120	120	120	100	100	110	110	110	100
	(MJ)	0.4	0.4	0.5	0.5	0.3	0.5	0.5	0.5	0.5	0.5	0.5
Fat	(g)	1	2	2	2	2	1	2	1	2	2	1
Carbohydrate	(g)	17	19	18	19	21	17	18	18	18	18	22

(a) as non-starch polysaccharides
(b) Department of Health, *Dietary Reference Values for Food Energy and Nutrients for the United Kingdom*, HMSO, 1991
(c) as a percentage of Estimated Average Requirement

Table B11
Nutritional value of household food by income group, 1996

		\£595 and over	\£310 and under \£595	\£150 and under \£310	Under \£150	\£150 and over	Under \£150	OAP
		A	B	C	D	E1	E2	
		Households with one or more earner				Households without an earner		
		(i) Intake per person per day
Energy	(kcal)	1730	1730	1840	1840	2080	1890	2220
	(MJ)	7.3	7.2	7.7	7.7	8.7	7.9	9.3
Total protein	(g)	62.7	61.8	64.6	63.8	71.9	64.7	75.9
Animal protein	(g)	38.6	37.8	39.3	38.9	44.4	39.3	47.6
Fat	(g)	77	76	81	82	92	83	98
Fatty acids:								
saturated	(g)	30.5	29.9	30.8	30.7	36.1	31.5	38.8
monounsaturated	(g)	27.4	27.3	29.2	29.9	32.5	30.1	35.1
polyunsaturated	(g)	13.9	13.6	14.9	15.4	16.6	15.0	17.0
Cholesterol	(mg)	220	214	224	230	270	245	303
Carbohydrate	(g)	208	211	229	225	258	237	274
of which:								
total sugars	(g)	84	84	86	90	117	99	127
non-milk extrinsic sugars	(g)	44	45	49	53	67	62	79
starch	(g)	123	127	128	135	142	138	147
Fibre [a]	(g)	12.5	12.0	12.0	11.7	14.6	12.1	14.7
Calcium	(mg)	790	780	800	790	940	820	960
Iron	(mg)	9.9	9.7	9.8	9.6	11.4	10.1	11.9
Zinc	(mg)	7.5	7.3	7.7	7.6	8.6	2.0	9.1
Magnesium	(mg)	230	220	222	218	265	227	269
Sodium	(g)	2.42	2.55	2.60	2.59	2.77	2.63	2.98
Potassium	(g)	2.59	2.47	2.53	2.53	3.07	2.61	3.03
Thiamin	(mg)	1.42	1.41	1.41	1.38	1.62	1.40	1.66
Riboflavin	(mg)	1.55	1.52	1.55	1.54	1.85	1.62	1.95
Niacin equivalent	(mg)	26.1	25.4	26.1	27.7	29.5	26.2	30.4
Vitamin B6	(mg)	1.9	1.9	1.9	1.9	2.3	2.0	2.2
Vitamin B12	(μg)	4.2	3.9	4.2	4.0	5.1	4.7	5.3
Folate	(μg)	243	234	239	238	292	250	303
Vitamin C	(μg)	66	55	49	47	71	49	59
Vitamin A:								
retinol	(μg)	500	500	550	550	710	640	850
β-carotene	(μg)	1820	1670	1570	1550	2050	1470	2050
total (retinol equivalent)	(μg)	810	780	810	810	1050	890	1190
Vitamin D	(μg)	2.84	3.09	3.27	3.33	3.81	3.48	4.53
Vitamin E	(mg)	9.92	9.91	10.78	11.17	11.99	10.81	12.10
		(ii) As a percentage of Reference Nutrient Intake [b]
Energy [c]		90	85	88	87	95	91	99
Protein		156	144	146	141	147	145	142
Calcium		126	118	118	113	129	119	125
Iron		101	93	93	89	114	98	122
Zinc		103	96	97	96	102	98	105
Magnesium		97	88	85	83	93	87	88
Sodium		181	181	177	174	173	179	170
Potassium		92	83	81	80	89	84	79
Thiamin		185	174	168	164	184	167	181
Riboflavin		151	139	137	135	152	142	152
Niacin equivalent		205	188	187	184	204	189	205
Vitamin B6		170	159	161	157	176	162	161
Vitamin B12		338	304	311	291	343	348	324
Folate		144	131	129	127	145	135	139
Vitamin C		190	151	130	121	172	125	136
Vitamin A (retinol equivalent)		143	131	131	130	159	142	172
		(iii) As a percentage of food energy
Fat		40.4	39.9	39.4	40.2	39.7	39.3	39.9
of which:								
saturated fatty acids		15.9	15.6	15.0	15.0	15.6	15.0	15.8
Carbohydrates		45.1	45.8	46.5	45.9	46.5	47.0	46.4
		(iv) Contribution to selected nutrients from soft and alcoholic drinks and confectionery
Energy	(kcal)	130	110	110	110	130	90	80
	(MJ)	0.5	0.5	0.5	0.4	0.6	0.4	0.4
Fat	(g)	2	2	1	1	2	1	1
Carbohydrate	(g)	20	18	19	18	18	18	14

(a) As non-starch polysaccharides
(b) Department of Health, *Dietary Reference Values for Food Energy and Nutrients for the United Kingdom*, HMSO, 1991
(c) as a percentage of Estimated Average Requirement

Table B12
Nutritional value of household food by household composition, 1996

		Households with										
No of adults		1		2					3	3 or more		4 or more
No of children		0	1 or more	0	1	2	3	4 or more	0	1 or 2	3 or more	0
		(i) Intake per person per day										
Energy	(kcal)	2130	1570	2140	1650	1610	1490	1481	2060	1980	1590	1740
	(MJ)	8.9	6.6	9.0	6.9	6.8	6.3	6.2	8.7	8.3	6.7	7.3
Total protein	(g)	75.9	54.0	76.0	59.4	55.8	49.8	52.2	75.0	65.6	54.6	62.1
Animal protein	(g)	46.8	32.7	47.1	36.2	33.8	29.6	31.6	46.8	38.3	34.4	39.4
Fat	(g)	92	68	95	73	71	65	63	93	84	72	82
Fatty acids:												
saturated	(g)	36.4	26.5	36.8	28.4	28.0	25.8	25.4	35.3	31.2	27.2	30.1
monounsaturated	(g)	32.8	24.5	34.0	26.4	25.6	23.5	22.8	33.5	30.3	26.2	29.6
polyunsaturated	(g)	16.2	12.1	17.3	13.0	12.6	11.6	10.5	17.1	16.3	13.3	16.0
Cholesterol	(mg)	286	190	277	205	192	173	191	272	225	212	235
Carbohydrate	(g)	264	197	260	201	200	187	188	247	258	194	202
of which:												
total sugars	(g)	116	78	112	78	80	72	69	97	86	82	83
non-milk extrinsic sugars	(g)	68	45	65	41	45	40	39	55	50	51	47
starch	(g)	148	119	148	124	119	115	119	151	172	112	119
Fibre [a]	(g)	14.8	9.9	15.0	11.3	10.8	9.5	9.7	13.7	11.9	9.9	11.1
Calcium	(mg)	960	740	930	760	740	690	670	880	800	700	730
Iron	(mg)	12.0	8.4	11.8	9.3	8.9	8.0	8.2	11.1	9.8	8.4	9.3
Zinc	(mg)	9.1	6.4	9.0	7.1	6.7	5.9	6.2	8.8	8.0	6.3	7.4
Magnesium	(mg)	275	190	271	210	199	177	177	254	220	187	210
Sodium	(g)	3.10	2.27	2.99	2.46	2.33	2.10	2.08	2.96	2.48	2.12	2.46
Potassium	(g)	3.0	2.2	3.1	2.4	2.2	2.0	2.1	2.9	2.5	2.2	2.4
Thiamin	(mg)	1.69	1.20	1.67	1.34	1.26	1.15	1.23	1.62	1.41	1.17	1.34
Riboflavin	(mg)	1.91	1.41	1.84	1.47	1.43	1.31	1.34	1.70	1.52	1.37	1.47
Niacin equivalent	(mg)	30.8	21.9	31.0	24.2	22.8	20.3	21.8	30.4	26.2	22.6	25.6
Vitamin B6	(mg)	2.2	1.7	2.3	1.8	1.7	1.6	1.7	2.2	2.0	1.7	1.9
Vitamin B12	(µg)	5.6	3.5	5.1	3.6	3.6	3.3	3.4	5.2	4.1	3.6	4.6
Folate	(µg)	300	205	295	222	211	193	203	273	238	207	235
Vitamin C	(µg)	66	42	68	51	47	39	41	57	50	44	53
Vitamin A:												
retinol	(µg)	760	420	710	710	448	424	401	683	539	449	672
β-carotene	(µg)	2000	1130	2090	1530	1450	1150	1500	1860	1550	1130	1680
total (retinol equivalent)	(µg)	1100	610	1060	710	690	620	650	990	800	640	952
Vitamin D	(µg)	4.03	2.75	4.08	3.13	2.76	2.49	2.72	3.80	2.99	3.00	3.16
Vitamin E	(mg)	11.64	9.01	12.4	9.7	9.3	8.6	7.8	11.9	11.5	9.7	11.3
		(ii) As a percentage of Reference Nutrient Intake [b]										
Energy [c]		97	88	96	83	83	77	76	93	94	76	80
Protein		150	154	148	142	145	133	142	149	144	129	126
Calcium		133	118	128	117	116	107	103	125	113	99	105
Iron		120	79	115	88	87	79	80	107	89	77	88
Zinc		110	94	106	95	90	80	82	105	101	79	91
Magnesium		95	88	92	87	87	78	78	89	83	74	75
Sodium		188	182	181	180	179	162	157	185	167	148	157
Potassium		85	87	86	83	85	78	82	83	79	73	70
Thiamin		191	167	187	169	163	149	157	182	166	140	153
Riboflavin		157	147	148	137	138	127	130	141	134	123	125
Niacin equivalent		214	185	209	183	176	158	168	205	185	163	176
Vitamin B6		168	166	170	157	156	145	158	168	164	141	147
Vitamin B12		360	311	332	286	299	280	292	347	302	276	312
Folate		145	130	142	127	128	117	124	136	128	115	120
Vitamin C		159	126	163	138	134	111	117	142	131	119	135
Vitamin A (retinol equivalent)		166	114	158	121	121	109	114	152	130	105	149
		(iii) As a percentage of food energy										
Fat		39.1	39.0	40.1	39.8	39.8	39.6	38.4	40.4	38.1	40.6	42.2
of which:												
saturated fatty acids		15.4	15.2	15.5	15.4	15.6	15.6	15.4	15.4	14.2	15.4	15.6
Carbohydrate		46.6	47.2	45.7	45.8	46.4	47.0	47.6	45.0	48.7	45.7	43.5
		(iv) Contribution to selected nutrients from soft and alcoholic drinks and confectionery										
Energy	(kcal)	100	100	100	100	100	100	100	100	110	90	90
	(MJ)	0.5	0.4	0.5	0.5	0.5	0.4	0.5	0.4	0.5	0.3	0.4
Fat		2	1	2	2	2	2	2	1	1	1	1
Carbohydrate		17	20	20	20	20	18	20	19	19	18	14

(a) as non-starch polysaccharides
(b) Department of Health, *Dietary Reference Values for Food Energy and Nutrients for the United Kingdom,* HMSO, 1991
(c) as a percentage of Estimated Average Requirement

Table B13

Contribution made by selected foods to the nutritional value of household food: national averages

per person per day

	Energy	Fat	Fatty Acids Saturated	Fatty Acids Poly-unsaturated	Total sugars [a]	Starch [b]	Fibre [c]
	kcal	g	g	g	g	g	g
Milk and milk products	187	8.9	5.4	0.3	17.7	0.1	...
of which: whole milk	77	4.7	2.9	0.1	5.5	-	-
low fat milks	71	2.2	1.4	0.1	7.9	-	-
yoghurt	14	0.3	0.1	...	2.5	-	-
Cheese	59	4.9	3.0	0.2	...	-	-
Meat and meat products	263	18.0	6.8	2.1	0.8	4.7	0.2
of which: carcase meat	67	4.7	2.0	0.4	-	-	-
poultry, uncooked	42	2.7	0.8	0.5	-	-	-
bacon and ham	34	2.5	0.9	0.4	...	-	-
offal	...	...	...	...	-	-	-
Fish	28	1.3	0.3	0.4	...	0.8	...
Eggs	20	1.5	0.4	0.2	-	-	-
Fats	223	24.5	7.5	6.8	0.3	...	...
of which: butter	41	4.6	3.0	0.2	-	-	-
margarine	38	4.2	1.1	1.0	...	-	-
low fat and dairy spreads	61	1.4	1.6	2.4	...	-	-
vegetable and salad oils	65	7.2	0.8	3.1	-	-	-
Sugar and preserves	97	...	...	...	25.4	...	...
Vegetables	198	5.1	1.6	1.4	6.7	27.8	4.7
Of which: fresh potatoes	66	0.1	...	0.1	1.0	14.3	1.0
fresh green vegetables	5	0.1	...	0.1	0.6	0.1	0.4
other fresh vegetables	15	0.2	...	0.1	2.7	0.2	0.9
frozen vegetables	28	0.8	0.7	0.2	0.5	4.0	0.8
canned vegetables	20	0.1	...	0.1	1.4	2.3	0.9
Fruit	79	1.5	0.3	0.4	15.4	0.5	1.4
Of which: fresh fruit	41	0.3	...	0.1	9.3	0.4	1.1
fruit juices	14	-	...	...	3.5	-	...
Cereals	642	13.7	5.4	2.2	19.4	100.7	5.7
Of which: white bread (standard loaves)	104	0.7	0.1	0.2	1.3	20.9	0.7
brown and wholemeal	53	0.6	0.1	0.2	0.5	9.8	1.2
cakes, pastries and biscuits	168	7.2	3.5	0.8	10.7	14.0	0.7
breakfast cereals	67	0.5	0.1	0.2	3.5	11.3	1.4
Other foods	56	2.4	0.8	0.8	6.2	1.3	0.2
Total food GB	**1852**	**81.6**	**31.6**	**14.8**	**92.3**	**135.9**	**12.4**
Total food UK	**1855**	**81.8**	**31.7**	**14.8**	**92.3**	**136.3**	**12.4**
Soft drinks	45	-	-	-	12.1	-	-
Alcoholic drinks	28	...	...	...	0.6	-	-
Confectionery	37	1.5	0.9	0.1	5.3	0.3	0.1
Total food and drink GB	**1962**	**83.2**	**32.5**	**14.9**	**110.3**	**136.2**	**12.5**
Total food and drink UK	**1965**	**83.3**	**32.5**	**14.9**	**110.3**	**136.6**	**12.5**

(a) includes sucrose, glucose, fructose, lactose and other simple sugars, as their monosaccharide equivalents
(b) as its monosaccharide equivalent
(c) as non-starch polysaccharides

Table B13 continued

per person per day

	Calcium	Iron	Sodium (d)	Vitamin C	Vitamin A (e)	Vitamin D
	mg	mg	mg	mg	µg	µg
Milk and milk products	366	0.2	172	2.7	122	0.2
of which: whole milk	131	0.1	63	0.7	62	...
Low fat milks	190	0.1	87	1.0	31	...
yoghurt	27	...	12	0.2	2	...
Cheese	96	...	113	-	52	...
Meat and meat products	27	1.4	518	1.9	183	0.4
of which: carcase meat	2	0.4	20	-	1	0.2
poultry, uncooked	1	0.1	16	-	5	0.1
bacon and ham	1	...	184	0.1	-	0.1
offal	...	...	...	...	...	...
Fish	17	0.2	71	...	3	0.6
Eggs	8	0.3	19	-	26	0.2
Fats	5	...	154	0.1	197	1.3
of which: butter	1	...	42	-	49	...
margarine	1	...	40	-	42	0.4
low fat and dairy spreads	3	...	71	0.1	105	0.8
vegetable and salad oils	-	-	-	-	-	-
Sugar and preserves	4	0.1	4	0.5	0.1	-
Vegetables	50	1.7	254	20.0	228	...
of which: fresh potatoes	4	0.3	9	6.1	-	-
fresh green vegetables	8	0.2	1	2.3	11	-
other fresh vegetables	13	0.3	9	5.1	165	-
frozen vegetables	6	0.3	14	3.6	27	-
canned vegetables	11	0.4	117	0.9	13	-
Fruit	18	0.4	13	27.5	10	-
of which: fresh fruit	11	0.2	3	13.5	7	-
fruit juices	4	0.1	4	13.3	1	-
Cereals	207	5.2	1011	1.6	19	0.6
of which: white bread (standard loaves)	49	0.7	247	-	-	-
brown and wholemeal	19	0.6	134	-	-	-
cakes, pastries and biscuits	37	0.7	136	...	7	...
breakfast cereals	10	1.7	136	1.3	-	0.5
Other foods	24	0.5	288	0.5	14	...
Total food GB	**820**	**10.1**	**2616**	**54.7**	**855**	**3.3**
Total food UK	**820**	**10.1**	**2622**	**54.4**	**853**	**3.4**
Soft drinks	6	...	15	4.6	8	-
Alcoholic drinks	4	0.1	3	-	...	-
Confectionery	8	0.1	9	-	2.4	-
Total food and drink GB	**838**	**10.3**	**2643**	**59.3**	**865**	**3.3**
Total food and drink UK	**838**	**10.3**	**2649**	**59.0**	**864**	**3.4**

(d) excludes sodium from table salt
(e) retinol equivalent

Appendix C

Supplementary Tables for the Eating Out Survey

List of supplementary tables

		page
C1	Consumption of individual foods, 1994 - 1996	115
C2	Consumption of food eaten out by age and gender, 1996	117

Table C1 Consumption of individual foods eaten out, 1994 to 1996

grams per person per week, unless otherwise stated

		Consumption		
		1994	1995	1996
Ethnic foods		**28**	**26**	**32**
of which:	Chinese dishes	10	9	13
	Curry	13	12	10
	Indian dishes	3	3	7
Meat and meat products		**109**	**108**	**99**
of which:	Bacon, gammon or ham	5	6	6
	Steak	5	5	3
	Hamburger or cheeseburger	16	17	13
	Meat pies (pastry and potato based)	21	19	15
	Roast beef, pork, lamb, and chops	5	4	4
	Meat based dish (e.g. casserole, lasagna, chilli con carne)	19	17	12
	Sausages (including sausage rolls, toad in the hole)	19	19	19
	Chicken or turkey (roasted or fried)	15	16	21
Fish and fish products		(a)	(a)	**23**
of which:	White fish	(a)	(a)	11
Cheese and egg dishes and pizza		**27**	**26**	**28**
of which:	Cheese pie or pastry	5	3	5
	Pizza	11	10	12
	Eggs	4	5	6
Potatoes and vegetables		(b)	(b)	**179**
of which:	Potato chips	(b)	(b)	69
	Boiled or mashed potatoes	21	18	21
	Roast or sautéed potatoes	12	11	11
	Jacket potatoes	12	9	8
	Other potato dishes	8	7	5
	Peas, sweetcorn or mange tout	12	11	10
	Green vegetables	13	11	11
	Carrots	8	8	7
	Tomatoes	2	3	5
	Beans (not green, e.g. broad beans, baked beans, chick peas)	13	13	14
	Vegetable products (e.g. mushy peas, nut roast, humous)	9	7	8
Salads		(a)	(a)	**17**
Rice, pasta and noodles		**20**	**18**	**24**
of which:	Rice	10	9	12
	Pasta or noodles	10	9	12
Soup	(ml)	**18**	**16**	**17**
of which: Vegetable based soup (including tomato)	(ml)	12	11	10
Baby food		...	...	...
Breakfast cereal		**1**	**1**	**1**
Fruit (fresh and processed)		**17**	**17**	**18**
of which:	Apples	5	4	5
	Bananas	3	3	3
Yoghurt		**6**	**4**	**5**
Bread		**13**	**14**	**14**
of which:	Bread roll, french stick, or baguette	5	5	5
	White bread toasted or untoasted	4	5	5

115

Table C1 continued

Sandwiches			36	37	35
of which:	Meat based sandwich		11	11	11
	Fish based sandwich		7	7	6
	Cheese based sandwich		8	8	7
	Egg based sandwich		3	3	3
	Poultry based sandwich		4	4	4
Rolls			25	26	24
of which:	Meat based roll		11	11	11
	Fish based roll		3	3	3
	Cheese based roll		5	5	5
Sandwich/roll extras			9	10	7
of which:	Salad fillings (e.g coleslaw, mayonnaise)		7	7	5
Miscellaneous foods			16	16	17
of which:	Butter		4	4	4
	Savoury sauces (e.g. gravy, tomato ketchup)		8	8	7
Other additions			18	15	15
of which:	Milk based additions (e.g. custard, cream)		14	12	12
Ice creams, desserts and cakes			57	49	51
of which:	Ice creams		8	7	8
	Cream cakes or buns, and dairy desserts (e.g. cheesecake, trifle)		7	6	7
Biscuits			6	5	12
Crisps, nuts and snacks			10	9	12
of which:	Crisps and potato snacks		8	7	9
Beverages		(ml)	383	389	392
of which:	Coffee	(ml)	223	212	219
	Tea	(ml)	149	164	161
Soft drinks including milk		(ml)	310	330	336
of which:	Mineral water	(ml)	16	24	23
	Pure fruit juices	(ml)	24	26	22
	Fruit juice drink or squash	(ml)	39	38	43
	Carbonated drink	(ml)	197	208	216
	Milk as a drink	(ml)	16	15	19
	Milk-based drinks (e.g. milkshake)	(ml)	10	10	12
Alcoholic drinks		(ml)	539	535	483
of which:	Low alcohol beer or cider	(ml)	4	4	7
	Beers	(ml)	295	281	251
	Lagers and continental beer	(ml)	178	183	167
	Ciders and perry	(ml)	20	22	21
	Wine - full strength	(ml)	22	24	24
	Wine or spirit with mixer, low alcohol wine	(ml)	14	15	8
Confectionery			21	19	23
of which:	Chocolate coated bar or sweet		12	11	12

(a) comparable data not available in 1994 and 1995

Table C2 Consumption of food eaten out by age and gender, 1996

grams per person per week, unless otherwise stated

	Infants	Children			Males				Females				
	Infants under 1	1 to 3	4 to 6	7 to 10	11 to 14	15 to 18	19 to 50	51+	11 to 14	15 to 18	19 to 50 not pregnant	19 to 50 pregnant	51+
Ethnic foods	-	6	25	20	30	15	57	19	31	13	43	41	18
Meat products	9	78	122	141	173	152	165	69	116	111	74	67	40
Fish dishes and products	7	15	23	29	24	11	28	23	15	23	22	9	21
Cheese/egg dishes and pizza	...	11	25	38	61	46	42	16	42	30	26	32	13
Potatoes and vegetables	24	109	244	299	309	229	217	143	245	183	156	126	115
Salads	-	6	6	8	10	9	22	14	15	12	27	15	15
Rice, pasta and noodles	5	12	56	49	32	23	31	8	45	7	27	12	9
Soup (ml)	3	8	2	6	9	5	22	23	10	21	19	18	16
Baby food	-	...	-	-	-	-	-	-	-	-	-	-	-
Breakfast cereal	...	2	-	...	...	1	2	1	1	1	1	-	1
Fruit (fresh and processed)	11	21	26	21	13	6	23	10	21	21	22	17	12
Yoghurt	3	8	9	10	3	2	6	1	8	2	7	13	4
Bread	4	8	3	7	14	13	24	14	8	19	15	19	8
Sandwiches	1	13	11	12	10	45	65	26	27	64	43	25	17
Rolls	2	2	2	10	23	45	47	16	21	61	26	10	8
Sandwich/roll extras	...	1	1	1	4	6	12	4	5	14	11	9	3
Miscellaneous foods	2	6	8	12	20	17	24	14	16	22	19	12	13
Other additions	3	11	30	28	16	8	15	16	13	7	12	9	13
Beverages (ml)	-	5	5	5	27	90	831	375	17	183	518	272	238
Ice creams, desserts and cakes	5	37	90	109	97	48	46	32	98	52	49	24	38
Biscuits	-	17	13	17	20	14	15	6	17	22	12	4	6
Crisps, nuts and snacks	1	7	9	14	26	36	17	2	46	30	11	9	1
Soft/milk drinks (ml)	28	279	336	415	788	939	423	88	728	848	360	353	92
Alcoholic drinks (ml)	-	-	-	1	13	380	1304	813	-	174	304	23	86
Confectionery	1	15	21	34	95	86	25	4	110	69	18	12	2

Appendix D

Supplementary Tables for Regional Data

List of supplementary tables

		page
D1	Household food expenditure by region, 1994 – 1996	119
D2	Household food consumption by region, 1994 – 1996	121
D3	Regional nutrient contributions made by selected foods, 1994 – 1996	
	Energy	123
	Fat	124
	Saturates	125
	Vitamin C	126
	β-Carotene	127

Table D1 Average household expenditure on food and drink by region, 1994-96

pence per person per week

	Regions of England							England	Wales	Scotland	Great Britain
	North	Yorkshire and Humberside	North West	East Midlands	West Midlands	South West	South East and East Anglia				
MILK AND CREAM:											
Liquid Wholemilk, Full price	41.3	44.9	42.4	40.3	43.5	42.7	39.8	41.6	43.1	43.6	41.9
Welfare and school milk	0.2	0.3	0.4	0.2	0.4	0.4	0.3	0.3	0.2	0.4	0.3
Low fat milks	50.6	56.1	58.6	60.1	51.1	57.7	56.9	56.3	58.3	51.2	56.0
Dried and other milk, including dairy desserts	15.7	11.7	12.6	14.5	12.2	10.5	14.8	13.5	12.1	9.1	13.0
Yoghurt and fromage frais	21.0	24.3	24.0	25.8	24.3	25.9	27.1	25.4	23.0	23.6	25.1
Cream	3.3	3.6	3.5	4.3	3.5	6.9	5.1	4.5	4.0	3.4	4.4
Total milk and cream	**131.9**	**140.8**	**141.6**	**145.6**	**135.1**	**144.1**	**143.9**	**141.6**	**140.6**	**131.3**	**140.6**
CHEESE:											
Natural	33.5	39.9	37.6	48.3	48.3	50.6	49.7	45.6	41.4	40.3	44.9
Processed	4.6	5.5	5.7	4.7	4.4	3.9	4.7	4.8	4.3	7.0	5.0
Total cheese	**38.1**	**45.5**	**43.3**	**53.0**	**52.6**	**54.5**	**54.5**	**50.4**	**45.7**	**47.3**	**49.9**
MEAT:											
Beef And Veal	60.9	56.5	56.5	56.2	60.0	50.8	51.7	54.8	53.0	77.5	56.8
Mutton And Lamb	16.0	18.7	29.0	19.1	27.0	21.8	30.4	25.7	28.1	11.6	24.6
Pork	23.4	28.5	25.8	30.5	30.6	27.0	27.0	27.5	29.8	20.5	27.0
Total carcase meat	**100.4**	**103.7**	**111.3**	**105.8**	**117.7**	**99.5**	**109.1**	**108.0**	**110.9**	**109.6**	**108.3**
Bacon And Ham uncooked	38.8	33.5	37.8	32.3	34.8	33.2	28.9	32.7	37.4	38.2	33.5
Poultry, uncooked	53.9	52.3	55.7	53.7	59.4	59.3	63.2	58.6	60.2	52.9	58.2
Other meat and meat products	166.7	157.5	167.7	166.1	155.5	142.7	170.1	163.7	167.5	193.9	166.7
Total meat	**359.8**	**347.0**	**372.4**	**357.8**	**367.3**	**334.7**	**371.4**	**363.1**	**376.1**	**394.6**	**366.7**
FISH:											
Fresh	10.4	12.9	16.7	12.6	14.9	13.8	17.7	15.4	13.5	22.3	15.9
Processed and shell	9.2	8.6	10.3	8.9	9.3	12.6	13.6	11.3	9.9	12.0	11.2
Prepared, including fish products	34.3	35.7	26.5	26.5	28.0	24.2	27.5	28.3	21.2	19.9	27.1
Frozen, including fish products	18.9	16.7	17.4	20.8	18.7	18.9	20.4	19.2	22.5	13.6	18.9
Total fish	**72.9**	**73.9**	**70.9**	**68.8**	**70.9**	**69.5**	**79.1**	**74.1**	**67.1**	**67.9**	**73.1**
EGGS	18.5	16.9	16.5	16.5	17.3	18.3	18.7	17.8	16.8	17.7	17.7
FATS:											
Butter	10.8	9.0	9.9	9.3	9.6	11.9	11.7	10.6	12.2	11.8	10.8
Margarine	5.7	5.9	4.4	4.7	5.1	4.4	3.7	4.5	3.8	4.0	4.4
Vegetable & Salad oils	11.0	11.8	13.6	14.7	16.4	15.4	13.1	13.6	16.8	11.5	13.6
Low fat and dairy spreads	4.3	4.6	4.9	6.3	5.2	6.1	6.9	5.9	5.6	5.2	5.8
Other fats	3.4	3.6	2.6	3.3	3.0	2.6	2.6	2.9	2.7	2.6	2.9
Total fats	**35.1**	**34.9**	**35.4**	**38.4**	**39.2**	**40.5**	**37.9**	**37.5**	**41.2**	**35.1**	**37.5**
SUGAR AND PRESERVES:											
Sugar	8.7	10.3	10.0	10.1	11.7	11.6	9.7	10.1	11.6	9.5	10.2
Honey, preserves, syrup and treacle	8.0	7.3	6.5	7.6	7.6	9.3	8.1	7.8	7.8	7.6	7.8
Total sugar and preserves	**16.7**	**17.6**	**16.4**	**17.7**	**19.3**	**20.9**	**17.7**	**17.4**	**19.4**	**17.1**	**17.9**
VEGETABLES:											
Potatoes	32.7	31.8	33.2	31.4	32.8	31.6	34.0	33.0	37.7	28.4	32.8
Fresh green	21.3	23.7	21.0	27.8	27.2	27.0	32.0	27.4	25.3	16.4	26.3
Other fresh	47.1	49.3	48.1	52.3	51.5	59.2	63.7	55.9	52.5	43.5	54.6
Frozen, including vegetable products	22.6	23.4	23.8	27.4	27.9	25.4	28.3	26.3	27.6	24.7	26.3
Other processed, including vegetable products	74.5	69.1	69.9	73.2	71.1	63.8	68.6	69.5	68.2	68.6	69.4
Total vegetables	**198.1**	**197.2**	**196.0**	**212.1**	**210.47**	**207.0**	**226.7**	**212.1**	**211.3**	**181.5**	**209.3**

Table D1 *continued*

pence per person per week

	Regions of England							England	Wales	Scotland	Great Britain
	North	Yorkshire and Humberside	North West	East Midlands	West Midlands	South West	South East / East Anglia				
FRUIT:											
Fresh	60.5	65.7	67.4	72.0	72.0	81.8	88.1	76.9	72.3	67.8	75.8
Other, including fruit products	13.3	14.0	13.8	16.9	16.1	18.4	17.9	16.3	15.2	13.3	16.0
Fruit Juices	13.1	14.7	14.7	17.7	16.6	20.1	22.8	18.7	17.2	14.7	18.2
Total fruit	**87.0**	**94.4**	**95.9**	**106.6**	**104.8**	**120.4**	**128.8**	**111.9**	**104.7**	**95.4**	**110.0**
CEREALS:											
White bread	22.7	25.2	28.3	23.2	26.9	20.1	19.0	22.7	29.5	20.9	22.9
Premium and softgrain bread	5.9	3.6	4.1	4.6	4.2	4.3	5.3	4.7	4.3	6.7	4.9
Brown bread	7.4	7.0	7.6	6.2	6.4	8.2	6.5	6.9	7.4	6.3	6.9
Wholemeal bread	8.1	8.2	8.1	8.0	7.5	9.7	8.3	8.3	8.4	6.4	8.1
Other Bread	30.9	26.5	25.7	25.9	23.5	22.4	26.1	25.8	22.5	37.0	26.6
Total bread	75.0	70.6	73.7	67.9	68.5	64.8	65.3	68.3	72.1	77.2	69.3
Flour	2.6	3.0	1.8	3.1	3.2	2.8	2.6	2.7	2.3	1.4	2.5
Cakes	37.7	35.2	39.3	38.4	34.9	34	37.0	36.8	30.2	32.3	36.0
Biscuits	41.9	35.5	34.9	36.0	34.8	36.6	33.4	35.1	36.6	41.3	35.8
Oatmeal And Oat products	1.3	1.2	1.1	1.1	1.3	1.4	1.1	1.2	1.2	3.0	1.4
Breakfast Cereals	32.0	35.8	33.8	36.7	33.3	37.1	35.3	35.0	33.2	31.84	34.6
Other cereals	64.8	62.1	62.1	70.0	61.0	57.7	75.3	67.5	56.6	68.5	67.0
Total cereals	**255.3**	**243.2**	**246.7**	**253.1**	**236.9**	**234.4**	**250.1**	**246.6**	**232.1**	**255.6**	**246.6**
BEVERAGES:											
Tea	17.2	17.1	19.1	18.1	21.3	17.3	18.0	18.3	19.5	16.1	18.2
Coffee	23.7	23.5	22.5	22.9	22.6	25.7	22.4	23.0	22.1	23.0	22.9
Cocoa and drinking chocolate	0.7	0.9	0.8	1.1	1.3	1.3	1.0	1.0	1.1	0.6	1.0
Branded Food Drinks	2.3	2.4	2.2	3.2	3.6	2.9	2.8	2.8	2.8	1.3	2.7
Total beverages	**43.9**	**44.0**	**44.6**	**45.3**	**48.7**	**47.3**	**44.3**	**45.1**	**45.5**	**41.0**	**44.8**
MISCELLANEOUS											
Soups canned, dehydrated and powdered	9.6	10.1	11.9	8.0	9.2	8.8	9.3	9.6	9.1	14.5	10.0
Other foods	62.1	66.0	65.3	73.4	67.8	76.7	81.8	73.5	68.1	65.2	72.4
Total miscellaneous	**82.5**	**82.5**	**82.5**	**82.5**	**82.5**	**82.5**	**82.5**	**82.5**	**82.5**	**82.5**	**82.5**
TOTAL FOOD:	**1317.2**	**1319.8**	**1345.8**	**1383.8**	**1368.7**	**1364.6**	**1450.5**	**1388.8**	**1366.5**	**1352.1**	**1384.2**
SOFT DRINKS:											
Concentrated	6.6	8.4	9.8	9.2	10.7	10.0	10.5	9.7	7.9	7.2	9.4
Unconcentrated	23.6	21.2	23.6	22.6	25.2	17.2	23.8	22.9	25.2	32.4	23.9
Low calorie, volume as purchased	13.9	9.8	14.4	14.0	14.9	10.3	14.7	13.6	16.9	22.6	14.6
Total soft drinks, (volume purchased)	**44.1**	**39.5**	**47.9**	**45.8**	**50.8**	**37.4**	**48.9**	**46.3**	**50.0**	**62.2**	**48.0**
ALCOHOLIC DRINKS:											
Lager and beer	29.2	25.6	35.0	31.6	25.5	23.9	29.2	29.0	25.5	29.9	28.9
Wine	35.4	33.8	43.7	46.3	36.3	43.8	49.0	43.5	33.1	36.1	42.2
other alcoholic drinks	25.0	26.2	34.3	34.2	37.3	34.7	31.8	32.2	38.1	49.1	34.1
Total alcoholic drinks	**89.6**	**85.5**	**112.9**	**112.1**	**99.2**	**102.4**	**109.9**	**104.7**	**96.6**	**115.0**	**105.2**
CONFECTIONERY:											
Chocolate confectionery	23.0	18.6	17.9	22.3	20.8	18.1	19.6	19.7	25.8	18.9	20.0
Mints And Boiled Sweets	5.6	5.9	5.2	6.0	5.8	5.5	6.1	5.8	4.9	5.5	5.7
Other confectionery	1.4	1.3	1.2	1.5	1.8	1.2	1.3	1.3	1.8	1.7	1.4
Total confectionery	**30.0**	**25.8**	**24.2**	**29.9**	**28.4**	**24.8**	**27.1**	**26.9**	**32.4**	**26.1**	**27.2**
TOTAL FOOD AND DRINK	**1480.9**	**1470.7**	**1530.8**	**1571.5**	**1547.1**	**1529.2**	**1636.4**	**1566.8**	**1545.4**	**1555.3**	**1564.5**

Table D2 Average household consumption of food and drink by region, 1994-1996

grams per person per week

	\multicolumn{7}{c}{Regions of England}				
	North	Yorkshire and Humber-side	North West	East Midlands	West Midlands	South West	South East/ East Anglia	England	Wales	Scotland	Great Britain
MILK AND CREAM:											
Liquid Wholemilk, Full Price	788	854	769	794	839	806	736	780	798	850	788
Welfare and school Milk	56	30	42	25	20	34	22	29	52	35	31
Low fat milks	968	1074	1116	1188	1014	1108	1085	1084	1114	1038	1082
Dried and other milk, including dairy desserts	139	107	126	138	106	84	121	119	106	75	113
Yoghurt And Fromage Frais	110	132	123	135	123	128	130	127	111	116	125
Cream	14	14	14	16	13	23	19	17	14	12	16
Total Milk and cream	**2075**	**2211**	**2190**	**2296**	**2115**	**2183**	**2113**	**2156**	**2195**	**2126**	**2155**
CHEESE:											
Natural	79	94	87	111	105	109	103	100	94	86	98
Processed	10	12	12	10	9	8	9	10	9	15	10
Total cheese	**89**	**106**	**99**	**122**	**114**	**117**	**112**	**110**	**103**	**101**	**108**
MEAT:											
Beef And Veal	135	120	115	121	124	107	107	115	117	148	118
Mutton And Lamb	37	45	68	44	67	52	73	61	67	22	58
Pork	71	82	67	84	91	73	72	76	83	49	74
Total carcase meat	**243**	**247**	**250**	**250**	**283**	**232**	**252**	**252**	**267**	**218**	**250**
Bacon And Ham Uncooked	101	85	88	75	88	75	62	76	88	75	77
Poultry, uncooked	211	205	216	209	234	235	229	223	235	175	219
Other meat and meat Products	464	416	418	402	376	347	368	390	431	459	398
Total meat	**1019**	**953**	**972**	**936**	**981**	**889**	**911**	**941**	**1021**	**927**	**944**
FISH:											
Fresh	23	26	31	24	28	25	32	29	26	43	29
Processed and shell	15	14	15	12	12	17	19	16	17	20	17
Prepared, including fish products	63	76	57	53	56	49	52	56	46	36	55
Frozen, including fish Products	50	45	44	52	47	46	49	48	53	33	47
Total fish	**151**	**161**	**147**	**141**	**143**	**137**	**152**	**149**	**142**	**132**	**148**
EGGS	2.17	2.01	1.85	1.81	1.85	1.88	1.79	1.87	1.75	1.86	1.86
FATS:											
Butter	36	32	36	33	35	42	41	38	44	40	38
Margarine	51	57	41	44	46	39	33	41	34	37	40
Vegetable & Salad Oils	41	49	39	63	49	49	57	51	53	47	51
Low fat and dairy Spreads	62	69	77	80	90	79	71	75	90	65	74
Other fats	27	29	19	23	22	17	15	19	18	16	19
Total fats	**217**	**237**	**211**	**244**	**241**	**227**	**217**	**225**	**240**	**206**	**224**
SUGAR AND PRESERVES:											
Sugar	125	150	147	146	168	149	128	141	160	131	141
Honey, preserves, syrup and treacle	44	44	36	43	39	46	42	42	41	41	42
Total sugar and Preserves	**169**	**194**	**184**	**188**	**208**	**195**	**170**	**183**	**201**	**173**	**183**
VEGETABLES:											
Potatoes	850	834	840	842	906	842	729	806	965	712	807
Fresh green	208	234	187	268	264	262	257	243	234	147	234
Other fresh	455	459	423	485	473	520	515	484	466	386	474
Frozen, including vegetable products	186	202	188	217	221	199	213	206	216	192	206
Other processed, including vegetable products	431	407	382	395	370	333	346	369	358	337	366
Total vegetables	**2130**	**2136**	**2020**	**2207**	**2234**	**2156**	**2060**	**2108**	**2239**	**1774**	**2087**

Table D2 *continued*

grams per person per week

	Regions of England							England	Wales	Scotland	Great Britain
	North	Yorkshire and Humber- side	North West	East Midlands	West Midlands	South West	South East/ East Anglia				
FRUIT:											
Fresh	559	611	604	672	661	728	743	679	647	577	668
Other, including fruit Products	70	79	76	90	86	89	81	81	80	73	80
Fruit Juices	186	224	215	261	233	280	283	253	242	204	247
Total fruit	**815**	**914**	**895**	**1023**	**980**	**1097**	**1107**	**1013**	**969**	**854**	**995**
CEREALS:											
White bread	384	402	413	401	454	323	312	367	463	374	373
Premium and softgrain bread	79	49	53	65	59	61	75	65	57	94	67
Brown bread	85	80	86	75	73	94	72	78	82	69	78
Wholemeal bread	97	98	92	108	94	116	102	101	97	83	99
Other Bread	168	144	140	140	127	118	127	134	121	187	138
Total bread	813	772	784	790	807	711	689	745	819	807	755
Flour	63	75	46	81	87	67	63	67	54	32	63
Cakes	133	134	142	138	125	115	125	130	106	104	126
Biscuits	162	146	135	144	142	145	132	140	147	149	142
Oatmeal And Oat products	10	12	10	11	14	13	10	11	9	19	12
Breakfast Cereals	127	143	136	149	134	147	136	138	132	120	136
Other cereals	234	242	229	255	235	219	306	262	218	251	258
Total cereals	**1542**	**1524**	**1482**	**1568**	**1544**	**1417**	**1461**	**1493**	**1485**	**1482**	**1492**
BEVERAGES:											
Tea	38	38	41	38	44	36	39	39	41	33	39
Coffee	18	17	15	17	16	20	16	16	16	15	17
Cocoa and drinking chocolate	2	2	2	3	4	3	3	3	3	2	3
Branded Food Drinks	5	5	4	6	7	6	6	5	5	2	5
Total beverages	**62**	**62**	**63**	**63**	**71**	**65**	**64**	**64**	**65**	**52**	**63**
MISCELLANEOUS											
Soups canned, dehydrated and powdered	78	73	87	58	64	56	59	66	70	117	71
Other foods	311	337	362	380	365	419	442	395	353	317	383
Total miscellaneous	**389**	**410**	**449**	**438**	**429**	**475**	**501**	**461**	**423**	**434**	**454**
SOFT DRINKS:											
Concentrated	83	100	105	110	115	112	114	109	87	79	105
Unconcentrated	560	494	503	517	567	358	425	472	565	569	486
Low calorie, volume as purchased	286	208	274	282	292	198	258	258	338	375	273
Total soft drinks, volume as purchased	**929**	**802**	**883**	**908**	**974**	**668**	**798**	838	988	1025	864
ALCOHOLIC DRINKS:											
Lager and beer	205	176	227	218	174	149	182	190	176	190	189
Wine	97	90	115	121	93	113	116	109	88	89	106
other alcoholic drinks	46	51	64	65	81	70	58	62	77	69	63
Total alcoholic drinks	**349**	**317**	**407**	**403**	**348**	**334**	**356**	**360**	**342**	**348**	**358**
CONFECTIONERY:											
Chocolate confectionery	45	36	34	42	40	36	36	37	47	36	38
Mints and boiled sweets	14	15	12	15	14	12	14	14	11	13	14
Other confectionery	2	3	2	3	3	2	2	2	3	4	2
Total confectionery	**61**	**54**	**48**	**60**	**58**	**50**	**52**	**54**	**62**	**52**	**54**

Table D3 Regional contributions to nutrient intake made by selected foods, 1994 – 1996

per person per day

	\multicolumn{7}{c}{Regions of England}			
	North	Yorkshire & Humberside	North West	East Midlands	West Midlands	South West	South East/ East Anglia	England	Wales	Scotland
ENERGY (kcal)										
Milk and milk products:	184	194	188	199	184	193	185	189	190	187
whole milk	79	85	77	79	84	80	73	78	80	85
low fat milks	64	70	71	77	65	72	71	70	72	69
yoghurt	14	17	16	17	16	17	17	17	15	15
Cheese	46	54	50	63	62	63	60	58	55	54
Meat and meat products:	290	269	270	265	270	246	251	261	281	266
carcase meat	70	70	70	70	80	65	71	71	75	63
poultry, uncooked	35	33	35	35	39	39	38	37	38	28
bacon and ham	44	39	40	35	30	35	31	35	41	36
sausages, uncooked	26	25	23	27	26	26	25	25	24	33
Fish	32	34	28	28	28	27	29	29	27	23
Eggs	24	22	20	20	20	20	19	20	19	20
Fats:	218	239	208	244	239	223	217	224	236	204
butter	38	34	37	35	36	44	43	40	46	42
margarine	53	60	43	47	48	41	34	43	36	39
low fat and dairy spreads	49	55	62	64	74	62	57	60	72	50
vegetable and salad oils	48	58	46	74	57	58	67	61	63	55
Sugar and preserves	87	101	97	98	110	101	88	95	106	90
Vegetables:	207	194	190	203	206	189	180	191	205	181
fresh potatoes	70	68	69	69	74	69	60	66	79	59
fresh green vegetables	5	5	4	6	6	6	6	6	5	3
other fresh vegetables	14	14	13	15	15	16	16	15	15	12
frozen vegetables	25	26	24	27	27	24	26	26	26	27
canned vegetables	23	22	20	20	19	17	17	19	19	17
Fruit:	62	71	68	80	77	85	85	78	75	65
fresh fruit	33	36	36	40	39	44	44	40	39	34
fruit juices	10	12	12	14	13	16	16	14	13	11
Cereals:	624	618	593	643	626	587	610	612	598	595
white bread (standard loaves)	122	127	131	127	145	104	100	117	149	118
brown and wholemeal breads	56	55	55	57	52	65	54	55	55	47
cakes, pastries and biscuits	176	166	161	169	160	156	153	160	153	155
breakfast cereals	63	71	67	73	66	73	67	68	65	59
Other foods	49	53	49	52	52	55	56	53	55	53
Total food	**1822**	**1849**	**1762**	**1896**	**1873**	**1790**	**1781**	**1811**	**1846**	**1737**
Soft drinks	42	42	44	45	48	37	41	43	43	43
Alcoholic drinks	24	23	29	29	26	26	27	27	26	28
Confectionery	38	33	30	37	36	32	32	33	40	32
Total food and drink	**1927**	**1947**	**1865**	**2009**	**1984**	**1885**	**1881**	**1913**	**1955**	**1840**

Table D3 *continued*

per person per day

FAT (g)	North	Yorkshire & Humberside	North West	East Midlands	West Midlands	South West	South East/ East Anglia	England	Wales	Scotland
Milk and milk products:	8.8	9.1	8.6	9.2	8.6	9.2	8.7	8.8	8.9	8.9
whole milk	4.8	5.2	4.7	4.8	5.1	4.9	4.5	4.7	4.8	5.1
low fat milks	2.0	2.2	2.1	2.3	1.9	2.3	2.2	2.1	2.2	2.2
yoghurt	0.3	0.3	0.3	0.3	0.3	0.3	0.4	0.3	0.3	0.3
Cheese	3.8	4.5	4.1	5.3	5.2	5.3	5.1	4.8	4.6	4.5
Meat and meat products:	20.2	18.7	18.7	18.4	18.8	17.2	17.4	18.1	19.4	18.4
carcase meat	4.9	4.9	4.9	4.9	5.6	4.6	5.0	5.0	5.2	4.3
poultry, uncooked	2.2	2.1	2.2	2.3	2.6	2.5	2.5	2.4	2.4	1.8
bacon and ham	3.4	3.0	3.1	2.7	3.0	2.7	2.3	2.7	3.1	2.7
sausages, uncooked	2.1	2.0	1.8	2.1	2.0	2.1	2.0	2.0	1.9	2.6
Fish	1.6	1.7	1.4	1.4	1.3	1.3	1.4	1.4	1.3	1.0
Eggs	1.7	1.6	1.5	1.4	1.5	1.5	1.4	1.5	1.4	1.5
Fats:	24.0	26.2	22.8	26.8	26.3	24.5	23.8	24.6	25.9	22.4
butter	4.2	3.8	4.2	3.8	4.0	4.9	4.8	4.4	5.1	4.7
margarine	5.9	6.7	4.8	5.2	5.3	4.5	3.8	4.7	4.0	4.3
low fat and dairy spreads	5.3	6.0	6.7	6.9	8.0	6.7	6.1	6.5	7.8	5.4
vegetable and salad oils	5.3	6.5	5.1	8.2	6.4	6.4	7.5	6.7	7.0	6.1
Sugar and preserves	...	...	...	...	...	...	...	...	...	...
Vegetables	5.2	4.5	4.6	5.1	5.0	4.6	4.4	4.7	4.8	4.8
Fruit	1.1	1.3	1.1	1.5	1.4	1.4	1.6	1.4	1.3	1.1
Cereals:	13.7	12.9	12.4	13.6	12.7	12.4	12.5	12.7	12.2	12.8
white bread (standard loaves)	0.8	0.9	0.9	0.9	1.0	0.7	0.7	0.8	1.1	0.8
brown and wholemeal bread	0.6	0.6	0.6	0.6	0.6	0.7	0.6	0.6	0.6	0.5
cakes, pastries and biscuits	7.6	7.1	6.8	7.3	6.9	6.7	6.5	6.8	6.7	6.8
breakfast cereals	0.4	0.5	0.4	0.5	0.5	0.6	0.5	0.5	0.4	0.3
Other foods	1.9	2.3	2.0	2.3	2.0	2.3	2.4	2.2	2.2	2.2
Total food	**82.0**	**82.8**	**77.2**	**85.1**	**82.8**	**79.7**	**78.7**	**80.3**	**81.8**	**77.5**
Soft drinks	-	-	-	-	-	-	-	-	-	-
Alcoholic drinks	...	...	...	...	...	...	...	...	...	...
Confectionery	1.6	1.3	1.2	1.5	0.8	1.3	1.3	1.3	1.7	1.3
Total food and drink	**83.6**	**84.1**	**78.4**	**86.6**	**84.2**	**81.0**	**80.0**	**81.6**	**83.5**	**78.8**

Table D3 *continued*

per person per day

SATURATED FATTY ACIDS (g)	North	Yorkshire and Humberside	North West	East Midlands	West Midlands	South West	South East/ East Anglia	England	Wales	Scotland
Milk and milk products:	5.4	5.7	5.3	5.7	5.3	5.7	5.4	5.5	5.5	5.5
whole milk	3.0	3.3	2.9	3.0	3.2	3.1	2.8	3.0	3.0	3.2
low fat milks	1.3	1.4	1.3	1.5	1.2	1.4	1.4	1.3	1.4	1.4
yoghurt	0.1	0.2	0.2	0.2	0.2	0.2	0.2	0.2	0.2	0.2
Cheese	2.4	2.8	2.6	3.3	3.2	3.3	3.1	3.0	2.9	2.8
Meat and meat products:	7.7	7.1	7.2	7.0	7.2	6.5	6.7	6.9	7.4	7.1
carcase meat	1.9	1.9	2.0	2.0	2.3	1.9	2.1	2.0	2.1	1.8
poultry, uncooked	0.7	0.7	0.7	0.7	0.8	0.8	0.8	0.7	0.7	0.6
bacon and ham	1.3	1.1	1.1	1.0	1.1	1.0	0.9	1.0	1.2	1.0
sausages, uncooked	0.8	0.8	0.7	0.8	0.8	0.8	0.8	0.8	0.7	1.0
Fish	0.4	0.4	0.3	0.3	0.3	0.3	0.3	0.3	0.3	0.2
Eggs	0.5	0.5	0.4	0.4	0.4	0.4	0.4	0.3	0.4	0.4
Fats:	7.8	8.1	7.3	7.8	8.0	7.8	7.4	7.6	8.1	7.2
butter	2.8	2.5	2.8	2.6	2.7	3.3	3.2	2.9	3.4	3.1
margarine	1.7	1.9	1.4	1.5	1.5	1.3	1.1	1.4	1.1	1.2
low fat and dairy spreads	1.3	1.5	1.7	1.8	2.0	1.7	1.6	1.6	2.0	1.4
vegetable and salad oils	0.5	0.7	0.5	0.9	0.7	0.7	0.8	0.7	0.7	0.6
Sugar and preserves	...	...	...	...	...	...	...	...	...	...
Vegetables	1.5	1.3	1.3	1.5	1.5	1.4	1.3	1.4	1.4	1.4
Fruit	0.3	0.3	0.3	0.3	0.3	0.3	0.4	0.3	0.3	0.2
Cereals:	5.5	5.1	4.9	5.4	4.9	4.9	4.9	5.0	4.8	5.1
white bread (standard loaves)	0.1	0.2	0.2	0.2	0.2	0.1	0.1	0.1	0.2	0.1
brown and wholemeal bread	0.1	0.1	0.1	0.1	0.1	0.1	0.1	0.1	0.1	0.1
cakes, pastries and biscuits	3.7	3.4	3.3	3.5	3.3	3.2	3.1	3.3	3.2	3.3
breakfast cereals	0.1	0.1	0.1	0.1	0.1	0.1	0.1	0.1	0.1	0.1
Other foods	0.6	0.7	0.6	0.8	0.7	0.7	0.7	0.9	0.8	0.7
Total food	**32.1**	**32.0**	**30.2**	**32.5**	**31.9**	**31.4**	**30.5**	**31.2**	**31.9**	**30.7**
Soft drinks	-	-	-	-	-	-	-	-	-	-
Alcoholic drinks	...	...	...	...	...	...	...	...	...	...
Confectionery	0.9	0.7	0.7	0.9	0.8	0.8	0.7	0.8	1.0	0.7
Total food and drink	**33.0**	**32.7**	**30.9**	**33.4**	**32.7**	**32.1**	**31.3**	**31.9**	**32.9**	**31.5**

Table D3 *continued*

per person per day

VITAMIN C (mg)	North	Yorkshire and Humberside	North West	East Midlands	West Midlands	South West	South East/ East Anglia	England	Wales	Scotland
Milk and milk products	2.8	2.6	2.8	3.1	2.5	2.5	2.6	2.7	2.6	2.5
Cheese	-	-	-	-	-	-	-	-	-	-
Meat and meat products	2.4	2.1	1.9	1.9	1.7	1.8	1.7	1.8	2.1	2.6
Fish	...	...	...	...	...	...	...	...	...	...
Eggs	-	-	-	-	-	-	-	-	-	-
Fats	0.1	0.1	0.1	0.1	0.1	0.1	0.1	0.1	0.1	0.1
Sugar and preserves	0.5	0.5	0.4	0.5	0.5	0.5	0.5	0.5	0.5	0.5
Vegetables:	20.2	19.8	19.0	21.6	22.0	20.7	20.4	20.4	21.3	16.9
fresh potatoes	6.5	6.2	6.3	6.5	7.2	6.5	5.4	6.1	7.4	5.6
fresh green vegetables	2.2	2.3	1.8	2.7	2.7	2.6	2.5	2.1	2.2	1.4
other fresh vegetables	4.6	4.5	4.3	4.9	4.9	5.3	5.5	5.0	4.6	4.1
frozen vegetables	3.1	3.4	3.5	3.8	4.0	3.4	3.8	3.6	3.8	3.1
canned vegetables	0.8	0.9	0.7	1.0	0.8	0.8	0.9	0.9	0.8	0.6
Fruit:	21.3	24.7	23.6	27.2	25.2	29.3	30.1	27.1	25.6	22.3
fresh fruit	11.2	12.5	11.8	12.9	12.5	14.0	14.8	13.4	12.5	11.1
fruit juices	9.5	11.4	11.0	13.3	11.9	14.3	14.4	12.9	12.3	10.4
Cereals:	1.0	1.1	1.1	1.2	1.0	1.0	1.1	1.1	1.0	0.9
white bread (standard loaves)	-	-	-	-	-	-	-	-	-	-
brown and wholemeal bread	-	-	-	-	-	-	-	-	-	-
cakes, pastries and biscuits	...	...	...	0.1	...	...	...	...	...	...
breakfast cereals	0.7	0.8	0.8	0.9	0.8	0.8	0.8	0.8	0.8	0.7
Other foods	0.3	0.4	0.5	0.4	0.5	0.4	0.5	0.4	0.5	0.6
Total food	**48.7**	**51.3**	**49.4**	**56.0**	**53.5**	**56.3**	**56.8**	**54.1**	**53.6**	**46.4**
Soft drinks	5.6	5.2	5.6	5.9	6.2	4.7	5.3	5.5	5.7	5.8
Alcoholic drinks	-	-	-	-	-	-	-	-	-	-
Confectionery	-	-	-	-	-	-	-	-	-	-
Total food and drink	**54.3**	**56.6**	**55.0**	**61.9**	**59.7**	**61.0**	**62.1**	**59.6**	**59.3**	**52.2**

Table D3 *continued*

per person per day

β-CAROTENE (μg)	North	Yorkshire and Humberside	North West	East Midlands	West Midlands	South West	South East/ East Anglia	England	Wales	Scotland
Milk and milk products	46	47	44	49	45	48	45	46	46	47
Cheese	24	28	26	33	33	33	32	31	29	28
Meat and meat products	25	22	24	19	20	16	20	21	24	26
Fish	2	2	2	2	2	2	2	2	2	2
Eggs	-	-	-	-	-	-	-	-	-	-
Fats:	85	91	93	96	105	100	91	94	106	87
butter	22	20	22	20	21	26	25	23	27	25
margarine	16	19	14	15	16	15	12	14	12	15
low fat and dairy spreads	45	51	56	59	66	58	52	55	65	47
vegetable and salad oils	-	-	-	-	-	-	-	-	-	-
Sugar and preserves	1	1	1	1	1	1	1	1	1	1
Vegetables:	1309	1392	1349	1450	1373	1412	1376	1381	1424	1096
fresh carrots	849	923	871	923	856	939	842	873	948	676
frozen vegetables	143	161	181	181	195	158	186	178	183	141
fresh green vegetables	56	58	46	67	66	67	70	63	55	41
canned vegetables	88	84	78	84	75	70	71	76	73	71
Fruit:	37	41	45	49	46	48	54	48	43	41
fresh fruit	29	32	36	39	37	38	44	39	34	35
fruit juices	4	5	4	5	5	6	6	5	5	4
Cereals	21	21	20	24	20	19	22	21	19	21
Other foods	47	53	52	41	45	47	48	47	47	47
Total food	**1596**	**1699**	**1656**	**1764**	**1690**	**1726**	**1692**	**1691**	**1741**	**1396**
Soft drinks	42	49	52	54	56	54	55	53	44	40
Alcoholic drinks	...	...	...	...	...	...	...	...	...	...
Confectionery	4	3	3	4	4	3	3	3	4	3
Total food and drink	**1642**	**1751**	**1710**	**1821**	**1750**	**1783**	**1750**	**1747**	**1789**	**1439**

Glossary

Glossary of terms used in the Survey

Adult A person of 18 years of age or over, however, solely for purposes of classifying households according to their composition, heads of household and diary-keepers under 18 years of age are regarded as adults.

Average consumption For the main Survey, the aggregate amount of *household food obtained for consumption* by the households in the sample divided by the total number of persons in the sample. For the eating out extension, the aggregate amount of *eating out consumption* by the people in the extension sample divided by the number of people in the extension sample.

Average expenditure For the main Survey, the aggregate amount spent by the households in the sample divided by the total number of persons in the sample. For the eating out extension, the aggregate eating out expenditure by the people in the extension sample, divided by the number of people in the extension sample.

Average price The aggregate expenditure by the households in the sample on an item in the Survey Classification of foods, divided by the aggregate quantity of that item purchased by these households. It is therefore, more strictly an 'average unit value'.

Child A person under 18 years of age; however, solely for purposes of classifying households according to their composition, heads of household and diary-keepers under 18 years of age are regarded as adults.

Composite meals and snacks For the eating out extension, these are defined as meals or snacks for which a cost can only be given for a number of foods together. A cost is given for the whole meal, and the individual components are recorded for use in calculating consumption and nutritional values.

Convenience foods Those processed foods for which the degree of preparation has been carried to an advanced stage by the manufacturer and which may be used as labour-saving alternatives to less highly processed products. The convenience foods distinguished by the Survey are cooked and canned meats, meat products (other than uncooked sausages), cooked and canned fish, fish products, canned vegetables, vegetable products, canned fruit, fruit juices, cakes and pastries, biscuits, breakfast cereals, instant coffee and coffee essences, baby foods, canned soups, dehydrated soups, ice-cream, and all frozen foods which fulfil the requirements of the previous sentence.

Eating our consumption Individual consumption outside the home of all food and drink not obtained from household stocks, regardless of who paid for the food or drink.

Eating Out expenditure Individual expenditure on all food and drink purchased for *eating out consumption,* whether for consumption by the purchaser or others or both. Expenditure on food and drink for 'business' purposes, i.e. that which is to be reclaimed as business expenses, is not included.

Eating Out extension   An additional section of the National Food Survey which asks half of the main survey households to record their *eating out consumption* and *eating out expenditure*.

Garden and allotment produce, etc   Food which entered the household without payment, and was consumed during the week of participation in the Survey. It includes supplies obtained from a garden, allotment or farm, or from an employer, but not gifts of food from one household in Great Britain to another if such food has been purchased by the donating household. (See also *Value of garden and allotment produced, etc*).

Household   For the Survey purposes, this is defined as a group of persons living in the same dwelling and sharing common catering arrangements.

Household food obtained for consumption   Food purchases from all sources (including purchases in bulk) made by households during their week of participation in the Survey and intended for human consumption during that week or later, plus any *garden or allotment produce, etc* which households actually consumed while participating in the Survey, but excluding sweets, alcohol, soft drinks and meals or snacks purchased for *eating out consumption*. For an individual household, the quantity of food thus obtained for consumption, or estimates of nutrient intake derived from it, may differ from actual consumption because of changes in household stocks during the week and because of wastage. Averaged over a sufficiently large group of households and a sufficiently long period of time, increases in household stocks might reasonably be expected to differ only slightly from depletions.

Income group   Households are grouped into eight income groups (A1, A2, B, C, D, E1, E2 and OAP) according to the ascertained or estimated gross income of the head of the household or of the principal earner in the household (if the weekly income of the head is less than the amount defining the upper limit to income group D). Households without an earner (E1 and E2) are those with no person normally working more than ten hours a week, however of these, *Pensioner Households* and those with at least one person unemployed for less than a year are not counted as households without an earner.

Intake   See Food obtained for consumption.

Main Survey   The core part of the National Food Survey, for which the main estimates of *average consumption* and *average expenditure* for *household food obtained for consumption* are derived.

Meals   For the eating out extension, a meal is an eating occasion which cannot be described by a single food item code, but which includes a main dish. In addition a meal must be served and consumed on the premises of one of the following types of outlet: respondent's workplace, school, restaurant, public house, catering facilities on trains, buses or aeroplanes, meals on wheels or other catering facilities such as hospitals, football grounds, etc. A meal is distinct from a meal occasion, which is defined as breakfast, mid-day or evening meal or other eating or drinking occasion and may comprise a meal or drink or snack or any combination of these.

Net balance The net balance for an individual (a member of the household or a visitor) is a measure of the proportion of the individuals' food needs which are met by meals eaten in the home by that individual during the Survey week. Each meal is given a weight in proportion to its normal importance, the relative weights currently used being breakfast 3, mid-day meal 4, evening meal 7. These weights were changed during 1991; previously, separate weights for tea (2) and supper (5) were used if two evening meals were taken; now a light tea or supper is disregarded in this calculation. The net balance is used when relating nutrient intakes to reference intakes (based on age and sex etc).

Nutrients In addition to the energy value of food expressed in terms of kilocalories and megajoules (4,184 megajoules = 1,000 kilocalories), the food is evaluated in terms of the following nutrients:

> Protein (animal and total), fat (including the component saturated, monosaturated and polyunsaturated fatty acids), carbohydrate (including total sugars, non-milk extrinsic sugars and starch), fibre (as non-starch polysaccharides), calcium, iron, zinc, magnesium, sodium, potassium, vitamin A (retinol, B-carotene, retinol equivalent), thiamin, riboflavin, niacin equivalent, folate, vitamins B6, B12, C, D and E, cholesterol, copper, manganese, phosphorus, biotin and pantothenic acid.

Pensioner households (OAP) Households in which at least three-quarters of total income is derived from state retirement pensions or similar pensions and/or supplementary pensions or allowances paid in supplementation or instead of such pensions. Such households will include at least one person over the state retirement age.

Person An individual of any age who, during the week of the Survey, spends at least four nights in the household ('at home') and has at least one meal a day from the household food supply on at least four days, except that if he/she is the head of the household, or the diary-keeper, he or she is regarded as a person irrespective of the above conditions.

Price index A price index of Fisher 'Ideal' type is used; this index is the geometric means of two indices with weights relating to the earlier and later periods respectively or, in the case of non-temporal comparisons (e.g. regional, type of area, income group and household composition), with weights relating to the group under consideration and the national average respectively.

Quantity index This index is also of the Fisher 'Ideal' type. The price and quantity indices together thus account for the whole of the expenditure difference between the two periods or groups being compared.

Real price The price of an item in relation to the price of all goods and services. The term is used when referring to changes in the price of an item over a period of time. The real prices quoted in this report are obtained by dividing the *average price* paid at a point in time by the Index of Retail Prices (All Items) at that time.

Regions The standard regions for statistical purposes, except that East Anglia is combined with the South East region.

Seasonal foods Those foods which regularly exhibit a marked seasonal variation in price or in consumption; for the purposes of the Survey these are deemed to be eggs, fresh and processed fish, shellfish, potatoes, fresh vegetables and fresh fruit.

Snacks For the eating out extension, snacks are all eating out occasions other than those classified as meals (but including any eating out occasion referred to as snack by the respondent even if this also fulfils the meal definition). They may be from any outlet and contain any food item or combination of items.

Value of consumption Expenditure plus *value of garden and allotment produce, etc.*

Value of garden and allotment produce, etc The value imputed to such supplies received by a group of households is derived from the average prices currently paid by the group for corresponding purchases. This appears to be the only practicable method of valuing these supplies, even though if the households concerned had not had access to them, they would probably not have consumed as much of these foods, and would therefore have spent less on them than the estimated value of their consumption (though they might have spent more on other foods). Free school milk and free welfare milk are valued at the average price paid by the group for full price milk. (See also *Garden and allotment produce, etc.*).

Symbols and conventions used

Symbols   The following are used throughout:

. - = nil

... = less than half the final digit shown

na or blank = not available or not applicable

Rounding of figures   In tables where figures have been rounded to the nearest final digit, there may be an apparent slight discrepancy between the sum of the constituent items and the total shown.

Additional Information

Analyses of Survey data providing more detail and, in some cases, more-up-to-date information than published in this report are available directly from the Ministry of Agriculture, Fisheries and Food. These analyses are of three main types:

i)   Compendium of supplementary NFS results

ii)   Standard analyses

   Quarterly national averages - available approximately 10 weeks after the end of each survey period

   Analyses of components of selected food codes

iii)   Ad hoc analyses

   Ad hoc analyses can be undertaken to meet the special requirements of organisations, subject to resources being available

Some of the figures in this and previous reports are available from the CCTA Government Information Service on the World Wide Web at the address:-

   http://www.maff.gov.uk

Further details regarding additional Survey information are available from:

   National Food Survey Branch
   Ministry of Agriculture, Fisheries and Food
   Room 513, West Block
   Whitehall Place
   London SW1A 2HH

   Telephone: 0171-270 8562/3